HONEST DOVER'S FANCY.

Words by John Masefield. 1904.
Air: "Greenwich Park." 1698.

Campden town
Is quiet after London riot;
Campden street
Is kindly to the feet;
Campden wold,
So bonny to behold,
Is merry with the blowing wind & glad with growing wheat.

Campden fields
Are covered up with buttercup,
And bluebells slight
That tremble with delight;
Cuckoos come
When blossom's on the plum
And blossom's on the apple trees in petals red and white.

Campden woods
Are ringing with the blackbirds singing
Thrill! thrill! thrill!
O merry orange bill!
Sweet! sweet! sweet!
Says the chaffinch in the wheat;
All the pretty birds that are do delicately trill!

Dover's Hill
Has bramble bushes full of thrushes;
Tall green trees
That set a heart at ease;
Soft green grass
Where little rabbits pass
To nibble yellow buttercups amid the honey bees.   V.—41

The Simple Life

GVI 188
LD ·8·

Fiona MacCarthy

The Simple Life

C. R. Ashbee in the Cotswolds

University of California Press
Berkeley and Los Angeles

First edition 1981
University of California Press
Berkeley and Los Angeles

Library of Congress Catalog Card Number 80-53299
ISBN 0-520-04369-3

Designed by Alan Bartram
Made and printed in Great Britain by
Robert MacLehose and Company Limited
Printers to the University of Glasgow

Contents

Illustrations appear between pages 88 and 89

List of Illustrations

15 The Guild of Handicraft, group photograph probably taken in 1906 or 1907.
16 The carvers at work at the Guild of Handicraft.
17 The woodshop on the second floor of the old Silk Mill.
18 The Guild's blacksmiths.
19 The machine shop.
20 Cottages at Catbrook designed by C. R. Ashbee and built for the Guild craftsmen.
21 Broadwood piano designed by C. R. Ashbee and decorated by the Guild of Handicraft.
22 Houses in Cheyne Walk, Chelsea, by C. R. Ashbee.
23 Double-handled silver dish designed by C. R. Ashbee and made by the Guild of Handicraft, 1902.
24 Silver dish with looped handle designed by C. R. Ashbee and made by the Guild of Handicraft, 1900.
25 Jewelled finial for comb designed by C. R. Ashbee and made by the Guild of Handicraft, c. 1903.
26 Pendant jewel in the form of a peacock designed by C. R. Ashbee and made by the Guild of Handicraft, c. 1903.
27 and 28 Painted music cabinet and curved seat made by the Guild of Handicraft for the Grand Duke of Hesse's Palace at Darmstadt, about 1898, designed by M. H. Baillie Scott.
29 Brooch in enamelled gold designed by C. R. Ashbee, c. 1903.

PHOTOGRAPHIC ACKNOWLEDGMENTS
Jacket illustration, Victoria and Albert Museum.
1 and 2 Felicity Ashbee; 3 and 4 Victoria and Albert Museum; 5 King's College, Cambridge; 6 Sheffield City Libraries; 7 and 8 Campden Trust; 9 and 10 Victoria and Albert Museum; 11 *Craftsmanship in Competitive Industry*; 12 King's College, Cambridge; 13 and 14 Art Workers' Guild; 15 descendants of Walter Edwards, Guild silversmith; 16 and 17 Campden Trust; 20 *Craftsmanship in Competitive Industry*; 21 Art Workers' Guild; 22 Victoria and Albert Museum; 23 Worshipful Company of Goldsmiths; 24 Victoria and Albert Museum; 25 Art Workers' Guild; 26, 27, 28 and 29, Victoria and Albert Museum.

We are grateful to Tim Hill for his expertise in copying photographs in the collections of the Victoria and Albert Museum and the Art Workers' Guild; to Alan Crawford for illustrations 2, 5 and 12; and to Robert Welch for illustration 15.

Prologue

The search for the New Life has been a potent element, constantly recurring, endearingly persistent, in the intellectual life of the last century in Britain. Surprisingly enough, since the British countryside has been in almost all ways a traditionalist stronghold, the venue for the New Life, the chosen setting for the many progressive communities established between the 1880s and the early 1900s, was predominantly rural. Bound up with the strong impulse to reshape accepted attitudes to politics, religion, labour, education, sex, aesthetics, food, drink, dress, and all the other institutions ripe for reformation, has almost always been the idea of escaping: abandoning the city, symbol of oppression, to try the simpler, freer, more creative country life.

The Simple Life was never for the simple-minded. It has tended to be a very complicated concept. By the year 1901 or 1902, when C. R. Ashbee began contemplating moving the Guild of Handicraft from Whitechapel to Gloucestershire, the idea that rural life was true and natural existence, binding men together in their communal dependence on the rhythm of the seasons, a theme greatly in favour both with Romantic poets and Victorian novelists, had combined with a more political awareness that the land was the birthright of the people. The Back-to-the-Land movement, obviously influenced by an idealized, nostalgic view of rural life and values, was also motivated by a more aggressive spirit, the idea that the people were reclaiming their lost rights.

In this, it echoed both Carlyle and Ruskin: Carlyle's view that man's spirit was squandered in the city, his energies dispersed, his loyalties fragmented; Ruskin's passionate assertion that cities were so ugly because they were so evil, dominated by capitalist greed and the 'cash nexus', and men of any visual sensitivity must flee from them. From Ruskin came the concept of the working fellowship, so powerfully developed in the writings and the lectures of William Morris and popularized by many Socialist tracts, in particular by Blatchford's best-selling *Merrie England*. This persuasive piece of Socialist propaganda, first published in 1894 and reprinted many times over the next two decades, attacked violently the 'every-man-for-himself principle' that dominated the capitalist scheme of things, proposing in its place a more tolerant and equitable system of working in small self-contained communities. The idyll of life as it should be, the rural vision which encouraged the great flight from the city to the country at the end of the last century, focused on an England which was mainly agricultural, in which the economy was self-supporting and in which the people, freed from the pressures of their role as labourers in the workshop of the world, would work in a spirit of joy and camaraderie, at one with their fellows and at one with their surroundings. Central to this vision was the generous, hopeful theory, especially important in the Arts and Crafts communities, that the labourers of Britain, stunted in the city, would, in a new setting of dignity and harmony, develop their creative instincts to the fullest. Essential to the idea that the good life was man's birthright, and the good life more attainable in country than in city, was the concept that the right life allowed men sufficient leisure to develop all their faculties, a late Renaissance doctrine of the total human being.

In spite of its insistence on man's right to joyfulness, the Simple Life movement was in some respects a solemn one. Getting back to the land had an element of duty. The proselytizing writers of the period put it over as a kind of a crusade, a sacred charge. Perhaps the intensity had dissipated somewhat since Ruskin's early plans for St George's Farm, near Sheffield, set up in 1876, in which the recruits, who were mostly Sheffield shoemakers, were entrusted with being 'Life Guards of the New Life . . . more in a spirit of a body of monks gathered for missionary service, than of a body of tradesmen gathered for the promotion even of the honestest and usefullest trade'. But certainly in much of the Simple Life to come, the ruralist ventures of the next half century – the agricultural colony at Starnthwaite, for instance, established by H. V. Mills in the early 1890s; such Anarchist communities as Clousden Hill and Norton; the Tolstoyan colonies of the later 1890s at Purleigh in Essex and Whiteway in the Cotswolds; the Arts and Crafts Guild movement, in which Ashbee's role was crucial, right on to Garden Cities and Eric Gill at Ditchling – the spiritual impulses were obviously strong.

It was with a sense of spiritual awakening, gleefully described by Malcolm Muggeridge in the first volume of his autobiography, *The Green Stick,* that a party of his Tolstoyan neighbours from Croydon, most of them clerks, schoolmasters and shop assistants with no experience of fending for themselves under primitive conditions, set out on bicycles, with very little money, to found the communist colony at Whiteway. (They bought the land, but then, with good Back-to-the-Land logic, to demonstrate their hatred of the principle of property, they burned the title deeds in a ceremonial bonfire.) For Ashbee, an old man in 1938, with the exodus from Whitechapel to Campden long behind him, the phrase 'Back-to-the-Land' still had strong reverberations. It was one of the cries of what he called the 'Happy Nineties', remembering the optimism and excitement, almost the intoxication, of the time when escaping to the countryside had seemed so very urgent: 'For those of us living in the East End', recalled Ashbee, 'it had been neither a political tag, nor an agricultural commonplace; it was a matter of necessity, instinct, life.'[1]

One of the main concerns of Simple Life was unravelling the complicated strands of human intercourse, so that human beings, whatever their age, sex, class or education, could communicate freely and directly. This aim, in theory so admirably sensible, in practice of course was very perilous indeed, and no doubt some of the euphoria of the period sprang from the novelty, and the inherent dangers, of many of its social experiments. Lytton Strachey, for instance, in a letter to his mother written from Cambridge in 1903, described the excitement of the atmosphere at King's, where the whole college was 'wracked by the social work and agnosticism question' and the University was being flooded by 'so-called "working-men" ', imported by George Trevelyan for the day and needing entertainment at various meals.[2] Besides the old-established relationships between the scholar and the artisan, the gentleman and tradesman, the Simple Life involved a rethinking of such patterns as master and man, husband and wife, and the sexual relationships of either, and both, sexes. Honest living, as its protagonists discovered, had innumerable pitfalls. But a surprising number persevered.

In the ideal egalitarian community, in which so-called working men were encouraged to read Plato, who did the actual labour? This was a constant puzzle which the people of the Simple Life were called upon to solve. For, inevitably, in a movement whose ancestry was traceable back to Gerrard Winstanley and the Diggers on St George's Hill in Weybridge in the mid-seventeenth century, the element of manual labour could be formidable. The aim of self-sufficiency in healthy rural settings, keeping pace with the harmonious recurrence of the seasons, involved a great deal of simple spadework. The question of who should do the digging, the shovelling and hoeing, the humping and the loading essential to agricultural endeavour, was discussed ad infinitum, often rather heatedly. At Brook Farm, the most famous of the many Simple Life communities founded in the 1840s in America, all tasks were shared out between all members. No distinction was made between manual and intellectual work: both were paid at the same rate. Few people could quarrel with this democratic theory. But, as Nathaniel Hawthorne was to find when he joined Brook Farm, and as many British intellectuals discovered later, a day in the fields could be appallingly hard work, especially to those unused to manual labour. Cultivation of one's market garden left one much too tired for cultivation of the mind. Although the less resilient Oxford and Cambridge farmworkers made a fairly quick retreat from the potato trenches, some grappled with these problems with admirable stamina, and amongst the books once owned by Edward Carpenter, most famous of all English simple lifers, is a touching little pamphlet, much-thumbed and annotated, entitled *Successful Gardening or How to Make £100 a Year on an Acre*. This booklet, which is full of helpful, practical instructions – 'A word here', says the author, 'as to your Dung Heap' – guides the horticultural novice through the routines for each season, and includes substantial sections on Poultry and The Pig.

The Simple Life involved a rethinking of aesthetics, 'the absence of *things*' which Janet Ashbee noted when she went to visit Edward Carpenter at Millthorpe. The plain, uncompromising character of many simple lives of the period was a basic question of necessity: sometimes the Simple Life was a struggle for survival. But it was also, at many different levels of wealth and sensibility, a conscious attempt to clear away encumbrances, the accumulation of meaningless traditions, to free body and spirit for the things in life which mattered. Not so far removed from the undyed wool garments of the citizens of Thomas More's Utopia were the natural clothes of a somewhat self-conscious shapelessness preferred by so many simple lifers. (Edward Carpenter even had a Saxon tunic made for him but, rather to his friends' relief, it seems he did not wear it.) The clothes of Simple Life, the Norfolk jackets and the djibbahs, lasted on for many years as the uniform, if one dare use the word in such non-conformist circles, of progressive public schools.

The country cottage cult, which sprang from Simple Life ideas, had a profound effect on the building and decoration of the period. It owed a lot to William Morris's description in *News from Nowhere* of an imaginary England of the future: an England which is now 'a garden, where nothing is wasted and nothing is spoilt, with the necessary dwellings, sheds and workshops scattered up and down the country, all trim and neat and pretty'. Trimness, prettiness and neatness, for those who could afford it, were ideals to be aimed for, and the belief that buildings should be unpretentious, functional and indigenous to their natural surroundings dominated the work of the homely school of architects, such Simple Life practitioners as Gimson and Voysey, Baillie Scott and Prior. (In the end, with the irony which is so rife in almost every aspect of attempts at simple living, the rural style of building became a kind of cliché, a feature of the suburbs of almost every town.)

The basic character of the Simple Life interior, as it first developed, bore a strong resemblance to that of the Shaker communities in New England at the end of the eighteenth century, with their regulation green painted bedsteads, blue and white bedcovers, ladder-back chairs and simple useful tables. The well-known green stained furniture in clumpy peasant style designed in the 1860s by Ford Madox Brown, and made by Morris Marshall Faulkner & Co., was the precursor of innumerable sets of countrified chairs and beds, oak dressers and oak settles, conscientious furniture for conscientious clients, produced by rural (or quasi-rural) craftsmen. The tradition was continued, with added commercial acumen, by Heal & Son, purveyors of Simple Oak Furniture to Garden City dwellers; and it can indeed be followed through to Habitat pine kitchens c.1969.

Then, as now, the Simple Life idea has always appealed more to the educated classes than the working population who, understandably, have often failed to see the point of it. The country cottage cult was particularly strong amongst intellectual women of the 1890s. For instance, Charlotte Wilson, Girton-educated anarchist and feminist, an aficionado of the style – so much so that many people believed she had invented it – held famous Fabian gatherings in her farmhouse kitchen, a room in which no cooking ever seems to have been done.

Simple Life, of course, in the end got out of hand. As Simple Life manuals came pouring from the publishers, as Schools of Simple Life and Peasant Arts abounded (to Mrs Ashbee's horror, there was even one in Chelsea), the movement exploded in pretences and absurdity. But it was a heroic period while it lasted, and in all its ironies and forlorn hopes, extremely poignant.

It has left a classic figure of modern English literature, Dr Trelawney, the visionary leader of a mysterious progressive sect in Hampshire, in Anthony Powell's *Music of Time*. For me, there is no more evocative or moving epitaph to the Simple Life than the description of Dr Trelawney, at the summit of his powers in the decade of frenzied social experiment before the First World War, leading his disciples, in their artistic clothes made from rough material in pastel colours, with long loping strides through the scrubland around Aldershot.

C. R. Ashbee, though less mystic and alarming, came out of the same mould.

In pursuit of the Simple Life, I have had help and information from innumerable people, amongst whom I should particularly like to thank the following: Edward Barnsley, Shirley Bury, Frank Deakin, William Gaunt, Blaise Gillie, Nina Griggs, Joan Hague, Henry Hart, Robin Holland-Martin, Ray Leigh, W. E. A. Lewis, Meg Nason, Joseph Nuttgens, Dr Patrick Nuttgens, Dr Janet Roscoe, Sir Gordon Russell, Robert Welch.

I am especially indebted to Felicity Ashbee for her constant interest and encouragement, as well as for permission to quote from the so far unpublished *Ashbee Journals*; and also to Alan Crawford, who has been extremely generous in sharing the results of his own research on C. R. Ashbee's life and work.

1

From Whitechapel to Camelot
1888 to 1901

In the spring of 1902, when the Back-to-the-Land movement was at its height, an exodus began to Chipping Campden in the Cotswolds. It was an exodus of East End London tradesmen – jewellers, silversmiths, enamellers, printers, carvers, modellers, blacksmiths, cabinet-makers, polishers and gilders – escaping from the rushed and crowded life of the big city to a simple rural idyll of craftsmanship and husbandry which was, at the time, many good socialists' dream. This extraordinary idealistic movement was to have a lasting impact not only on the lives of the 150 London immigrants, the men, women and children of the Guild of Handicraft, and their leader, the architect, Charles Robert Ashbee, but also on the nature of the little town they came to. At Campden, things could never be at all the same again.

The Guild had first been formed fourteen years earlier, in Whitechapel. Ashbee at that time was only 25. As well as being a promising architect-designer, he was also an intense idealist and activist, the product of an era in which many of the children of the prosperous well-settled middle classes underwent a quite dramatic *crise de conscience* and, mustering the qualities of courage and efficiency which would otherwise have fitted them for army, church or Empire, channelled all their energies in a different direction: into improving the conditions of the poor.

Ashbee's early life provides an excellent case history of this peculiarly British mid-Victorian phenomenon. He came from a rich, successful bourgeois family. His mother was a Hamburg Jewess, daughter of a merchant of considerable substance, and his father, Henry Spencer Ashbee, businessman and bibliophile, was senior partner in the London branch of his father-in-law's firm. The family lived a life of discreet luxury in Upper Bedford Place in Bloomsbury, and Charles, the only son, was sent to Wellington, a school which did not suit him and from which he emerged apathetic and uncertain.

His father, it appears, was determined he should join the family exporting business, Charles Lavy & Co. But he much disliked this prospect, and instead, encouraged by his mother, applied to go to Cambridge. Though his father, according to the legend in the family, gave him £1000 and from then on washed his hands of him, he never had much reason for regretting his decision. For his time at Cambridge was in some ways his salvation, providing the basis for his whole life's work to come.

At Cambridge, in the 1880s, came conversion, a total change of outlook, an almost religious fervour. Life at King's swept over him, as it was to engulf E. M. Forster (1) ten years later, after much the same bewildered misery at public school. He was fortunate to find a group of friends almost immediately who shared his intellectual enthusiasms and encouraged his sense of social commitment. Among them was James Headlam, later well known as James Headlam-Morley, the diplomatic historian; Arthur Berry, mathematician, who became Secretary of the

(1) E. M. Forster, the novelist, arrived at King's from Tonbridge in 1897. In 1946, the college made him an Honorary Fellow, and he lived there till he died at the age of 91.

(2) Goldsworthy Lowes Dickinson (1862–1932), humanist, historian, pacifist and Hellenist, author of *The Greek View of Life*, *A Modern Symposium* and so on. He embodied for Ashbee 'the ultimate and perfect type of friendship – the friend always at hand, from whom nothing is hid' – until the day he died. His aesthetic appreciation, however, was never quite up to Ashbee's standard: faced with the works of Steer, for instance, he said in desperation 'One can only hold one's tongue and pray about it'.

(3) Roger Fry (1866–1934), art critic and artist. At Cambridge, he and Ashbee had one of those passionate romantic friendships indigenous to King's. But their attachment faded out in later life. The last time they met was

at Lowes Dickinson's funeral when both were in their late sixties. Though Ashbee had hoped for a significant reunion, it proved an uncomfortable occasion: 'It was too hard for both of us', he wrote later: 'it is the peak moments of life one ever wants to recapture'. (*Ashbee Journals*, 1934)

(4) Edward Carpenter (1844–1929), poet, prophet, market gardener and sandal-maker. Unflagging champion of the working classes and courageous protagonist for homosexual love.

(5) Not that F. D. Maurice (1805–72) was in many respects an ordinary clergyman. He was leader of the Christian Socialist faction, and his views were very radical. He was particularly concerned with education; he founded Queen's College in Harley Street, in order to give proper education to governesses, and was instigator of the Working Men's College, set up for the improvement of the artisan.

Cambridge University Extension and then Vice-Provost of King's; and Arthur Laurie, son of the Professor of Education in Edinburgh, who was to espouse the cause of Henry George. At King's, Ashbee found extraordinary liberation: here were people, at last, whom he could talk to. Well into the night, he discussed eternal verities, ethics, truth and beauty. He read Plato, he read Ruskin and began developing his tastes in art and architecture. These were to become two ruling passions.

The greatest of his friends among his King's contemporaries were, first, Goldsworthy Lowes Dickinson (2) and later Roger Fry (3). Lowes Dickinson described Ashbee in 1884, when he had finished his first year at Cambridge, as 'a long youth, enthusiastic, opinionated',[1] recollecting that he started a society for discussion, which was to spread throughout the world, and which in fact collapsed after his first term. (He also impressed Dickinson by making a hole in one of the college eights by leaping over-optimistically into it. This incident, too, had its many parallels later on in Ashbee's life.)

It was while he was at Cambridge that he first met Edward Carpenter (4). Of all the people who influenced his way of thinking, Edward Carpenter was by far the most important. Ashbee's tendency to hero-worship, always quite acute, was at its most intense in relation to Carpenter, who was of an age to be a father figure to him. When they met, Edward Carpenter was in his early forties. His background was prosperous, like Ashbee's, with strong naval connections; his father was a naval officer, his grandfather had even been an admiral. He, too, had been to Cambridge; he had taken orders and been curate to F. D. Maurice (5) in London. But then his life had altered very startlingly. It happened on a certain memorable journey back from Cannes, as Carpenter recounts it in his memoirs: 'it suddenly flashed upon me, with a vibration through my whole body, that I would and must somehow go and make my life with the mass of the people and the manual workers.'[2]

This mysterious vibration had sent him north to Sheffield. He had given his dress clothes away – an act of some significance, marked by italics in Carpenter's account of it – and determinedly made friends with Sheffield railway-men and porters, clerks, signalmen, ironworkers and coach-builders, not forgetting Sheffield cutlers. He claims to have felt at home with them immediately; it seemed he had arrived at, or at least got within sight of, the world which he belonged to, his natural habitat. Carpenter's new-found eagerness for sharing in the manual labour of the world, which surely must have seemed a most peculiar aberration to those who had been manual labourers for years, prompted him to buy himself three fields at Millthorpe, a small village in Derbyshire, not far from Sheffield, and to throw himself into a full programme of hard labour, working for hours and whole days together out in the open field or garden. He describes himself digging drains with pick and shovel, and much of his time seems to have been spent driving carts along the roads of Derbyshire: going to the coalpit to fetch coal, travelling to Chesterfield to load manure, and setting off for Sheffield market at six in the morning with fruit and vegetables which he sold at his own stall. This exhausting routine was subsequently modified, since it left no time and still less energy for writing, but Carpenter never lost his belief that a moderate amount of manual labour is essential for human self-respect.

As well as market-gardening he embarked on making sandals. The design for these was based on a pair of Indian sandals which Harold Cox (6), another Carpenter disciple, had sent him from Cashmere. Carpenter had enjoyed wearing them, striding down the Derbyshire lanes in his new sandals with a feeling of elation at having freed his feet from the tyranny of shoe-leather, and after taking lessons from a boot-maker in Sheffield, he got quite good at making Indian-style sandals for friends and friends of friends. From then on indeed sandals became an essential feature of the life of the intelligentsia in England, worn alike by high-thinking men and women (7), symbolizing liberal thought and rational pleasures.

When Ashbee first met Carpenter, he was in the centre of a ferment of activity, a leading figure in the multitude of movements for reform which were getting under way in the early 1880s. As one of the founding

(6) Harold Cox (1859–1936). A man of extremes. Soon after leaving Cambridge as senior optime in the Mathematical Tripos, he went to work as an agricultural labourer, setting up a co-operative farm in Surrey, where, as Bernard Shaw reported, his only successful crop was radishes, which he made into jam.

Cox began life as a Liberal and radical, friend of Sidney Webb and secretary of the Cobden Club, but changed his mind completely and in middle age became violently anti-Socialist and anti-liberal.

(7) Evelyn Sharpe (b. 1903, leading Civil Servant, later Baroness of Hornsey) was a typical customer of Carpenter's: 'I read Edward Carpenter's books when I was young; I wore his sandals on my summer holidays, waiting months for them while he made them with his own hands'. (Edward Carpenter: *In Appreciation*, ed. Gilbert Beith, George Allen & Unwin, 1931)

(8) Precursor of the (less eccentric) Fabian Society.

members of the Fellowship of the New Life (8), he was much concerned not just with the idea of universal manual labour but also with the need for humane diet and rational dress, democratic ideals and communal institutions. As one of the main propagandists for the Simple Life, he had links with a great many of the groups of early Socialists and Anarchists, Feminists and Suffragists, Humanists and Naturalists, Sexologists, Theosophists and Psychical Researchers, which were burgeoning just then. (When Goldsworthy Lowes Dickinson once asked him rather anxiously how he related mysticism to Socialism he replied he liked to hang out his red flag from the ground floor and then go up above to see how it looked.[3])

In 1886, Ashbee had gone with Lowes Dickinson to hear Carpenter lecture at the Hammersmith Branch of the Socialist League. This was the group which William Morris formed after he resigned from the Social Democratic Federation, and the meeting took place in the little hall converted from a coach-house alongside William Morris's own house in Hammersmith. After the lecture, which was on 'Private Property', they had been asked to supper at Morris's long table, for further revolutionary talk. The infectious excitement of the evening was graphically described by Ashbee. Lowes Dickinson, he said, drew Morris out on the first principles of Socialism, and a splendid conversation followed across the table, with the others all listening intently and now and then putting in a word:

Old Morris was delightful, firing up with the warmth of his subject, all the enthusiasm of youth thrilling through veins and muscles; not a moment was he still, but ever sought to vent some of his immense energy. At length banging his hand upon the table: 'No' said he, 'the thing is this, if we had our Revolution tomorrow, what should we Socialists do the day after?' 'Yes, what?' we all cried. And that the old man could not answer: 'We should all be hanged because we are promising the people more than we can give them!'[4]

Still discussing revolution, the two young men walked back across the park to Goodge Street with Bernard Shaw, a Socialist supporter who had also been to supper with the Morrises. Neither of them knew him, but Lowes Dickinson described him as the wittiest and most brilliant talker he had ever met.[5]

For Ashbee, all his life, Carpenter stood for all that he loved most about those early days at Cambridge. His sudden urgent sense of all life's opportunities. His new perception of the joys of love and friendship: reading the *Phaedo* with Goldsworthy Lowes Dickinson and communing with eternity; wandering with Roger Fry along the Backs by moonlight, quoting verses from Walt Whitman (9) and feeling that the highest spiritual communion between man and man is that between friend and friend. This highly emotional attitude to friendship, the man to man relationship, was very much a part of Edward Carpenter's philosophy. The idea of Comradeship, not as a substitute but as a viable alternative to marriage, was propounded in many of his writings: in *Narcissus and other Poems,* his first collection, and in his vast tone-poem *Towards Democracy.* This was in progress while Ashbee was at Cambridge. In *Towards Democracy,* a thundering denouncement of the conditions of the British working classes and a plea for a return to the simple rural life, he glorified the somewhat unsuspecting figure of the unsophisticated British workman – from thick-thighed young bricklayers to oily, grimy stokers – and put forward the intoxicating theory that it was with the young working men of Britain, splendid in body and also pure in spirit, that hope for England's regeneration lay.

Carpenter had an unusually persuasive manner. As even *The Times* obituary put it, 'He was well-served, as he himself used smilingly to admit, by his aptitude for propounding dangerous themes with a suavity that had a reassuring effect'.[6] (Such was his aura of respectability that, as a young man, Queen Alexandra had summoned him to Windsor to interview him as prospective tutor to her two sons, the Duke of Clarence and Prince George, who later became King George V: fortunately, perhaps, the post did not materialize.) Carpenter's views on the need to break down the barriers of class, and get truly in touch with working people, made a profound impression on Ashbee. Carpenter came to stay with him at King's in 1886, and he wrote in his diary:

After supper we had a delightful walk through the green cornfields in the afterglow. He unfolded to me a wonderful idea of his of a new free-masonry, a comradeship in the life of men which might be based on our little Cambridge circle of friendships. Are we to be the nucleus out of which the new Society is to be organized?[7]

Carpenter's alluring vision of a new civilization, built by such a band of comrades, also much affected Ashbee's closest friends, Roger Fry and Goldsworthy Lowes Dickinson. They shared Ashbee's admiration for Carpenter. ' "It is a joy" said Goldy', (the three of them were standing dreaming on St John's Bridge one evening in the sunset) ' "to think

(9) Whitman's *Starting from Paumanok,* especially the last stanza, 'O camerado close !', was a constant inspiration to Carpenter and friends.

that such a man exists – that he is not in a novel".'[8] They all, at various times, went to stay with him at Millthorpe and Goldsworthy Lowes Dickinson became, for one hard summer, an agricultural labourer, hoeing, digging and ploughing till his back ached on Harold Cox's experimental farm near Farnham. (The place was called Craig Farm, but so appalling did he find it, it appears as Crankie Farm in the book he wrote about it.) Even Fry, temperamentally the least susceptible of the three friends to the Carpenter charisma, was soon describing Edward Carpenter as quite one of the best men he had ever met.

How to reconcile the freedom and culture of life as lived in Cambridge with self-supporting labour: 'that is the question which vexes me', wrote Edward Carpenter to Ashbee in 1886.[9] It was a conundrum which vexed Ashbee greatly too, and which was indeed to worry the more intellectual factions of British socialism for many years to come. Ashbee's first attempt to solve it, after he left Cambridge, was to go and live in Whitechapel. He had made up his mind to be an architect, and while he did his training went to live at Toynbee Hall, the pioneer East London settlement founded by the famous social reformer, the Reverend Samuel Barnett, 11 years before.

'The tide of fashionable philanthropy', as Ashbee was later to describe it, 'was then at its height.'[10] Toynbee Hall was thronging with titled people, politicians, cabinet ministers, eminent artists, university professors, bishops and relatively humble sightseers from the provinces, eager participants in the salvation of the poor. These visitors, many of whom would keep their carriages waiting in the slums outside, went home after dinner to more salubrious surroundings. But there was a nucleus of young university graduates in residence, which Ashbee was to join.

They were earnest young men, anxiously preoccupied with the iniquities of a society which countenanced the spending of £2,500 on the Lord Mayor's Banquet, £400 of which was for the turtle soup alone, when the unemployed were starving. The reformers all had their own ideas of how to change things. Ashbee's first move was to found a Ruskin reading class. A contemporary drawing shows Ashbee interpreting Ruskin's *Crown of Olives* to a group of young East End workmen in an attic room in Whitechapel.

Ashbee, full of Edward Carpenter's injunctions to get to know the people, came to London intent on coming face to face with proletarians, although at first the British Working Man, referred to in his Journal by the code-name 'B.W.M.', very much alarmed him. However, soon, after some valiant forays to such B.W.M. strongholds as West Ham and

Deptford, giving lectures on Ruskin, he began to find his feet and grow in confidence. 'I felt myself getting nearer to these men and beginning to understand the Whitmanic position', he wrote only a few weeks after he arrived in London: 'Ruskin is little known, but immensely appreciated, and they enjoyed the fiery humour of "Fors" (10) . . . but where I have to differ with any of them I held my own, and the "B.W.M." is no more a terror for me.'[11]

The Ruskin class in Whitechapel in fact was the beginning of the Guild of Handicraft. 'Ruskin', as Ashbee very soon reported in a letter to his friend Roger Fry, 'goes down like anything.'[12] Ashbee's handful of pupils found the works of Ruskin so immediately inspiring that the reading class led to a practical experiment, and a small class developed for the study of design. Soon there were thirty men and boys involved in painting, modelling, plastercasting, gilding, all enthusiastically bringing to fruition a characteristic Arts and Crafts creation: a round decorative panel, depicting a large galleon, for the Dining Room at Toynbee Hall. This Guild craft, alias this ship of skill (for Ashbee had a passion for a double meaning), became a kind of symbol for the Guild as it set sail.

Guilds of handicraft proliferated in the late nineteenth century. Some, like Ashbee's Guild in Whitechapel, were relatively large and professional in standard, some were very small-scale, some were hopelessly inept. They were very much the symptom of their time, the thinking person's protest in an age of increasing mass-production and a worsening environment. The Guilds looked back, with varying degrees of sense and eccentricity, to better days before industrialization when craftsmen took pride in their work and found joy from it. Ruskin's own Guild of St George was set up in the 1870s to carry out on English ground 'those laws and methods of life fully known, tried and already carried out at Venice, Florence and other great cities at the time of their best life'.[13] (This particular experiment, a curious amalgam of shoemaking and farming, was less than a success.) There were many Guilds to follow: Guilds from Birmingham to Bristol, Edinburgh to Barnstaple, working ladies' guilds and peasant arts societies, all of them, to a greater or lesser extent, founded to establish a better way of working and in many cases also a whole new way of living.

There was then a feeling current – an idea which was to surface again

(10) *Fors Clavigera*, Ruskin's rousing series of monthly epistles to the workmen and labourers of Great Britain.

and again, and is indeed still with us – that men were out of tune with their surroundings. Industrialization had destroyed all creativity. Division of labour took away responsibility. Capitalism, the tyrannical 'cash nexus', had a terrible effect on the British workman's soul. These were theories strongly voiced by both Carlyle and Ruskin. As a young man still at Oxford, William Morris read Ruskin's *Stones of Venice* and realized that this was the new road on which the world should travel. His monumental energies from then on were directed to the betterment of life through revival of the handicrafts. From Morris's convictions, from his lectures and his writings and the many crafts he practised, sprang the whole of the Arts and Crafts movement and the Guilds.

Ashbee's Guild of Handicraft, which like other guilds reflected the particular ideals and predilections of its founder, was based on both the mediaeval guilds of England and the craft guilds of the Italian Renaissance. An additional element, which set Ashbee's Guild apart from the many less flamboyant followers of William Morris, was its dependence on the theories of Carpenter: his yen for simple useful things produced by honest toil; his hope that British working man could build a new society; most of all, his burning faith in the reforming zeal of comradeship. Ashbee's own homosexual instincts made him especially receptive to Carpenter's prophetic view of homosexuality, which he expounded on all possible occasions, much to the confusion of his more conventional Socialist colleagues who saw the whole thing as an embarrassing red herring trailed in the path of democracy. Carpenter's belief in 'homogenic love', a mystic condition in which the sexual urges were to be transformed into the purer love of comrades working together in the common cause, needless to say appealed very much to Ashbee. To some extent at least, he shared Carpenter's strange vision of homogenic love as 'the basis or at least one of the motors of social reconstruction'.[14] Though Ashbee, perhaps wisely, did not say too much about it in the vicinity of Toynbee Hall and Mile End Road, homogenic love was an important element in his early plans for the formation of the Guild. Some Guildsmen were identified as more obviously 'homogenic' than others, by which he seemed to mean more responsive to the friendship and support of other men, a link in the ever-growing chain of comradeship. These were the men in whom he put his highest hopes.

Whether or not they saw themselves as furthering the cause of Comradeship, the Guild had the support of many of the major artists and designers of the time: for instance, Burne-Jones (11), Holman Hunt (12), and Alma Tadema. Hubert von Herkomer, on reading the Guild circular, wrote hearteningly to Ashbee, telling him to try it (although going on to say 'It reads a little too idyllic, and I should take objection to your anxiety to save all the lost geniuses in East London.')[15] Walter Crane and Lewis F. Day were both encouraging; Mackmurdo, who had founded his own more dilettante Century Guild four years before, wrote to say 'I am delighted your experiment is progressing . . . This is worth all our wordy theories'.[16] William Blake Richmond, well-known painter and designer, responded with enthusiasm to an invitation from Ashbee to come to Mile End Road and lecture to the Guildsmen: 'I will come and speak to your people from the bottom of my heart.'[17] Only William Morris, when Ashbee went to see him, threw 'a great deal of cold water' on the scheme, but this is not perhaps surprising because Morris, by then ageing, had come to believe in revolution or nothing, and may too have felt some natural antagonism towards a young enthusiast proposing to put so many of his own precepts to a practical test.[18] Ashbee was not deterred by Morris's discouragement. With his characteristic resilience, a quality which stood him in good stead throughout the history of the Guild, he pushed the

(11) Ashbee lunched with Burne-Jones and his daughter Margaret to discuss Whitechapel plans. It was a picturesque occasion: 'He sitting stately at the head of his table, in blue and silver-grey beard peaked Velasquez-like, with blue shirt Morris-like, and silver studs and amethyst set in silver . . . She fairy-like, very lovely . . . sort of all frizzy in white muslin, and hair harmonious.' (*Ashbee Memoirs*, July 1887)

(12) Holman Hunt was an early patron of the Guild. Ashbee admired him but found him rather daunting: 'No man ever seemed to me so much the man of genius, but yet he is just like his pictures, parenthetical, dwelling in minute or beautiful detail, speaking in a weird and dreamy way'. (*Ashbee Memoirs*, July 1887)

(13) Barnett was himself a man of great determination, as was shown by Mrs Barnett in her biography of her husband: 'so wholly was his mind under control that on one occasion when I was so ill that death seemed imminent, in spite of his deep love and agony of anxiety, he surprised the nurses and astounded my sister by steadily reading *Ivanhoe*'.

(14) Only two (Nos. 38 and 39) remain today. Nos. 71 to 75, a group which included the house Ashbee designed for himself and his wife on his marriage, were destroyed by a parachute mine in 1941. No.37, the Magpie and Stump, which was probably Ashbee's most innovatory and interesting building, designed for his mother and also used as his own office, was demolished by Wates in 1969.

inauguration plans on rapidly, and the Guild with its attendant School of Handicraft was opened formally in 1888.

Ashbee's Guild was more ambitious than many guilds to come. From the start, there was a special emphasis on education. The interdependence of the Guild and School, with the Guildsmen doing the teaching and the pupils being gradually absorbed into the Guild, was an essential part of Ashbee's scheme. The idea that training in art and design should be carried on alongside actual production became so well known it almost turned into a truism, but at that time it was fairly revolutionary.

Ashbee's Guild was also especially enterprising, one could almost say intrepid, in the range of handicrafts it undertook. The Guild soon severed its Toynbee Hall connections – Ashbee being pathologically unsuited to answering to committees, let alone the Reverend Samuel Barnett (13) – and, in 1891, moved into its own workshops in Essex House in Mile End Road. Here its activities multiplied rapidly. By the end of the century, Guild craftsmen were working in copper, brass and iron; making silver and jewellery, some of it enamelled; cabinet-making, modelling and carving, and carrying out whole restoration and decoration schemes. In 1898, after William Morris's death, Ashbee took over Morris's famous Kelmscott presses, with most of Morris's printers, and set up his own Essex House Press in Whitechapel. By then the reputation of the Guild was very high.

Ashbee's own work as an architect had been developing concurrently. His life at this time was almost breathlessly progressive. Indeed much of it seems to have been spent bicycling between Whitechapel and Chelsea, where he had his architectural office. His practice was apparently typically high-handed: 'He would not deign to call upon his clients', wrote Phoebe Haydon, his ever-faithful secretary, 'they had to come humbly to him, Earl Beauchamp, the Countess of Lovelace, Mrs Holman Hunt, Mrs Godlee, Hugh Spottiswoode'.[19] Maybe his clients were impressed with Ashbee's nonchalance, thinking it the sign of the real true artist-architect. In any case, they came. His practice was not large but rarefied and rather intellectual. He designed new buildings, most notably a collection of town houses in Cheyne Walk in Chelsea (14), and he also specialized in restoration. From the point of view of the fortunes of the Guild, the practice was of course a considerable blessing, since all possible work on Ashbee's buildings – fixtures and fittings, decorations and furniture – was sent to Mile End Road.

Work came in to the Guild from many sources. From other architects, especially those who had worked as Ashbee had in G. F.

Bodley's (15) office. From artists in sympathy with the ideas of the Arts and Crafts movement: for instance, the Guild made the original repoussé copper frame for Holman Hunt's painting 'May Morning on Magdalen Tower', and G. F. Watts commissioned a small suit of armour to assist him with the figure of the Knight in 'The Court of Death'. The Guild had built up a considerable mailing list of private customers, friends, relations, craft-conscious individuals, many of whom bought Guild work fairly regularly from the Essex House showroom or, later, from the shop which the Guild opened in 1899 at 16A Brook Street, on the corner of Bond Street. The Guild exhibited in London and abroad; articles about the Guild and pictures of Guild work began to appear often in *The Studio, Art Journal, Art Workers' Quarterly* and in their foreign counterparts, those artistic magazines which deluged down on Europe in the 1890s. These, too, brought in commissions, and in 1898 the Guild was asked to make the massive collection of furniture and metalwork which Baillie Scott designed for the Grand Duke of Hesse's Palace at Darmstadt. This important job was very good for Guild prestige, but a visit to Whitechapel by the royal clients in full pomp, with courtiers and 'Gold Sticks in Waiting' in attendance – as Ashbee described it, a real scene from Lewis Carroll – left the Guild apprentices, who were well indoctrinated with democratic principles, extremely unimpressed.

It was one of the continuous ironies of this and other comparable socialist endeavours that, democratic as they were in outlook, their prosperity, even their existence, was dependent on the whims of the rich. Ashbee recognized this: once, when asked to make a necklace costing £200 or £300, he remarked that it seemed wasteful to spend

(15) G. F. Bodley (1827–1907), great Victorian Gothic architect and one of the first patrons of Morris & Co. He was one of those men who believed in proper *structure*: 'A wall', he once said, 'that is not a good wall is not worth painting'. Ashbee joined him as a pupil in 1886, working alongside the 'gentle and pious' Ninian Comper (1864–1960, later Sir Ninian), the well-known church architect, whose main preoccupations even then were saints and clergymen and whose speciality was drawing angels.

(16) For instance, Arthur Cameron, soon after his election, was court-martialled by his fellow-Guildsmen for 'foul talk' and had his Guild membership suspended, although he was still allowed to work in the Guild workshops. After a year, his case was reconsidered and he was re-elected to the Guild.

the price of a pleasant small house on just one necklace. But it was a fact of life with which he seemed to come to terms. His customers and clients, with a very few exceptions, did not really interest him, but he managed to put up with them, saving his energies for the work he really cared about: the building of the Guild into a strong community with a life and social purpose of its own.

The Guildsmen had been recruited very much at random. Ashbee, with his distrust of principles of trade and commerce, was naturally wary of craftsmen with a trade background, and in the early days at least, hardly any of the craftsmen had had conventional training. Will Hardiman, one of the first of Ashbee's silversmiths, was rescued from a cat's meat barrow in Whitechapel. The history of W. A. White, another early metalworker, though not so lurid, was scarcely more distinguished: he was working in a cheap bookshop in the City when he came to Ashbee's class at Toynbee Hall. Ashbee had always been prepared to back his hunches. Ned West, for instance, an apprentice taken on in 1898, had had few recommendations; his drawing showed little promise, his mother was a terror, his family associations were unfortunate, 'and altogether', as Ashbee admitted later, 'the choice was most unwise'.[20] But he liked the boy's face, and this was enough for Ashbee. To him, the impression of sincerity was everything. His ideal method of selection (and who has found one better?) was to grasp the man's hand to see what mettle he was made of, simultaneously gazing searchingly into his eyes.

To Ashbee, each individual craftsman was important. This was the whole basis of the Guild, its raison d'être. Ashbee saw his task (sometimes easier said than done) as freeing the creative instincts of the craftsman, eliciting his potential talent, and encouraging him to design as well as making. The making of the object and the making of the man went together, as he frequently explained to anyone who cared to listen. The craftsman should set his own individual standard; the workshop should set a standard in society. Not all the craftsmen working at the Guild were Guildsmen, but after a specified period of service they became eligible for election. The Guildsmen were jointly responsible for policy, to the extent of disciplining their own members (16), and a small proportion of every Guildsman's wages was invested in the Guild. After the Guild became a Limited Company in 1898, a labour director was elected annually by the Guildsmen. Ashbee claimed this as the first example of official representation of labour on the Board of a registered company, insisting that these small steps towards self-government were of utmost importance to society at large.

In the life of the Guild of Handicraft, there was great emphasis on corporate activities. Believing that the work was less important than the workman, convinced too that the best craftsmen were also the best citizens, Ashbee put enormous efforts into an intensive programme of leisure-hour activities. The life-style of the Guild, as it gradually developed, was an extraordinary amalgam of Ashbee's own tastes and preoccupations; partly English mediaeval, partly Elizabethan, with elements of Cambridge and the British public school.

The craftsmen listened to Guild lectures: Alma Tadema on *Sculpture*, William Morris on *Gothic Architecture* (17), W. B. Richmond on *The Dignity of Handicrafts*. Edmund Gosse and Kegan Paul, Walter Crane and Holman Hunt all came to talk in Whitechapel within the first few years. Regularly, the craftsmen held convivial Guild suppers. Led by Ashbee, they sang folk-songs and catches, and acted in Guild masques. They formed a Guild cricket team: the Essex House XI. Some even wore a special Sports Club uniform, a resplendent combination of scarlet scarves and blazers embroidered with white pinks. The white pink, which grew profusely in the garden at Essex House, was taken as the emblem of the Guild.

The life of the Guild, which had been uncompromisingly masculine, altered when in 1898 Ashbee got married. His young wife Janet came from Sevenoaks in Kent. Ashbee was always scornful about Janet's antecedents, but this was silly of him: they were very like his own. Janet's father, F. A. Forbes, was a cultivated stockbroker and her mother, who was Scottish, had been brought up in St Petersburg. It was a comfortable background, cosmopolitan and musical, perhaps a bit complacent, but this did not prevent Janet from understanding and embracing, almost as if by instinct, the ideas of the Guild.

In the context of the ever-growing chain of Comradeship, one may well ask how Ashbee ever managed to get married. But he did not see the two things as irreconcileable. He wrote to Janet with rather

(17) William Morris apparently found the technicalities of lecturing with slides a little nerve-wracking. See his letter to Ashbee in 1889: 'By the way you must understand I know nothing about such things so I hope you will get someone to help me. I will come (and thanks) to dinner: but I must certainly be on the spot before the lecture begins so as to arrange properly'.

(18) In fact, the only one of these relationships which hurt her was Ashbee's only known overtly physical affair with Chris, a young soldier. This was much later, just before the First World War.

touching honesty shortly before their marriage explaining how his love
for his men and boy friends had up to now been the guiding principle
in life. 'Some women', he said 'would take this and perhaps rightly as
a sign of coldness to their sex, and they would shrink from a man who
revealed himself thus, and fear a division of affections. That depends
upon the woman. I have no fear that you will misunderstand and
thus, not fearing, feel that it were almost superfluous for me to tell you
that you are the first and only woman to whom I have felt that I could
offer the same loyal reverence of affection that I have heretofore given to
my men friends. Will not the inference be obvious to you? There may
be many comrade friends, there can only be one comrade wife.'[21] He
had certainly chosen well with Janet. The inference did in point of fact
seem fairly clear to her, at least at the beginning of the marriage, and she
gladly accepted her role as the chief comrade, taking all the rest of the
comrades in her stride. This was partly, one might say, a kind of naïve
hopefulness: Janet, after all, was only 19 when she married. She had a
particularly literal nature and so long as Ashbee's love for them was
spiritual not physical, perhaps she did not see the comrades as a
threat (18).

Right from the beginning, when the Guild men and boys had been
asked down to Kent for Ashbee's wedding, no doubt causing consternation to the Forbes's well-heeled neighbours, Janet had been
immersed in Guild life and Guild concerns. The Ashbees spent their
wedding night at Essex House, and after they had moved into the house
in Cheyne Walk, built needless to say to the bridegroom's own design,
which Janet's father gave them as a wedding present, Janet paid a
regular visit each mid-week to the Guild in Whitechapel, where she
busied herself calling on the Guildsmen's wives and organizing sewing
parties, eating pies and raisin puddings at the Guildsmen's Wednesday
suppers and joining in the sing-songs, wandering around the workshops to learn the craft techniques, transcribing the translation
and proofing the pages for the Essex House edition of Cellini, contributing to all the Guild activities and plans.

From the time of Ashbee's marriage, the Journal he had kept
throughout his adult life – a somewhat erratic record of events, interspersed with reflections on Art and Life and Friendship – became a
combined enterprise. Janet's succinct manner of expression and her
sharper powers of observation much improved the Journal, counter-
balancing her husband's rather ponderous excursions. (Janet complained, not totally unfairly, that he sounded as if he wrote through
cotton wool.)

Janet was also the author of *The Essex House Alphabet*, a considerable tour de force incorporating all the Guild craftsmen and apprentices from A to W, from Arthur Cameron to W. A. White. Its consistent tone of affectionate banter reflects endearingly the spirit of the workshops and the Ashbees' own relationship with the Guild craftsmen. It begins:

A stands for Arthur the Cameron (19) bold,
Our great Cockney Craftsman in silver and gold,
With his hair and his eyes and his gestures and shape
He is just chuka-chuka the Music Hall Ape!

A's also for Alfred (20), our gay Volunteer,
(The effects of whose drilling do not yet appear);
From his great curly fringe to his long curly toes
He's the wild Man of Poplar, as every one knows.

B is for Bray (21), the young Cabinet maker,
The sweetest, demurest, most obstinate Quaker;
If you saw him at work through his window turned South
You would hardly think Butter would melt in his mouth.

B's also for Binning (22) our old Kelmscott Comp,
Who tells you of Morris with awe and with pomp;
Suggest anything new, and it's 20 to 1
He'll answer you gravely: It cannot be done.[22]

It was not long before Arthur and Alfred, Bray and Binning, Cyril Kelsey, Charley Downer and the rest of the Guild craftsmen were involved in the most ambitious project in Guild history: the scheme to move the whole Guild away from Whitechapel. Possibly the idea of the exodus from London had always been in the back of Ashbee's mind. At any rate, like Ruskin, he had always maintained passionately that good craftsmanship can only spring from good and healthy life. Whitechapel was far from an ideal environment. This was obvious to Ashbee, and even if it had not been, a letter he received back in 1888 from the pugnacious Canon Rawnsley (23), champion of the British countryside, could have left him in no doubt. The Canon, writing from the pure keen atmosphere of Keswick (where he had recently founded his own School of Industrial Arts on behalf of unemployed Lake District boatmen), said to Ashbee 'I wish you would start your classes anywhere but in Hell', explaining his view that the Art of clean living and pure breathing must precede the Art of decorating.[23] This was a view which Ashbee in the main accepted. Although in the early years he was preoccupied with getting the Guild going where its market was, in London, he rented a succession of country cottages for the Guild to use for communal weekends and holidays. Then, in 1901, when the lease of Essex House was coming to an end, he set about looking seriously for a new and much more rural base of operations. 'Good honest craftsmanship', wrote Ashbee, 'is better done the nearer people get into touch with the elemental things of life.'[24]

The choice of Chipping Campden was not an accidental one. In his search for the ideal country setting for the Guild, Ashbee looked systematically at 30 far-flung districts, considering such promising possibilities as Letchworth; the water mill at Sawbridge in Kent; and the deserted silk mill at Blockley, close to Campden, a building which William Morris too had contemplated over 20 years before, in the early 1880s, before he moved his textile works to Merton Abbey. The advantages of Campden for the Guild of Handicraft were pointed out by Robert Martin Holland (24), then a young director of Martin's Bank, a friend of Ashbee's and a firm supporter of his aims. His family

(19) Arthur Cameron, metalworker. Originally employed as Ashbee's office boy, but promoted to the workshops in 1891, becoming one of the most proficient of the Guild apprentices. His nickname, Chuka-Chuka, earned by his somewhat grotesque appearance, apparently embarrassed him, especially after his marriage, and he tried to persuade the Guildsmen not to use it.

(20) Alfred Pilkington, joinery apprentice, a fine fellow though, according to Janet, a maddening tease. He left the Guild in 1900 to join the Army in South Africa.

(21) Bray, the Cabinet maker, was elected a Guildsman in 1899 and served seven years.

(22) Thomas Binning, once William Morris's foreman compositor. Traditional socialist and aggressive trade unionist who, as father of the chapel, had forced the London Society of Compositors to accept their first woman member, Mrs Pine.

(23) Canon Rawnsley (1851–1920). Vicar of Crosthwaite, near Keswick, and a Canon of Carlisle. Muscular Christian and inveterate crusader. Notoriously lacking in patience and humility. Once when returning to the Lake District, his train missed its connection. The other passengers were resigned to waiting for the next train, but not Rawnsley. He fetched the station master who immediately put a special train at his disposal. He also managed to write 37 books.

lived nearby; he knew the district well, and saw how it would suit the Guild endeavour. His arguments seem to have soon won Ashbee over. The claims of Letchworth, Sawbridge and Blockley were forgotten. Campden was to be the Guild's new City of the Sun (25).

Campden seemed the ideal place, for two important reasons. It had practical advantages: the small town, which at the height of the wool trade had been prosperous, even boasting its own mayor and corporation, had now very much declined; there were houses lying empty, ready for the Guild to occupy; there was also an old silk mill, suitable to be converted into the Guild workshops. Campden's other leading virtue, which perhaps appealed to Ashbee, arch-romantic as he was, still more strongly than the prospect of low rents and empty houses, was its symbolic fitness: in spirit, Chipping Campden was as far from Mile End Road as it was possible to be. For Ashbee, who saw life in high chivalric terms, as a quest or a crusade, the possibility of settling his Guild of Handicraft in this unspoilt mediaeval wool town must have seemed impossibly alluring. He had written a romance for the Guild apprentices, a tale of high endeavour called *From Whitechapel to Camelot*. Now it seemed he could translate romance into reality: Whitechapel was still Whitechapel, and Camelot was Campden.

Whitechapel at that time, perhaps unfairly, was a byword for poverty and decadence. 'When the foreigner asks "Which is the worst district

(24) Robert Martin Holland (1872–1944). Later, most confusingly, Robert Holland-Martin, having changed his name by Royal Licence in accordance with the stipulation in his uncle's will. He became Chairman of Martin's Bank in 1925, and later Chairman of the Southern Railway. All his life he was an indefatigable collector: his mind was crammed with out-of-the-way facts, and his house overflowed with bizarre objects, to the despair of his wife and family. (Sometimes he left his purchases behind with the dealers from whom he had bought them, not daring to appear at home with any more of them.) He collected people with the same enthusiasm, inviting them recklessly for weekends with no thought at all of how they might mix.

(25)
In England whence Mount Vernon sprang,
Where Eveleigh wrought, where Chaucer sang –
Ay, here beneath her solemn skies
My City of the Sun shall rise.

C. R. Ashbee, *Echoes from the City of the Sun*, 1905.

The favourite Ashbee image of the City of the Sun, a concept also dear to the heart of Edward Carpenter, was based on Thomas Campanella's *Civitas Solis*, his portrayal of the ideal commonwealth, published in 1623.

(26) See the reference in Henry IV Part Two to Justice Shallow's greyhound which was 'outrun on the Cotsal': i.e. lost the race in the sports on Dover's Hill at Campden.

in London?"', wrote Samuel Barnett, 'the answer will probably be "Whitechapel".'[25] From the 1880s onward, the journalists and novelists and social statisticians had made Whitechapel notorious. The sinister activities of Jack the Ripper and the horrifying revelations at the inquests had helped to make Whitechapel a powerful symbol of lawlessness and vice and woe.

Chipping Campden, in full contrast, in those days seemed the quintessence of rural peacefulness and antique beauty. It was apparently even an anachronism in the time of Shakespeare: Shakespeare's antiquated Justice Shallow, epitome of bumbling country justice, was, so far as one can place him, a citizen of Campden (26). The coming of the railway in the mid-nineteenth century did little to dispel Campden's legendary sleepiness. The languor of the place was rapturously described by Algernon Gissing, brother of the novelist George Gissing, looking back at his first visit around 1890:

Once more I must in fancy stand at that truly Gloucestershire stile (above Campden wood) and drop down through the fields into the long silent street which has never lost for me that spell of enchantment under which it seemed to lie when I first entered it as a boy. No imagination was needed. Here was the old world itself, touched by a magic wand centuries ago and remaining spellbound. After hours of sunlight on these lonely hills with the skylarks and the plovers, late in the afternoon I saw below me this wide secluded basin, made as it seemed simply to catch the sun, and basking there in the radiance was the little grey town with a majestic church tower shining at one end of it. Gradually I descended into the hollow, and on entering that one wide street, swept by the sun from behind me, I tried to muffle my footsteps in the silence. At the market place I stood in silent astonishment. From end to end nobody was to be seen. My foot alone on the gilded pavement (all consisting then not of cement but of the dove-grey lias stone) had broken the quiet of immemorial sleep and my own sounds only had echoed around me. Between the church tower and the sun lay the antique town in one graceful curve of what seemed infinite detail and variety yet of matchless harmony. Built all of stone, turned absolutely to gold just then, this wide street widened still more midway to admit, as islands, the arched pillared and gabled Market Hall and the Gothically buttressed Guildhall. It was indescribable, simply a dream.[26]

The idea of a dream city was a popular one then, among Morris's disciples and the readers of *The Clarion*, people with visions of a reborn Merrie England, people who bought books like Robert Blatchford's *Sorcery Shop: A Fascinating Forecast of the City Beautiful under Socialism*. Utopian cities were much under discussion. What made Ashbee so remarkable was his determination actually to set out to discover one. To persuade 150 people to leave their homes in London and travel off to Gloucestershire was no mean feat.

The scheme had been broached to the Guildsmen by autumn 1901, and had at least one immediate strong supporter, Cyril Kelsey, a young metalworker, who wrote to Mrs Ashbee saying 'I do hope the Gloucester scheme will come off, it will be simply great'. He added (a comment which tells one a good deal about Ashbee and his standing with the Guild): 'They say at the Guild that it's pretty certain to come off as CRA always gets his way in the end, they also say it's in his book so it must be true.'[27] A few weeks later, intrigued by the prospect of the Cotswolds, Kelsey and his workshop friends set off secretly on bicycles from the Guild's weekend cottage at Drayton St Leonard to spy out the land at Chipping Campden, returning exhausted after a 96-mile ride. (27)

In November, the Guild's first official viewing party, composed of workshop foremen, went to Campden. Rob Holland and Mr Dease, the local landlord's agent, met them at the station and took them to lunch royally at *The Noel Arms*. ' "For", said Rob', as Ashbee recorded in his Journal, ' "it is advisable to keep the men in good humour" '. (Or, as Cyril Kelsey later commented more cynically, 'First make the foremen drunk and you'll get them to consent to anything!')[28]

Certainly the Foremen's Beanfeast, as it went down in legend, was totally successful. After lunch, in mellow mood, the party then got down to detail:

We went over the silk mill again, measured it up, peered through the green and bottle glass panes, studied the girth of the plumtree growing round the stonework, tipped the old mad woman with the ringlets, climbed up and down the empty 17th Century houses, explored the town hall and the reading room, asked endless questions, and finally in the words of the exceedingly stolid Bill Thornton, the foreman of the smithy, professed ourselves as 'very agreeably surprised'. There now, the country has charms after all, and it seems as if the Great Move were at last coming off.[29]

The next task, back in London, was to put it to the men. A crucial Guild meeting was held on 8 December. The question of the move to Campden was blown up and down, in and out, here and there; it

(27) Kelsey, in the end, never went to work in Campden. He had left the Guild by then to join the Army in South Africa.

gyrated 'like an autumn leaf' round the topic of wages and trade unionism, the relation of wages to dividend, the responsibilities and duties incumbent upon wages. 'Altogether', said Ashbee (who liked that sort of thing), 'an interesting and educative two hours',[30] the long and short of which was that it was decided a poll whould be taken in a fortnight's time.

It must have been a fortnight of suspense and great debate. For many of the men, the decision was not obvious. A few, like the Hart brothers from Hitchin, countrymen already, were keen to move to Campden, but the majority had lived in London all their lives and were understandably afraid of such uprooting. Besides, Whitechapel itself had its own positive amenities. It had vast social problems, awful poverty and squalor, but it also had considerable excitement and vitality. Charles Booth, in his monumental London survey, *Labour and Life of the People,* described the endless drama of the streets of Whitechapel, jostling crowds and noisy markets, music halls and entertainments. Some of Ashbee's Guildsmen, both the old ones and the young ones, must have been reluctant to leave the familiar bustle of East London, with its shellfish barrows, barrel organs, mobile shooting galleries, for the secluded, unknown town of Chipping Campden. A move so far from London, to however beautiful a Socialist City, must have seemed a wrench.

Some of the men had personal problems to contend with. Sim. Samuels, 'Sammy', the keen, quick, careful, cheerful little Jewish boy, who came to the Guild first of all as printer's devil but had quickly graduated to the jewellers' shop, could not bear to leave his family. A. G. Rose, the willing, affable (though not entirely trustworthy) cabinet-maker who had been in the Guild since 1890, claimed he just could not afford to move to Campden: 'I can assure you', he wrote to Ashbee later, 'that the idea of parting gives me great grief and pain. In fact I can hardly bear the thought of it, but I cannot possibly manage to move'.[31] For old Tom Jellife, the trade union veteran, a greatly respected old-style radical, the conflict was acute: he loved the Guild and what it stood for, but felt that his trade union organization, the Alliance, needed him to stay in London. He came to Ashbee with a very long face and said he had decided not to come to Campden. 'It was a question', said Ashbee, 'whether obstinacy or reason was going to win, and I knew his heart was with us.'[32] The tussle of loyalties was settled when the Guild elected Jellife their labour director for the year. His duty was clear. If his men went off to Campden, then labour's representative could hardly stay behind.

Some of the workshops were less confident than others. The jewellers, an important workshop in the Guild, with about a dozen men, were on the whole against the move. This was partly perhaps because most of them were town-bred, from London or from Birmingham, with two who came from Germany. But it seems that their reluctance was also tradesmen's wariness: the jewellers' was one of the last unionized of workshops, and they feared that in the country they would not be so secure. The printers, whom Ashbee had inherited from Morris with the Kelmscott presses, were very much divided: they disliked leaving London, but they had transferred to Ashbee some of the personal loyalty they felt for William Morris. The cabinet-makers, another major workshop, this time significantly almost wholly unionized, were all greatly in favour, and their enthusiasm was the decisive factor when, just before Christmas, the Guildsmen's votes were cast.

The Guild then had 40 men eligible for a vote. (Of the full 60 or 70 Guild workers at that time, the rest were either boys or temporary non-Guild labour.) Seven of the voting Guildsmen were, for one reason or another, absent, so the total was 33. When the poll was declared, there were 11 against going, and these, as Ashbee commented, were, with two exceptions, new members 'not fully inoculated with Guild ideas'.[33] Twenty-two voted to go. When the men had had their Christmas Eve sing-song in the library, the blacksmiths had triumphantly chalked up the result on the smithy door. Lewis Hughes, blacksmiths' apprentice, known as 'Jacko' (because of his resemblance to an organ-grinder's monkey), set off for Waterside, the guild cottage at Drayton St Leonard, walking eight miles through the snow to bring the news to Ashbee. 'I am glad', wrote Ashbee in the Journal for that Christmas, 'to think that the men themselves have decided that on the whole it is better to leave Babylon and go home to the land'.[34] He did not under-rate the job ahead of him: 'Now the real work of building up has to begin!'

2

Cockneys in Arcadia
1902

At the time of the move Ashbee was almost 39. No longer the 'long youth' described at Cambridge by Goldsworthy Lowes Dickinson; but just as enthusiastic, perhaps even more opinionated, now that he was nearing middle age.

He was by now a minor public figure: increasingly well known as an architect-designer, a name to conjure with, especially on the Continent. Ashbee was highly thought of for his Guild of Handicraft endeavours; a formidable spokesman for Arts and Crafts in England; one of the most vocal (though not one of the most popular) members of the Art Workers' Guild. He was much involved in new ideas in education, and was one of the prime movers in the first environmental pressure groups which were then getting under way: he founded the London Survey Committee (1), which set out on a great task of listing and recording all buildings of historic and architectural interest in London; and he had been one of the very early members of the National Trust.

'In appearance tall, handsome, debonair', wrote Archie Ramage who joined the Guild in 1902, the year they went to Campden, 'C.R.A. might have walked out of a Velasquez picture. His attractiveness was so singular that some people were repelled!'[1] The features which seem to have made the most impression on people who knew Ashbee were his very high domed forehead; his watchful brown-green eyes, which were very disconcerting to the shifty or the nervous; his large moustache and

(1) In 1899, Ashbee made the comment: 'The survey at the rate we were working – one volume in 2 years – would, with 40 volumes, be completed in 80 years, by which time the London of 1899 would be where the common sense people want it to be – used up for concrete'. In fact, in 1979, the Survey had reached volume 39, and a good deal of London had indeed been used for concrete. Ashbee was not at all far out.

little beard, which he had the habit of caressing between finger and thumb while he was thinking. He had a lovely smile, a smile of quite unusual splendour, which would suddenly beam out on people he approved of.

'He spoke in a tenor voice', said Philippe Mairet (Mairet arrived in Campden four years later), 'pronouncing his words excellently, if with a slightly affected precision'.[2] His manner was, Mairet noted, 'highly cultivated'. He was obviously a figure of enormous magnetism (2). He had boundless energy, and many of his qualities could truthfully be described as noble. (Nobility, for Ashbee, was the very highest praise.) But obviously, too, he was in some ways quite intolerable. He had a large measure of the quirkiness and oddness which often goes with visionary zeal. He was touchy and uneasy, especially with women. To people he despised, he could be very rude indeed.

Some of his peculiarities can no doubt be attributed to the solitude and tensions of his upbringing: his over-protective dominating mother; his rift with his father, compounded by the fact that his parents separated seven or eight years after he left Cambridge. After the separation he had gone to live in Chelsea, in the house in Cheyne Walk which he designed himself, with his mother and Agnes and Elsa, his two unmarried sisters. (Of the three Ashbee sisters, only one had ever married: perhaps, suggested Janet cruelly, they were too well educated.) The correct, nervously feminist, oppressive atmosphere of 37 Cheyne

(2) These characteristics never left him, as is shown in a quotation from a lecture by Major Keith-Roach who knew Ashbee in Jerusalem, where he was Civic Advisor from 1918–22: 'I met Ashbee and his wife first in 1919. The impact was tremendous...' Ashbee was a 'distinguished looking, loosely grown man in his middle fifties. An Italian eyed and sensitive-mouthed creature with some marked Semitic features, plus a brilliant smile, he walked about Jerusalem with the lope of a Bedu. He was maddeningly vague and unbelievably clever.' At lunch with the Ashbees 'conversation traversed a wide variety of subjects in two or three languages'. Nothing much had changed.

Walk might well have strained the nerves of a much robuster character. To a sensitive young man, it must have been a constant trial.

There was also, to add to his disquiet, the disorientating fact, which he was doubtlessly aware of, that his father H. S. Ashbee, ostensibly a rather dull conventional City businessman with a public image of exemplary probity, had a simultaneous mania for the strange and the exotic. In private, H. S. Ashbee was one of the most avid collectors of erotic literature the world has ever seen. His three-volume catalogue, *Notes on Curious and Uncommon Books* (*with copious extracts from the erotic works described*), published between 1877 and 1885 under the pseudonym 'Pisanus Fraxi', was an extraordinarily comprehensive survey, the first work of its kind to appear in English.

Some of the things which tended to set people against Ashbee, in particular his rather pontificating manner, were quickly countered by Janet when he married her: her natural spontaneity was totally disarming. She had a saving sense of humour and perspective, which carried her along through Ashbee's earnest enterprises. From her first appearance at the Guild Wednesday night suppers, at which Ashbee had been in the habit of discussing the topics of the day with his apprentices, determinedly keeping up the tone of the discussion, the atmosphere changed from constraint to warmth and cheerfulness. Her impact on Guild life was celebrated in a poem (not a very good one) written by the cabinet-maker A. G. Rose:

Hushed into silence is the ribald tongue,
When our Lady of the Guild doth pass along.
The flower-like odour that to dear woman clings
Into our workshop her sweet presence brings.[3]

Janet was 23 when the Guild decided to set off to the Cotswolds. This was much the same age as the young workmen and apprentices. With her thick brown hair and tawny skin and her sunbonnets and sandals, she still looked very girlish; but her steady grey eyes and her sweet protective manner, not to mention her unusually large bosom (about which she was always especially self-conscious), made her appear at the same time quite mature. Perhaps it was this mixture, part-sisterly, part-motherly, which made the young Guildsmen find Janet so attractive. All, apparently, adored her. 'Never had I seen so radiantly vivid a person, quick in movements, quick in speech, quick "in the uptake" ', wrote one of them.[4] She was unique, another of the younger Guildsmen commented, in her ability to appreciate all classes alike. 'She is a real "Yankee" in spirit and is wasted on British soil', as

Ashbee's friend Frank Lloyd Wright (3) wrote later.[5] Certainly Janet had true pioneering instincts, unusual reserves of optimism and resilience most important to the story of the Guild in Chipping Campden: without her maybe Ashbee would not have had the courage to set out on the Gloucestershire excursion at all.

Once the decision to move had been arrived at, in the best traditions of Guild democracy, the Guildsmen were faced with the sheer physical problems of evacuating Essex House, the handsome eighteenth-century mansion in Mile End Road which had been the Guild head-quarters since 1891. This was a complicated task, involving the trans-portation to the Cotswolds of twelve year's accumulation of the tools of varied trades, on top of the upheaval of forty or so East End craftsmen's households. But perhaps, after so many weeks of tension and uncertainty, the moment of decision came as a relief, and arrangements for the move went on efficiently and smoothly, with minimum of friction, over the next three months.

The Ashbees themselves had their own house to dispose of, the

(3) Frank Lloyd Wright (1869–1959), the architect. Ashbee met him in 1900 in Chicago, on one of his transatlantic lecture tours, and was one of the first people, certainly the first Englishman, to recognise Wright's genius. 'Wright is to my thinking far and away the ablest man in our line of work that I have come across in Chicago, perhaps in America', wrote Ashbee in his Journal: 'He not only has ideas but the power of expressing them, and his Husser House, over which he took me, showing me every detail with the keenest delight, is one of the most beautiful and individual of creations that I have seen in America'. He and Wright, in spite of occasional clashes of temperament, remained friends for many years, and Ashbee wrote the introduction to the 1911 German edition of Frank Lloyd Wright's work.

Wright, incidentally, throws interesting light on Ashbee's reception in Chicago, telling the story in his *Autobiography* of the Chicagoan at the Ashbee banquet who 'stood Ashbee as long as he could, and then got up on his indignant feet to say that Chicago wasn't much on culture now, maybe, but when Chicago *did* get after Culture, she'd make Culture hum!'

(4) J. A. McNeill Whistler (1834–1903), the painter. His ideal in decoration, as described by James Laver, was a plain wall with two pictures, both of them by Whistler. Ashbee's complex, fanciful Arts-and-Crafts style building could have hardly, one would have thought, been further from his taste.

(5) E. A. Walton (1860–1922) and his wife. Walton, the painter, was one of the original 'Glasgow boys' and now a friend and neighbour of the Ashbees. Ashbee designed a house for him in Chelsea and he painted portraits of Ashbee's wife and mother.

building in Chelsea – 74 Cheyne Walk – given to them on their marriage by Janet Ashbee's father. Janet's mixed emotions on the exodus from London come over poignantly in her entry in the Journal describing the arrival of an unexpected customer. The date is 6 March 1902:

As I came along Cheyne Walk the other day I saw the copper door open, and Minney parleying with a stranger. I arrived in time to usher into the hall an old gentleman in a cocoa coloured ulster and craped silk hat of that exactly cylindrical form affected by Parisians. I knew, from recollections of a Nicholson drawing, that it must be Whistler (4), whom the Waltons (5) have sent round to look at the house. He has since decided to take it.

Alas! our dear little 74 is soon to pass from us for two whole years; but one cannot expect to live in a Gothic house at Campden without a proportionate sacrifice!

It took me back almost within touch of Ruskin, and Hamerton, and the other people in the 'Ten O'clock' to have the little, horrid, cantankerous, curled, perfumed creature on the floor before me. I hope I did not show the antipathy he raised in me, a purely physical one I believe. He gave me the impression of an old, old man trying to be young and sprightly and aping the oddities of youth, or rather of an old monkey copying the affectations of a young man. He was much exercised at the reflected light which he declared was thrown by a grey brick wall outside our north window. But the artificial heat captivated him.

'You people over here', he grumbled, 'have a perfect mania for living in draughts.'

No doubt it is interesting that such a celebrity should occupy your house, but to think of him using the intimacies of the home that even three and a half years have made very dear to you, is dreadful. Let us hope he will refrain from painting on the walls sarcastic comments on the builder of the house, as he has been known to do before![6]

As Whistler prepared to move into 74 Cheyne Walk (a house which he was later to describe as 'a successful example of the disastrous effect of art upon the middle classes'[7]), the Ashbees themselves were busy in the Cotswolds. They visited Campden several times that spring, finalizing the arrangements for renting the Guild buildings and seeing to a hundred and one necessary details to make the 'exodus from Cockneydom' easier. They were occupied with stripping walls and peeling plaster, uncovering the hidden Gothic glories of Woolstaplers' Hall, the fourteenth-century building in the main street of Campden which the Ashbees would be living in themselves. The elder Mrs Ashbee, back in London, was searching the department stores for kitchenware, reporting breathlessly to Janet: 'There must have been a rush for white enamelled Milk Jugs and Basins for Kitchen use. Harrods had none and Peter Jones was out, so I went to the Army and Navy and found what I wanted and to my joy "made in England", cheaper than Harrods if they had them'.[8] Meanwhile, the Ashbees, in the intervals of battling with an 'enlightened speculative builder' who was threatening to pull down a group of Elizabethan Cotswold cottages – the first of many such skirmishes, apparently successful – had their minds very much on the arrival of the Guildsmen. 'It will be interesting', comments Ashbee in the Journal, 'to watch the result of the impact of the Cockney upon this little decaying town. But it IS a lovely place!'[9]

Chipping Campden then had about 1,500 inhabitants. Obviously, the town had seen much better days. Indeed the dusty robes of the mayor and corporation were now kept in a wardrobe at the local grocer's and lent out for amateur theatricals. Campden's years of glory were certainly long past. But perhaps it was not quite the wild un-civilized terrain that Ashbee tended to describe, the town no man of culture had ever before entered. Laurence Housman (6), for instance, a friend of the Ashbees, wrote to Janet saying in a rather jeering tone: 'I hear you fancy you have discovered Campden. It is an old Camping ground of mine, and is worth living near for its architecture and its old yew hedges and peacocks.'[10] Housman had first come to Campden when he began writing songs and plays for Joseph Moorat, a Campden

(6) Laurence Housman (1865–1959), endlessly controversial playwright, novelist, polemicist. He had in fact begun life as an illustrator, and his relationship with Ashbee started with a dispute over a decorative drawing of a fruit tree which Ashbee had accused him of plagiarizing from one of the Essex House Press books. The quarrel, however, seems to have been soon forgotten, and he and Janet Ashbee began a correspondence which was to last for over 50 years.

(7) Gordon Russell (b.1892, later Sir Gordon), craftsman, designer and furniture manufacturer, Director of the Council of Industrial Design from 1947 to 1959. His family firm, Gordon Russell Ltd, is at Broadway, 4 miles from Chipping Campden, and in 1925 Gordon Russell started building Kingcombe, his house on the hill above Campden village. Fifty years on he was still adding to the building and improving the landscaping, doing much of the construction work himself.

(8) Norman Jewson (1884–1975). He stayed in the Cotswolds all his life, joining Ernest Gimson and the Sapperton group of architects and craftsmen, and marrying Ernest Barnsley's daughter Mary.

resident, to set to music. He loved the place. However, he warned Janet that the natives were on the whole not very pleasant or very interesting.

Cultural desert or not, the town of Campden had its own set character very different from London. It was a relatively small and circumscribed society, ruled over as it had been for centuries by the joint forces of the landed gentry and the clergy. It was a place in which the hierarchy was a rigid one, with farmers, tradesmen and agricultural labourers in corduroys all keeping, more or less, to their appointed places. In Campden at that time there was very little sign of the aspiring middle classes, still less the radicals.

Chipping Campden however had more than its fair share of 'rum old orkard characters', the statutory figures in all accounts of village life as it once was in England, when the village lunatic, the village quack and the village politician still existed. Gordon Russell (7), who came to the Grammar School in Campden soon after the Guild move, records in his autobiography[11] such notable eccentrics as old Dolphin, the cottager who kept his small front room full of potting earth and sometimes cleaned the front of his house with a pail of water and a toothbrush, dressed in an ancient postman's hat and coat; and Malin, the saddler's boy, who got under his bench when anyone looked through the window; and Sykes, who started as a medical student and ended up driving cattle. There was also the old man who was reputed to have grown his own tobacco and nearly killed himself smoking it. Campden like other villages and small towns of the period, had its own large store of folklore and fables which helped to offset its isolation of position. The life of the community was very self-contained.

The focal point of country life was of course the local inn. Campden had several. One of the most popular, *The Swan*, where Mrs Skey fed her patrons on delicious backbone pie, was nostalgically described by Norman Jewson (8), a young architect who followed the Arts and Crafts trail towards the Cotswolds shortly after Ashbee and the Guild. He went on to explain the peculiar ethos of the English inn in those days, its cosiness and brightness mingled with a certain mustiness, and its role at the centre of an unswervingly masculine community:

The village inn was essentially a place where men of the locality could meet together on an equal footing, to discuss the things they were most interested in, sport, crops, local politics, and so on, over their pints of beer or cider. There they could play games, such as skittles, draughts and darts and enjoy the comforts of good fellowship in a cosy room, away from their wives and families. As a rule the bar was a low ceilinged cosy room with a brick, tiled or stone floor, the lower parts of the walls panelled or match-boarded, oak grained or painted. There was a wide fireplace with an open grate having hobs on each side of it and on the high mantel-shelf a pair of brass candlesticks, a few china ornaments such as toby jugs or Staffordshire figures and a clock, unless there was a hanging clock elsewhere in the room. Sometimes there were a few sporting prints or oil paintings of prize bulls, rams or stallions painted by some unknown travelling artist. Often, too, there was an engraving of the local landowner or a coloured lithograph of Queen Victoria.[12]

Country inns, with their entrenched conservatism, were of course in some respects anathema to Ashbee and the ideas of social progress he propounded. And no doubt, in the masculine fastness of *The Swan* and the other inns of Campden, news of the incursion of 150 socialists from London was regarded with suspicion, if not out and out hostility. The *Evesham Chronicle* looked on the brightest side of things, publishing a fulsome little article, 'Welcome News for Campden', a few weeks before the arrival of the Guild, asserting that 'Gloucestershire's gain is London's loss' and congratulating not only Mr Ashbee in having found such a delightful spot as Campden in which to settle, but also the inhabitants of Campden upon the fact that at last the charms of the old town had been discovered.[13] But Evesham, it has to be remembered, was nine miles from Chipping Campden, in those days quite a distance, and there is little to suggest any comparable enthusiasm in the town itself. At one level at least, the Guild was seen as an intruder: it emerged a long time later that, quite unknown to Ashbee, some local labourers had actually been evicted so that their cottages could be let more profitably to the Guildsmen. Some of the Campden shopkeepers, although in the long term they obviously stood to benefit from increased custom, were apparently at first so overtly unwelcoming that they charged a higher price to the outsiders (as, interestingly enough, almost fifty years before, an earlier generation of shopkeepers in Campden had overcharged the navvies working on the local railway). The district hierarchy of landowners, from the Earl of Gainsborough downwards, were predictably resentful, in such a static small society, of any event likely to upset the status quo.

The Guild arrived gradually, workshop by workshop. It was planned that the woodshop should come to Campden first, then the forge and metal shop and so on, until all the Guild craftsmen were in situ in the old Silk Mill, which was being leased at £40 a year. It was a good building for the Guild, as had been obvious to the foremen when they first measured it up the previous November, and the craftsmen quickly settled in. The ground floor was scheduled for the showroom, the drawing office and general offices and the Essex House Press. The first floor was for jewellery, silver and enamelling, and the second floor for cabinet making, woodcarving and french polishing. The smithy was set up in an outhouse, since the blacksmiths tended to make a lot of noise.

The mill stood in an acre and a half, a pleasant garden with the plum tree which had so impressed the men on the first visit. (The fate of the old mad woman with the ringlets was not apparently recorded.) The romantic character of the old grey stonework was carefully preserved in the process of conversion and, as Ashbee described it in an article he wrote at the time of the move, there could 'still be seen the green twinkle of the lattice windows of the old silk weavers'.[14] Although a stream ran beneath the mill, its original source of power, this was not adequate for the Guild workshops, so an oil-engine was installed in a large shed in the garden, where the circular saw, bandsaw and planer, the only machinery used by the woodworkers, were also kept. There was a cottage in the garden which the Guild took over, and six cottages nearby which the Guild had leased to sub-let to the men on a temporary basis, until they had found themselves more long-term homes. In addition, some houses were acquired by Guild shareholders, others were put in good repair and rented by the Guildsmen, and land was bought by individual Guild well-wishers to provide houses with small plots for the Guildsmen, advancing that fine theory that, in an ideal country, craftsmanship and husbandry go hand in hand.

For the younger men, the boys and bachelors, Ashbee took over another Campden building, Braithwaite House, to make a guest house or, as he termed it grandiosely, Hall of Residence. The Braithwaite House scheme was very typical of Ashbee: he saw it as an amalgam of the Cambridge residential college and, inspired by his recent visit to America, a transatlantic university fraternity house with its endlessly hospitable hail-fellow-well-met atmosphere. The Guild made him a loan of £100 (with interest at ten per cent) towards the cost of furnishing the house for its first 12 young Guild residents, and a certain Mrs Averill was appointed housekeeper. The intellectual standards may have disappointed Ashbee. Perhaps the conversation of Will Hart, the woodcarver in charge of Braithwaite House, or Teddy Horwood, jeweller, lacked the philosophical cut-and-thrust of Cambridge. But in other respects, Braithwaite, right from the beginning, was an evident success.

Nearby in Elm Tree House, in the main street of Campden, Ashbee established a small architectural office, the rural branch of his main London practice. There he generally had two assistants working with him, a pupil or two, and the very capable lady secretary who had been with him in London and whose legendary loyalty had prompted her to come and type for Ashbee in the Cotswolds.

The Guild Library and Guild Museum also moved to Campden. The Library had been accumulating since the early days of the Guild in Essex House and was very much a product of the age when East End benefactors were intent upon improving the minds and widening the literary horizons of the workman. It included most of the great names of English Literature: Shakespeare, Bacon, Wordsworth, Shelley. It also offered Guildsmen a rather heady mixture of Ashbee's chosen authors of the revolution: such socialist handbooks as Edward Carpenter's *Towards Democracy* and William Morris's *Songs of Liberty,* as well as that notorious study in anarchy, *Alice in Wonderland* by Lewis Carroll. The original Essex House Library had been augmented recently by the gift of 300 surplus volumes from the large and somewhat esoteric collection which Ashbee's father, H. S. Ashbee, had bequeathed to the British Museum. These books, mainly duplicates unwanted by the nation, some of a general literary character, some of them relating to the various artistic, antiquarian and topographical subjects unflaggingly pursued by H. S. Ashbee, were brought along to Campden and, perhaps in desperation, were temporarily housed in a room in Braithwaite House.

The Museum, which came later than the Library but which was founded in much the same spirit of philanthropy, on the principle that men will love the highest if they see it, was also an important element in the Guild life. In London, the gallery adjoining Essex House had been much used by the workmen, as well as the students and pupils of the School of Handicraft, and Ashbee noticed with satisfaction how much Guild craftsmanship, 'details of shape, metal, inlaying, carving, modelling or designing', was being influenced to the good by some specimen of work shown in the gallery.[15] Before the move to Campden, Ashbee had negotiated a loan of Works of Art and Handicraft from the Board of Education. With his usual fervent attention to detail, he had chosen the exhibits himself, with the assistance of an official at South Kensington, and they included inspiriting examples of all the crafts practised at Campden: lettering and printing, metalwork, inlay, damascene, niello, and so on. His idea was that these should go on show in Campden Grammar School, as an optimistic step towards the education not only of the Guildsmen but also of the town.

The scene was set. Ashbee at Chipping Campden had provided the Guild with near-ideal conditions, almost unlimited opportunities for cheerful fellowship and self-improvement. But the task of starting life in this Utopian Cotswold city was, for some of the Londoners, not altogether easy. They seem to have found the total quietness astounding, and as Ashbee commented in an article on Campden, 'one of the things that coming into the country people have felt most is the extra-ordinary disregard for time that country people have'.[16] Some of the Guild boys were particularly homesick, and Mrs Ashbee kept a kind maternal eye on Charley Downer, the young blacksmith, who had been upset to leave his family and was still very doleful when he got to Campden. He and his friend, Fred Brown, were staying at *The Rose and Crown* wondering whether or not to take the plunge and move into the Guest House. Janet was also anxiously watching three boys from the woodshop – George Colverd, Fred Cliff and Frank Dowsett – who were lodging temporarily at a neighbouring bakers' in Campden. 'So far', she confided in the Journal, 'all goes well with them. Frank's sedative influence can only do good to George, who came down three weeks ago prepared to hate Campden and all its ways but who I fancy is becoming reconciled'.[17]

Campden itself seemed to be working its own influence. Ned West, nicknamed 'Jimmy Green' (after the music hall buffoon), an apprentice metalworker and a bit of a figure of fun in the Guild workshops, made the mistake on his first morning of appearing in the streets of Chipping Campden dressed in formal city clothes. Ashbee uncharitably described him as 'dressed with customary look of shabby propriety, rather doubtful stiff linen, needy trousers a bit frayed at the heels, showy gilt studs and watch chain with a presbyterian cut about his black coat, his entirely superfluous cane in one hand, and in the other Darwin's *Origin of the Species*'.[18] But this was not for long. Within the next few days, to everyone's amazement, he had changed from the stiff linen into a scarlet bathing dress and was organizing the loafing village lads of Campden into a harriers' club and was leading them in long measured runs about the country. (The sad sequel to this story of startling transformation was that Jimmy Green, totally in character, presumably having over-run his strength, collapsed with enlargement of the heart, in a state of wild delirium, and had to be taken back to London by his mother.)

As summer came, the Guild got gradually established. New recruits were coming in. One of them was Alec Miller, an ardent young wood-carver from Glasgow who had read a book of Ashbee's (9) and been inspired to come and seek true democratic craftsmanship in Gloucester-shire. 'On a heavenly May morning in 1902 I walked for the first time into the little town of Campden', wrote Alec Miller later in his memoirs. He had come on a circuitous route by packet steamer from Glasgow to Belfast, then on to Dublin, then to Bristol. He travelled by train for the last 60 miles to Campden, delightedly watching the passing scenery: the lush valleys, flowering orchards, glimpses of the Severn and the rich farming land of Gloucestershire and Worcestershire. To a young man of 23 who had spent all his life in Glasgow where his father had a workshop in a slum back courtyard and who had himself started work when he was 12, it was like another civilization altogether:

I walked up Campden's one long street entranced and happy; a mile-long street with hardly a mean house, and with many of great beauty and richness. It was, after Glasgow and Scottish village architecture, as foreign as Cathay and as romantic as the architecture of fairy-tale illustrations. It all seemed unbelievable! Was I really in the twentieth century, or in the sixteenth? I was almost wholly ignorant of the history of architecture and building. I could not 'read' the history embodied in those stone-built houses, so rich, so substantial, and of such beautiful stone. I simply walked on and on, in an ecstacy of pleasure, with no thought but just wonder.

His wide-eyed descriptions of his first few weeks in Campden give a very good idea of the scale of the operation and the atmosphere of the old Silk Mill in those early days:

There were about forty men, and more kept coming as the shops were prepared for them. There were about twelve cabinetmakers, of whom three were youths, and there were ten silversmiths making all kinds of metal work, from electric light fittings to the most elaborate table silver and ecclesiastical silver work. Off their workshop was a smaller shop where men made enamels, things often of mysterious

(9) This was *Chapters in Workshop Reconstruction and Citizenship*: not, one might have thought, a title to make immediate converts. But Alec Miller had been instantly impressed by the curious appearance of the volume, which was tall for its width, with the pink linen cover much favoured by the private presses of the era. On this was stamped 'a design in black of chimneys, tall factory chimneys, the smoke of which was worked into a decorative pattern ... Was there some significance', Ashbee's new disciple wondered, 'or was it accidental that the cover design of "dark Satanic mills" had, by the skill of the designer (the author), been made almost into a thing of beauty?' This was a good question.

beauty. The process was intricate and hazardous; the strange and inexplicable difference between the enamel as it was put into the furnace (muffle) and when it was taken out, was a never-ending miracle to me. Then there were ten or twelve jewellers, work of which I was totally ignorant but which proved to be both interesting and beautiful; and three blacksmiths made iron-work screens, fire-irons, lamp fittings, garden gates, etc. All these workshops were in one building (the blacksmiths were actually a little separated – for quietness!) The office staff consisted of Mr. W. J. Osborn (manager) with two clerks, and there were three men engaged in outside work with the sawmill and power house, packing, and gardening, for there was a pleasant garden behind the mill building and it was tended by an old soldier, Alf Smith.[19]

In May, the first Guild meeting was held in Chipping Campden, in the workshops in the Silk Mill. Fifteen Guildsmen were present; Ashbee wrote the minutes. Among the urgent topics for discussion were plans for the formation of the Craftsman Club (a subject which had tended to dominate Guild meetings in London too), and the practicability of a half-crown levy on all Guild members to go towards expenses of the annual Guild Beanfeast, to be held at Rob Holland's family home, Overbury, 20 miles away.

In May, too, Janet was reporting that Sid Cotton, 'The Mad Hatter', cabinet-maker and Guild character, was already feeling enough at home in Campden to be 'Whitechapeling frightfully' with the local damsels. There were 'horrible tales of his embracings in the market place'.[20] Ted Horwood, a young jeweller, who two years earlier had been a quiet retiring boy who hardly ever spoke, blossomed out in Campden and became the wag of the party, whose constant badinage kept everybody cheerful: 'he is a kind laureate jester', wrote Janet, who viewed the new Ted Horwood with almost proprietorial approval, 'and his jokes on all important occasions become classics and are stored up among the archives'.[21]

Ashbee himself was getting into his accustomed stride, with a letter of complaint to Mrs Carrington, the vicar's wife, who had apparently been cross-examining the foreman of the metal shop about the theological opinions of some of the newcomers. 'Our people', he told her in no uncertain terms, 'are not accustomed to this and they do not like it. I hope therefore you will pardon the suggestion, which as member of the Church of England perhaps I may be permitted to make, that anything like an inquisitional search for souls is more calculated to drive them away from church than to attract them thither'.[22] Ashbee, who had his own interests in the souls of the Guildsmen, threw in a passing reference to his friend and tutor, the late Dr Creighton (10), calculated to confuse the opposition. It had not taken long for war to be declared between the Guild and the church factions in Campden.

Janet, meanwhile, was weighing up the local landowners, the Gainsboroughs, who lived two miles out of Campden (when not at their alternative estate in Rutland) in a characteristic English aristocrats' mixture of 'homely simplicity and feudal state'.[23] So far, she found the Gainsboroughs, a leading Catholic family, motto 'Tout rien ou bien', a rather unknown quantity. The Earl seemed a harmless, gentle sort of ceature, out for peace above all; the Countess a clear-headed, able woman, a manager but at the same time kind and motherly. The three Gainsborough daughters (one by the Earl's first wife) struck her as attractive and pretty-mannered: 'especially', she commented, 'the eldest, who has a peculiar charm I have not yet had time to analyse'. Of the three Gainsborough sons, who were still being educated, she had the highest hopes of the oldest, Viscount Campden, who had just returned from a voyage to Jamaica with the family's priest, the small, round Father May. Campden seemed to Janet 'an interesting boy and one of whom one could get very fond'. But although the Gainsboroughs at first sight seemed amiable, Janet thought it most unlikely that they would ever become intimate. The barrier of conventionality was too immense.

The real ruler of Campden was not in fact Lord Gainsborough but Louis Dease, his agent, a charming, down-at-heel, extremely devious Irishman. It was Dease who had received the Guild's original deputation the August before, when the Ashbees first arrived in Campden to negotiate the move, on their way home from one of the Guild River Expeditions. They had looked like tramps, still in their boating clothes, not only very sunburnt but also so grubby from their night on Worcester Station that they hardly liked to sit on Dease's spotless chintzes. Dease, who in his way was as eccentric as the Ashbees, had not turned a hair.

(10) Mandell Creighton (1843–1901). Ashbee's history tutor at Cambridge and later Bishop of London. The Ashbees had remained great friends of the Creightons, appreciating all the paradoxes this implied, and enjoyed visiting them at Fulham Palace, where the episcopal regime was of the grandest. Ashbee found one tea party especially congenial: 'when we went in to tea and were joined by Sidney Webb and his wife the conversation round the tea table became delightful. 'Tis a fine thing when you come to think of it and speaks well for English life, that the Socialist leader of the radical wing on the L.C.C. should come to take tea with the Conservative Bishop of London'. (*Ashbee Memoirs*, October 1899)

(' "Well" ', he admitted later, ' "I must confess I did think it rather a wild sort of scheme – but I HOPE I didn't show it?" !'[24]) From the beginning, acting in what appeared to be the Gainsboroughs' best interests, he had always co-operated with the plan. Dease knew everyone and everything in Campden. He was a familiar figure walking round the town in his well-cut coat with the frayed edges, his correct but shabby necktie, with his hat always a little on a tilt. He was said to be the worst liar in Campden, and the Ashbees found him very entertaining. 'The lies are such perfect verisimilitudes of truth, are delivered with such aplomb, reveal such sympathy and versatility that it would be bad taste not to be deceived by them', wrote Ashbee in the Journal. 'Thank Heaven at least that, since we are an aesthetic community for the most part, we have a Celt and not a Saxon to run the show'.[25] You could not believe a word Dease told you, but the situation could have been a great deal worse.

While the Ashbees were making up their minds about their neighbours, the inhabitants of Campden were undoubtedly becoming increasingly baffled by the Ashbees. It was hard for them to see just how the Ashbees fitted into the familiar highly stratified society. They had important friends, but they were not exactly gentlefolk. Yet nor could they be classified as anarchists or cranks.

The role of Mrs Ashbee was particularly puzzling, becoming more – not less – so as Janet began to involve herself in local life in all its detail. She made immediate friends with the Chipping Campden children. Though the Vicar's wife maintained that the children of the parish were entirely dull and stupid, and that teaching them was hopeless work, Janet, whose nature was perhaps more optimistic, found many of them bright and quick, responsive, affectionate and kindly. Soon, she was seeing the children every day, either visiting the school and joining in the classes, or taking them home to her own garden to learn songs or help her with the vegetables. Within her first few weeks at Campden, the children were bringing her plants and seeds, making the marrow bed, staking the tomatoes, planting Sweet Williams and pansies and inundating her with nosegays. She was forever having to refuse rabbits and kittens which the children brought as presents. Sometimes she took a whole crowd of them for rambles to Northwick Park or Broadway Tower, to the amazement of the solider citizens of Campden, who gazed out at Mrs Ashbee and her somewhat ramshackle train of followers as they passed by. She must also have surprised them by sitting in the graveyard, a favourite haunt of hers, either reading Socrates and Dostoevsky or listening avidly to two small village children,

Albert and Frank, reputedly the naughtiest boys in Campden school, who had an endless store of the most fantastic stories of ghosts and haunted houses and enchanted trees.

For Janet, the first five weeks in Gloucestershire went by in a flash, and seemed a total holiday. She could not believe that this was real life at Campden and not a sort of glorified treat. At the height of the lovely Cotswold summer, with the country around blazing with buttercups, the far-off blueness of the sky and the galloping patches of cloud off-setting the varying grey of Cotswold stone, she could hardly bear to pack her bags to go to London, even for a three-day visit. 'For the first time today', she wrote in her Journal for 3 June 1902, 'I felt that Campden was H O M E '.[26]

This was an exciting, very optimistic period in the history of the Guild. That summer in Campden, they felt that they had made it. They had left Whitechapel, finally and unequivocally, for this strange picturesque land of quiet grey-yellow stone villages, the country of Cotswold pennycress and milkwort; where a mole was known as an 'oont' or a 'woont', where a field was 'a ground', a stone wall was 'a mound' and a deaf man was called a 'dunch' or 'dunny'. A place where the favourite proverbs were 'As sure as God's in Gloucestershire' or ' 'Tis as long in coming as Cotswold berle', and where old Nezzy Plested, the Campden mason, told one: 'I've as many grandchildren as 'ud fill a green field'.[27]

Though Gloucestershire life was by no means all idyllic, being in fact in many ways extremely hard and wearing for the families of labourers only just surviving on a wage of 12 or 13 shillings a week, it had great compensations and charms unknown in London. The simple homely comfort of all but the poorest cottages. The friendliness and mutual support of the villages nearby, with centuries of intermarriage. The prevalence of nicknames, such as Bendy, Berry, Brassy, Brindle,

(11) Elbert Hubbard, the Sage of Aurora, otherwise known as Fra Elbertus. A large expansive man, more an actor than a craftsman, with his flowing hair, his painter's smock and velvet tam o'shanter, who represented (to many purists' disapproval) the extreme commercial wing of Arts and Crafts. His quasi-religious community of Roycrofters produced a succession of artistic books in William Morris style, but using presses worked by gas, and produced a monthly magazine *The Philistine* to which 100,000 American devotees subscribed. He was an amazing egotist. But even Elbert Hubbard was not proof against disaster: he drowned in the *Lusitania* in 1915.

Blubber, Buggins, Buster: these were given to men only. The honest, trusting atmosphere of villages where the doors of all the buildings – cottage, church and manor house – were left open without thinking. The traditions and festivities of harvest-time and Christmas time; May Day processions, mummers and Morris dancing, which still went on in many of the Cotswold villages. (It was only 50 years since the famous Dover's Games were an annual institution on Dover's Hill in Campden). When the Guild arrived in Gloucestershire, the local men were picturesquely dressed in corduroy or rough natural-coloured cloth with black beaver hats in winter and white straw hats in summer, and broad old-fashioned birds-eye scarves in many shades of blue. Though smocks were going out, there were still shepherds to be seen in them, and sheep still wore their sheep-bells as they wandered on the hills.

The romanticism of the move and its possibilities, symbolic as well as practical, seems to have been infectious. Alec Miller described how the whole atmosphere of the Mill and different workshops was 'charged with a spirit of co-operative and communal effort'. To him, the Guild seemed a place of real freedom: the freedom which arose from pleasure in one's work. 'There was presently opened to me in the Guild', he wrote in retrospect, 'an entrancing and wholly new kind of life, in which it is now difficult to separate the various elements – the strange and romantic beauty of the Cotswolds, the absorbing interest of work, the widening intellectual life into which we of the Guild were introduced, the sense that we were a group enthused by a common aim'.[28] Hopeful letters kept arriving from friends and Guild supporters, the most loyal of them sharing Ashbee's view that the Guild move was a pilot scheme of national importance, a pioneer experiment in ways of life and work which might in the end revitalise the whole of British industry.

One of the letters which reached Campden that first summer was from Elbert Hubbard, famous showman of the Arts and Crafts movement in America (11), 'well-known Crank, Socialist, Book Maker, Heretic and "Anarkist" with a "k"', as Janet had described him two years earlier when she visited his Roycroft craft community in East Aurora.[29] Now he wrote to thank her for her cheery letter giving him the news of the move to Chipping Campden. 'I am glad', he said, 'to know that you have gotten out of the city into God's country. It may be a little lonesome for some of your workers at first, but they will get used to it, and then they will have everything that they need'. He sent her 'a handgrasp over the miles' (Arts and Crafts men were particularly partial to handgrasps), and added a postscript: 'Let me congratulate you on your typewriter. I wonder what William Morris would have thought of that!'[30]

By the end of August the Essex House Press, the last workshop to reach Campden, was safely installed in the ground floor of the Silk Mill. By then much of the local hostility was waning and a pattern of Guild life was emerging. The craftsmen at the Silk Mill worked a 50-hour week. They clocked in at 7.00, taking a metal number from a board and dropping it into a box outside the office, watched by the timekeeper. Anybody late lost his first half hour's wages. The organization of the working day was not in itself especially revolutionary: even Ashbee had not managed to avoid the need for timekeeping. But what made the Guild workshops so unique was the atmosphere and the attitude to work. At 8.30, there was a half-hour break for breakfast; there were ten-minute tea breaks at 10.50 and at 4.0 when the men would wander round the garden or sustain themselves with beer and biscuits in the workshops. Ashbee himself, Osborn the manager and often Janet too would come in and share these tea breaks. They were sociable occasions, as described by Alec Miller: 'It was during these intervals that a new-comer like myself visited the different shops and saw new crafts in process. This in itself was a widening experience, and it was enlarged and expanded by the closer contacts and friendships with the crafts-men'.[31]

Even an uninformed visitor could hardly fail to be impressed by the sheer variety of crafts in progress simultaneously in the Silk Mill. But perhaps the fine distinctions of the Guild's attitude to craftsmanship were best appreciated by a man like Alec Miller who knew the differ-ence between the Guild tradition of making things as well as they could possibly be made and the usual trade criteria of speed and cheapness. At the Guild, there was a certain consistent way of working, which had gone on for so long it was now more or less unquestioned. Machinery was used where machinery was useful, but handwork was preferred whenever handwork would be better: better for the work and better for the workman. For instance, according to Guild principles of craftsmanship, a timber plank could reasonably be sawn by a circular saw, but any subsequent carving should be hand-carving; a silver plate could be rolled in the mill, but the actual dish or cup should not be spun but raised by hand. This attitude to work, not a frenziedly dogmatic one, more an accepted way of going about things, to some extent pervaded all the Campden workshops and helped to shape the Guildsmen's working day.

Work in the Silk Mill finished at 5.30, leaving the evenings free for the lectures and the sing songs which were part of the Guild ethos, long rambles on the wolds in groups led along by Ashbee, and strenuous cycle rides around the countryside discovering the strangest and remotest Cotswold villages.

The event of the summer was, without doubt, the Beanfeast. There had been other Beanfeasts back in London, where an annual outing had been a Guild tradition, but none on the scale of this one, meticulously organized by Rob Holland at Overbury Court, which was then owned by his uncle, Sir Richard Martin. The Guild drove over in several brakes from Campden, with a small cavalcade of Guild boys on bicycles. They reached Overbury in time for lunch before the day's events began. It was a very English programme: a cricket match between the Guild and Overbury tenants; a football match in which the Guild was vanquished (surprisingly, perhaps, because one of the Guild craftsmen left soon afterwards to take up professional football). The Guild was more successful at the rifle-range shooting, helped by the experience of several of the Guildsmen who had recently been fighting in the Boer War. There was everything to make a fine English country day: good food, cider and beer, a band and dancing in the barn. Rob Holland and his wife, in the time-honoured English landowners' manner, were hospitable and charming, cheering on the sportsmen, chatting with the older Guildsmen, making sure that everyone enjoyed themselves. And if any of the more doctrinaire among the craftsmen disapproved of such a scene of English feudal hospitality, nobody was churlish enough to say so. Ashbee himself in fact had never had much difficulty reconciling his love of the life-style of the English country gentry with semi-revolutionary Socialist thought.

The Guild had hardly settled into Chipping Campden before the first visitors began arriving. The steady stream of friends, supporters, lecturers and teachers, inquirers and researchers (many of them from America), not to mention chance arrivals and accidental sightseers, which had always been an element of Guild life and indeed was an integral part of its philosophy, was not in the least diminished by the move into the Cotswolds. And of course once they had got there, the visitors stayed longer. Ashbee welcomed the activity: he never saw the exodus to Campden as a flight into oblivion. Very much the opposite. He was conscious of the move as a social experiment: it needed to be seen as such by influential people. Besides, one of the basic Guild ideas was to enlighten the Guild craftsmen by keeping them in touch with the great men of the time.

The Guest Room at Braithwaite House seems rarely to have been empty, even that first year in Campden. Cecil Brewer (12) came to stay, and went back home feeling 'quite braced up but rather disgusted with office and London'.[32] He sent the boys in the Guest House a conciliatory present of a set of up-to-date American boot cleaning equipment, having committed a classic Campden faux pas in leaving his boots outside the door for cleaning. (Will Hart had simply put a brush and box of boot blacking into Brewer's boots, in the proper spirit of egalitarian tact.)

Walter Crane (13) arrived in Campden and made great friends with the Guild boys, who took him out bicycling along the Cotswold highways. This cheerful expedition ended in confusion, a comic confrontation which Ashbee described 25 years later still with the same delight:

In that remote age (1902) the English countryside was still fortunately free of cars; your bicycle could be punctured at peace by a nail from the cast shoe of any leisurely cart horse; and it was thought immoral in our remote Arcadia to go a-riding on the Sabbath. We had sinned. Crane and a large party of our lads, returning from a long ride, met the congregation in a black, slow, reproachful stream passing from their prayers. Crane, I remember, was clad in a loud, brown, almost maroon and snuff-coloured, check cutaway, and looked, with his scarlet tie, like some happy but slightly bewildered cockchafer in *King Luckyboy's picture-book*. The church as only a church in Cockayne could do, held up its hands in holy horror, and at that moment the Divine Nemesis overtook us, Crane was punctured and collapsed by the roadside.[33]

In the visitor's book, as he was leaving, Crane scribbled a caricature of this memorable scene.

William De Morgan (14) was another early visitor to Campden. He had had his own connections with the Cotswolds. Early in the 1880s, when he planned to build a pottery alongside Morris's textile works, he too had come to Blockley to look at the old Silk Mill, where they found the notices of the last reduction of wages before the Mill closed down in the late eighteenth century still pasted to the door. More recently, Ashbee had tried to persuade De Morgan to move with him to Campden. But De Morgan, who by then was dividing his time somewhat precariously between potteries in Florence and in Fulham, had declined, calling Ashbee a wicked chap for putting such temptations in his path and explaining that he was absolutely forbidden by financial considerations from thinking of it. 'If I could come to Campden', he wrote to Ashbee, 'it would be, I am sure, a Paradise regained, and one in which I could be merry in spite of some great blanks and the twenty-years between. My being time-worn and tile-worn now would not stick in the way, nothing would prevent it but mere impossibility. However I shall not find it all impossible to pay you a visit with the missus, if you will ask us when you are settled, and I hope you will add pots to your other outputs as I am sure they will be pretty ones'.[34]

The pots, as it turned out, never did materialize; but De Morgan's promised visit with the missus took place duly in September. The ever-inventive, whimsical De Morgan, an early incarnation of Professor Branestawm, was described by Ashbee as 'a most loveable man', with his delightful blue eyes and his brazil-nut shaped head, surmounted by 'a sort of tender curly tuft', and his 'little musical winning high-pitched voice'. His wife appeared equally humorous and fanciful: 'Each', said Ashbee, 'is constantly surprising the other by the piquancy, the whimsicalness of the last new jest, and then they both forget the sorrows of life and laugh. "How strange and wonderful it must be", said De Morgan as he hoisted the kitten up in the air, "to be a little hairy thing among

(12) Cecil Brewer (d.1918), known in the Guild workshops as the 'boy architect'. He was one of those fresh-faced Englishmen who look forever 23 and Ashbee had always been particularly fond of him, describing their first meeting as love at first sight. 'He is also one of those rare people', wrote Ashbee, 'who in the metier of the architect have true feelings, who see and understand what architecture means, love it and can design for it.' (*Ashbee Journal*, September 1902). He includes Brewer in his short-list of the 'real architects' then at work in England; the others being G. F. Bodley, Philip Webb, Lethaby and Harry Wilson and Charles Holden. Brewer's best-known work is the Mary Ward Building, Tavistock Place (designed with A. Dunbar Smith). He was Ambrose Heal's cousin and, just before the First World War, designed Heal's new shop in Tottenham Court Road. He and Heal were among the co-founders of the Design and Industries Association.

(13) Walter Crane (1845–1915), artist, craftsman, designer and inveterate committee man. A gentle, kindly person (with an overpowering wife); a heart-felt Socialist of the old aesthetic type, well described by William Rothenstein in *Men and Memories*: 'Like Morris, Crane was a Socialist; and Socialism meant to him, as it did to Morris, a seemlier life for the people; in a Socialist world, men as well as women would be becomingly dressed.'

(14) William De Morgan (1839–1917), potter and later, to everyone's surprise, best-selling novelist. Ashbee asked him, after the appearance of *Joseph Vance* in 1906, what it felt like to be a fashionable writer. ' "My dear boy", he piped in his high-pitched voice; "My publisher keeps sending me cheques, and I don't know what to do with them. It's all come too late, had it come a few years ago I might have saved my pottery" '. (*Ashbee Memoirs*, introduction to Chapter 3, 1938)

creatures of infinite power!" The kitten too had a sense of humour and pretended an equality with the Jumblies.'

The Ashbees took De Morgan to look at Campden Church, where he sat dreamily dangling his legs from the wall. In the distance was the droning hum of the threshing machine. Or was it Mr Carrington at his services inside? 'De Morgan's whimsicalness never forsakes him', wrote Ashbee happily, 'and he muttered, half audibly – "When it's continuous it's agriculture; when it's intermittent it's religion".'[35]

The height of the visit was a dinner party in which the De Morgans were courageous (or whimsical) enough to attack two new neighbours of the Ashbees, Sidney and Beatrice Webb (15). It was a sparkling contest, in which the umpire was the Earl of Gainsborough's ever-smiling agent, Louis Dease. De Morgan rashly challenged the practical workings of collectivist socialism as illustrated by the LCC. Mrs Webb 'tore and rent' him. Sidney Webb characteristically looked on admiringly, and with 'a satirical stoicism' picked up the bits.

The arrival of the Webbs in the Guild's chosen Cotswold backwater was a fine stroke of irony which Ashbee much appreciated. 'To think', he wrote in the Journal that September, 'that after having definitely shaken the dust of London from off one's shoes and having retired to

(15) Sidney Webb (1859–1947, later Baron Passfield) and his wife Beatrice (1858–1943). Since their marriage in 1892, at which they had exchanged rings inscribed 'pro bono publico', they had worked together on some massive literary enterprises. Their *History of Trade Unionism* has been published in 1894; *Industrial Democracy* in 1897: and they had now embarked on the even larger task of writing the history of local government. The first volume in the series appeared in 1906: the ninth, and last, in 1929.

(16) A prize example of their incompatability occurred a few years later when by chance the Webbs and Ashbees met on the journey back home from Pompeii, where the Webbs had been taking a well-earned holiday after three years' hard work on the Poor Law Commission.

'We discussed Pompeii', wrote Ashbee in the Journal (17 March 1909), 'but the Webbs and we must by virtue of our different natures always differ in certain fundamentals.'

' "Pompeian life" ,' Mrs Webb declared 'in her lucid and final way, "must always be repellent to me. They lived for pleasure – they had neither mysticism nor seriousness of purpose – they were sensual, and their art was mostly hideous. Why, the life of a town like Oldham, which would probably correspond roughly to Pompeii, with its well educated operatives taking part in municipal and industrial life, is a far finer thing than anything Pompeii developed".' 'Oldham indeed!' Ashbee commented despairingly: 'Put Oldham under a volcano for 2000 years and then compare its product and value with Pompeii.'

agriculture and homilies with no County Council or Municipal Socialism to trouble us any longer, there should suddenly arise and settle at Campden for the summer Sidney Webb and his wife'.[36] Their arrival caused a good deal of excitement in the town, at least amongst those citizens who knew who the Webbs were. ('For most of us here', maintained Ashbee, 'Mr Webb is merely Mr Webb and we do not read the leaders in "The Times" on the terrors of the New Regime'.) There was even an enthralling rumour that the Prime Minister himself had been seen calling at the ugly little house by the station which the Webbs, with typical Fabian indifference to aesthetics, had rented for a few weeks' working holiday. 'The rumour', said Sidney Webb to Ashbee, 'is entirely unfounded, but in light of the support that we are trying to give to the new education bill, it is distinctly interesting, and has evidently come through a member of your Guild who is an S.D.F. man'.[37]

Whether the Webbs were delighted or dismayed to find that an experiment in real live Socialism had arrived ahead of them in Campden one can only guess. Either way, they made the most of the situation, eager to know every detail of Guild theory and Guild working, worming every last statistic out of Ashbee who, in retaliation, seized the opportunity of 'sucking the brains' of the formidable Webbs. On all possible occasions, at lunch or supper, out on bicycles, such vital national topics as the housing question, the education bill and secondary and technical education in Chipping Campden were thrashed out. Ashbee admired the Webbs, though his compliments were often decidedly back-handed: Sidney Webb, who was almost grotesquely ugly, he described as 'a finer man than he looks'. Beatrice, Ashbee noted, perhaps with some alarm, was writing a journal amongst her other works 'into which everybody goes, but which, like all decently minded journals, is only to show itself posthumously'. Maybe then he and Mrs Webb would compare notes. 'For the moment', he concluded cryptically, 'I like her company more than I like her.'

Basically, of course, the Ashbees and the Webbs were poles apart. Their ideas of Socialism were fairly incompatible: the Ashbees' Socialism was romantic and emotional; the Webbs were a great deal harder-headed, much more rational and intellectual (16). But they seem to have found each other stimulating, even joining forces to taunt the working-classes in the course of a bicycle outing together to Northwick Park. 'Coming into the dining room', wrote Ashbee in the Journal, 'the ubiquitous butler pointed out a row of copper plaques, 17th-century grisaille, and putting one in my hand said "These are considered very beautiful, and the curious thing about it is, that the art is entirely lost". Webb seized the opportunity of paying a jest at the man's expense and said "Do you think, Ashbee, you could produce these at Campden?" and I handed it back to the butler, with an "Oh yes, we can do you any number if you will only let us have the pattern and give us time enough".' The man's look of blank and discomfitted astonishment was, said Ashbee, amusing: it was not so much the fact that the plate could be copied which so mystified the butler as the fact that the plate could be copied at such a one-horse town as *Campden*. ' "Really Sir!", he stammered, "One has to be very careful what one says!" '[38]

In spite of all the visitors and early autumn jaunts, work went on well. The Guild craftsmen were all reasonably busy, though the jewellers seemed to be less busy than the others. Ashbee himself was much involved with designs for a great Prayer Book to be printed by the Essex House Press the following year, by far its biggest project. At the same time, he was embarking on grandiose schemes with Lawrence Hodson, a Wolverhampton brewer, for a group of church buildings planned to form a new Christian centre in the Midlands: plans which, needless to say, involved a monumental interchange of letters on the past, present and future of the Church in England. In the autumn, Ashbee also had an exhibition at the Woodbury Gallery in London. A letter Janet wrote him when he was away from Campden shows how she, as well, was continuously busy: she ends happily, but sounding slightly careworn, 'Always yours in blissful solitary warmth peace untidyness nervestraining and continuous occupation'.[39] (A little later she was telling her friend Arthur Wauchope (17) that she felt ten years older since she came to Campden.)

The Guildsmen were occupied too with preparations for a Guy Fawkes carnival and torchlight procession. It was reported in the local paper that the Guild had invited the townspeople to co-operate, the first formal attempt to integrate the two communities and so an event of

(17) Arthur Wauchope (1874–1947, later Sir Arthur, Major-General and High Commissioner of Palestine and Trans-Jordan). Friend of Janet's and one of her constant correspondents. In spite of his spectacularly successful record of service to his king and country, his letters are disarmingly full of doubts and worries. He had once been a Fabian, he explains in one of them, 'and from that day to this, Janet, I've never been able to decide whether I think it best to topsy turvy the present beastly state of things, or tinker them'. (*Ashbee Journals*, 1907)

some significance. Though the weather was particularly inauspicious – it was, alas, according to the papers, a typical November day, dull, misty and moist, with rain which 'fell somewhat heavily at intervals and damped everything except the spirits of those who were busily at work getting everything ready for the night's display'[40] – Chipping Campden carnival went ahead undaunted, and apparently featured some members of the Guild dressed in nigger costume (which suggests that the cultural level of the Guildsmen was not perhaps as rarefied as Ashbee might have hoped).

It was almost a year since the momentous decision to move to Campden had been taken by the Guildsmen, almost a year since Jacko, the young blacksmith, had walked through the snow to take the news to Ashbee. Great changes had been made in the life of the Guild. It seemed to Ashbee the right time to recap on his principles, the basic aims and ideas which had brought the Guild to Gloucestershire: 'It is good', he wrote in his Journal that November, 'now and again to get one's mind clear on fundamentals and when one has done so, or thinks one has, to state them as axioms.'

'Here goes then:
(1) Machinery is necessary in modern production, so also is human individuality.
(2) The recognition of Ethical principles in economics postulates a good and bad in the productions of machinery.
(3) Machinery in so far as it destroys human individuality is bad, in so far as it develops it is good.'[41]

Ashbee saw his business as the production of works of handicraft that give joy in use. How does one measure joy? Ashbee insisted that while the marketable value of the products and the customer's reaction to them, 'the consumers' conception of joy', provides an immediate and obvious yardstick, the ultimate standard is set by the pleasure of the man who makes them. 'Take away the producer's joy', ran Ashbee's argument, 'destroy his interest, his care, his thought, turn him into a hack or a machine, in other words destroy his individuality and the work produced will not be so good'. The year in Campden had confirmed all Ashbee's basic theories; in fact it had given them a lot of extra force, for in the comparative isolation of the Cotswolds, the onus was more obviously on individual craftsmen. Here, if anywhere, it seemed, according to its individual standards, the Guild of Handicraft would thrive or fall.

The Ashbees had some visitors to stay for Christmas: Gwendolen and Gerald Bishop, Nanette Dalmas and 'a charming well-trained formal little girl', May Hart, who was described by Ashbee as Fred Partridge's 'young woman'.[42] Fred Partridge, a jeweller from Devon, had recently come to work with the Guild in Campden, but because his liaison with May was unofficial – certain bourgeois scruples operating even in Utopian Socialist communities – he had been put on parole to stay away from Ashbee's house party.

In retrospect, it was a significant small gathering that Christmas-time in Campden: May Hart and Gerald Bishop, in particular, were to be central figures in the complex personal dramas which were later to develop, perhaps inevitably, in the high-flown atmosphere of Ashbee's City of the Sun.

But for the time being, all seemed peaceful, all seemed festive. Fourteen neighbours' children, trained by Janet, went out to sing carols round the town, wearing red hoods and carrying coloured lanterns, with a few grown-ups, dressed in black and white, to shepherd them along. They took round collecting boxes, the proceeds of which would go to buy the children swimming tickets for the bathing lake the Guild was going to build in Campden in the summer.

One night the carol singers stopped at the composer Joseph Moorat's house and sang him his own carol, 'For the snow lay on the ground'. He came out, delighted, stood at the garden gate, and in his 'little chirpy husky voice', joined in.

3

The Building of the City
1903

The new year began with the first Guild play in Campden, a performance of *The New Inn* by Ben Jonson. These productions, which became an annual tradition – enjoyed more, one actor claimed (1), by the performers than the audience – were very much a part of Ashbee's basic Guild philosophy, conveniently providing scope for simultaneous cheery fellowship and teamwork and improvement of the mind.

The plays chosen were usually late Elizabethan or early Jacobean, and this too was a reflection of the Ashbee aspirations. He looked back with some nostalgia to the spirit of freedom and adventure in Elizabethan England, and with touching faith asserted that, once you got them acting in Jonson's plays or Shakespeare's, this Elizabethan spirit would rub off on his young craftsmen, pioneers of the ideal democratic modern state. Ashbee went to great lengths with the Guild plays, coaching the actors, correcting cockney accents and mispronunciations, improving awkward gestures. 'Every detail was watched', wrote one of the performers, full of admiration, 'and he set a high standard and was relentless in his correction, particularly of slovenly speech'.[1] Not only was Ashbee the producer and the manager, staging the plays starkly without scenery, in the manner of Poel (2) and the Elizabethan Stage Society, but he was also one of the leading actors, year after year tirelessly assigning a large and demanding part to himself.

Ashbee was in fact, by all accounts, an excellent actor with a fine

---

(1) This particular craftsman-actor, Philippe Mairet, went on to act professionally with the Old Vic.

(2) William Poel (1852–1934), revolutionary stage director who believed that the plays of Shakespeare and his contemporaries should be performed in conditions as near Elizabethan as was possible. He was a great protagonist for fast, clear verse-speaking, the technique which Ashbee tried to transmit to the Guild.

speaking voice, in spite of his tendency to affectation in normal conversation, and *The New Inn,* in which he took the part of Lovel, melancholy gentleman, was on the whole a great success. The village crowded into the first two performances and asked for a third, which the Guild gladly put on for them. There was also a matinee for the local gentry, through much of which the Earl of Gainsborough sat fast asleep, only waking with a start when Prudence the Chambermaid stamped her foot in Act IV and cried 'Be damned for ignorance!' 'But what', remarked Ashbee with surprising tolerance, 'can even the most conservative of peers do when he has to sandwich a Ben Jonson play between two County balls, and his daughters keep him on his legs and yawning till four in the morning!'[2]

Dozens of the Ashbees' friends came to Campden for the play: Gerald Bishop and his wife, Goldsworthy Lowes Dickinson and his sister and many others who were quartered out in lodgings all around the village. William Strang (3) brought his whole family, and the Strangs and Ashbees had a riotous week of it, as Janet described it, 'full of Scotch stories and Holbeinesque drawings.' It was a stimulating week, culminating in an argument which showed the best of Janet's very independent spirit. The account is in her Journal for 14 January:

Strang and I went out cycling one day, and he wanted to push my machine up a hill, a thing I never allow. I told him I always resented that arrogance in a man which says: See how strong I am! What is it to me if I wheel ten bicycles, or open 50 doors, or stoop for 100 handkerchiefs? It's a harping on the purely physical superiority that galls.

Strang fired up, and quite glared beneath his shaggy brows.

'Ye're wrahng!' he said hotly, 'altegither wrahng! It's no an assumption of supeeriority, it's just a way of paying back the debt of man to woman. Just look what you've been doing for me in hoaspitality all these days. An' I'm not even to be allowed to relieve you of your cycle!'

'But I'm an able bodied woman,' I retorted, 'you've done quite as much with your magnificent drawings and stories as I have in meals I didn't cook and beds I didn't make . . . where's the obligation?'

'There's always an oabligation,' he said; 'and I hope the time may come when you'll be glad to let a man do things for you. And,' he concluded with the conviction of the male, 'it'll be a bahd day for the wurrld when men no longer desire to help women, or when women refuse their services!'[3]

Among the visitors who came to Campden for the play was John Masefield (4). Only recently, after a romantic sojourn in America as labourer, tramp, pot boy and farm hand, he had worked his passage back to England and the previous autumn his first book of poems, *Salt-Water Ballads,* had been published in a very small edition. He was now, through the good offices of friends in Wolverhampton, Secretary to the fine art section of the Wolverhampton Art and Industrial Exhibition (5).

Masefield, in his persona of the young and struggling poet, with his background of adventure, was popular at Campden both with Ashbee and the Guildsmen. 'Our poet', wrote Ashbee in the Journal, 'during his long periods of speaking silence, when he is not weaving yarns, sits and twists two corkscrews of hair that suggests the understudy for a youthful Moses. His acquaintance with minor poets, ballad singers, raconteurs and the dear folk of the wanderlust, is wonderful. He will tell of them one after another with an imaginative delicacy that defies description'.[4] And Campden evidently very much appealed to Masefield. George Hart, the silversmith, had run excitedly to Ashbee during one of the intervals in *The New Inn,* telling him to look at Masefield through the curtains: '"I say, C.R.A. do look at old Masefield's eyes, they're shining like silver!" And they were that, and more.'[5] By the end of his stay, Masefield was full of schemes for coming to live with the boys in Campden, on 12s 6d a week.

(3) William Strang (1859–1929), painter and etcher. A noisy, fiery Lowland Scot with 5 children. The Ashbees enjoyed going to his jolly, breezy London house, where 9 or 10 people would sit down to a meal. While he was in Campden, Strang did a whole series of drawings of the Ashbees and the Guildsmen, but unfortunately these have now all been dispersed.

(4) John Masefield (1878–1967, later Poet Laureate). William Rothenstein met him too about this time, at the Strangs' house in Hamilton Terrace, where he was regarded as a figure of some mystery. 'Laurence Binyon was a familiar there, and one evening he came bringing a stranger, a quiet youth, with eyes that seemed surprised at the sight of the world, and hair that stood up behind like a cockatoo's feathers. As a youth he had run away to sea, Binyon whispered, and had had wondrous adventures; now he wanted to write; but he was very poor, and Binyon was helping him'. (*Men and Memories,* London, Faber, 1932).

(5) The City Art Gallery at Wolverhampton originated in this exhibition. The intention was to show the important work being done by artists outside the Royal Academy. It was one of the many enterprises of Lawrence Hodson, the Wolverhampton brewer, whose centre for the New Religion Ashbee was then working on. Although so altruistic, Hodson was not very likeable, being unnecessarily unkind to his fat and stupid wife whom he called 'Piggy.'

When he got home, he sent Janet a poem set in Campden, the first of a succession of Cotswold poems and stories. This was a bloody ballad in thick rural dialect: 'It fell in the mirk Februeer'. It is chiefly memorable for verse three, in which the hero makes his appearance:

Ashbee looked West; Ashbee looked East
He looked dourly up and down
Till he was ware of the Jamie beast
A galloping grimly towards the toun.

After the exertions and excitements of *The New Inn,* which had yielded £36 profit – £8 for expenses, £9 for coal for the poor of the parish, the remainder for the Bathing Lake – the Ashbees must have felt in need of a small holiday. They set off north via Wolverhampton, stopping off for Ashbee to continue his long debate with Lawrence Hodson on the future Church of England. Then they travelled to Millthorpe in Derbyshire to visit Edward Carpenter.

Janet had been to Millthorpe before, four years earlier, just after her marriage, when Edward Carpenter, described in her diary as a man of 'the greatest human interest and vitality',[6] had far exceeded her expectations. On this, her second visit, she found Carpenter a trifle greyer, a shade more dreamy and preoccupied, but still the same 'warm, magnetic creature'[7] who had captivated her before. By this time Edward Carpenter had become very much one of the grand old men of Socialism, a notable eccentric, variously described as the Complete Anarchist

(6) This was the George Merrill who pinched E. M. Forster's bottom and directly inspired his homosexual novel *Maurice.*

(7) Nobody in England went quite as far as Thoreau, the American transcendentalist, who lived for two years in a hut on the banks of Walden Pond in totally primitive conditions. 'I was never unusually squeamish', wrote Thoreau in his account of his experiences, 'I could sometimes eat a fried rat with a good relish, if it were necessary.'

(8) Henry Salt was another revolutionary graduate of King's. In the early 1880s, when he and his brother-in-law Jim Joynes were both masters at Eton, they were 'carried away on the rising tide of socialism'. To the dismay of the authorities, as recounted by Carpenter in his memoirs, 'they adopted vegetarianism, a thing almost unheard of at Eton except in the dubious connection of Shelley; they revolted in their personal habits from the luxury and indulgence of the life there; and they protested against the coursing of hares, and other inhumanities favoured by both boys and masters. It soon became clear to them they could not remain in surroundings so uncongenial . . .'

and Saint in Sandals. Locally, he had become more or less an institution, and villagers would come to ask for help with such complicated tasks as making wills or signing deeds. He was also on good terms with the farmers of the neighbourhood, although ironically, when the main aim of his life had been demolishing class barriers, they treated him with all the respect due to a gentleman.

With Carpenter, in ostentatious irregularity, lived George Merrill, a relatively recent arrival (6). He had come, romantically, from the slums of Sheffield pushing his possessions before him on a handcart. He was a volatile and humorous young man, highly domesticated and very good at cooking. (Janet wrote with much approval of his salmon and steak pies and blackberry tart.) To many of the free-thinking people of the time, the regime at Millthorpe seemed very close to heaven, and there are ecstatic descriptions of the household in many contemporary Socialist memoirs, praising the simple and temperate routine; the sunbaths and the windbaths, taken naked to the elements; the open-air hut by the stream, inspired by Thoreau (7), in which Carpenter wrote his inflammatory treatises, rejoicing to get the sentiment of the open free world wafting through his pages. Janet herself had been greatly impressed with the absence of 'Things' in the small plain house at Millthorpe. Mrs Havelock Ellis depicted, with delight, Edward and his 'factotum and friend' sitting together, one mending his shirt, the other darning a pair of socks: one of Carpenter's innumerable theories was that anything a woman does, a man can always share.

There were always a great many visitors at Millthorpe. Carpenter had a dangerous ambition to make Millthorpe a rendezvous for all classes and conditions of society: for parsons and positivists, printers and authors, scythesmiths and surgeons, bank managers and quarrymen, and all the rest. Homosexual, or anyway homogenic, men were always much in evidence. (Janet asked George once why some of the young labourers at Millthorpe were so fine to look at; he said it was because they had learned to be kissed.) Sometimes the gatherings were not totally successful, but Carpenter had considerable resources for enlivening the atmosphere. According to Henry Salt (8), a frequent visitor:

Various were the devices that he had in reserve when things began to get a bit dull. One of them was a queer performance of what was known as 'the thunderstorm', when he would sit with elbows resting on a table, and head on hands, and in that posture give forth a succession of dour growls and murmurs to represent the storm as it approached: then the lightnings – to wit, his eyes – would flash; and this was the best part of an entertainment which could hardly be said to add to the gaiety of nations. At other times, when there was a threat of awkward silences, he would indulge in mild forms of horse-play. A friend told me that William Morris, after a short stay at Millthorpe, referred to him as a 'dreary cove'.[8]

Millthorpe was at its most crowded in the summer, the season when the tourists and the cranks descend in dozens, as the Ashbees were themselves to find at Campden. But in January, Millthorpe was relatively peaceful and they had some good days walking on the moors with Carpenter, discussing the prospects for democracy, and eating the homely meals George Merrill made for them. They appreciated George: he and Edward, noted Janet, 'seem as fitted as a hermit crab and his shell'.[9] Then, with one of the volte-faces which the Ashbees managed easily, without which indeed their life would hardly have been practical (9), they left the Anarchist community at Millthorpe for the gentlest of gentlefolk at Hallingbury Place.

Hallingbury Place in Essex was the home of the Archer-Houblon family, a house where the old order had not changed for centuries. All was feudal, prosperous and calm. The Guild, two years before, had done some work at Hallingbury, the pièce de résistance of which was an elaborate modelled ceiling in the billiard room, combining all the coats of arms of Houblon intermarriages with the white pinks which were the emblem of the Guild. To celebrate the completion of the work the Guild went down to Hallingbury for a cricket match against the village XI, which the yokels appear to have won easily. 'When the match was done', as Ashbee described the scene, 'the brake was brought down to the pavilion on the beautiful green sward, the tea things unpacked and we had a generous meal in the evening sunlight.'[10] These festivities, in which the Guild mingled not only with the villagers, but also with all the Archer-Houblons, boys and girls, retainers, servants, the Hallingbury house party, and even the Archer-Houblon pets, seemed to Ashbee a golden day in the Guild history. He talked of revolution, but his heart was never in it because he deeply loved the old English aristocracy, typified for him by the gracious personage of Lady Alice Houblon (10). Lady Alice, who emerges from the Ashbee

(9) Ashbee did not think it in the least incongruous, having spent the day working on drawings for the Prayer Book, to end the evening with a mighty chapter of Rabelais.

(10) Goodhart-Rendel missed the point when he made his famous comment that if you took up Ashbee you were really in with the revolutionaries.

journals as a kind-hearted lady with a patronizing manner, seemed to Ashbee very near perfection, and any revolution which disposed of Lady Alice, or anybody like her, was for him unthinkable.

On the way to Hallingbury, as they passed through London, the Ashbees had a disconcerting experience, the implications of which were all too clear to them. The Journal entry is for 25 January 1903:

We were driving from St. Pancras to Liverpool Street, splashing through the slosh of a dismal deadening London day, and thanking our luck that we were out of it, when our cab was suddenly pulled up by police, and an army of unemployed marched, or rather slouched by. There must have been some thousand of them, they were in rows of fives, they carried the red banner of the S.D.F. and they were terrible and tragic to see. Clothes of all sorts, a few in the duds of the agricultural labourer, most in shabby frock coats, whilom shop tailor things, the cast off rags of a superior class. They were mostly men of middle age. I noticed few either young or very old, but all wastrel, ugly boneless, brawnless with rotten faces and miserable beyond words. The well trimmed police marched along side, there were collections with money boxes, and the procession ended with mounted officers, thus giving an official stamp to the whole thing, as though society were saying through its home secretary: We hereby recognize the Social Democratic Federation, observe how it gives you a display in the shape of an object lesson in modern industry and ethics. There have been many pageants in this time of coronations and Durbars . . . this is but another of them – pay for it.[11]

They found it a relief to get back to Chipping Campden. Ashbee was promptly pounced on to solve all the little problems which had arisen in the workshops in his absence. The greatest commotion was, as usual, in the metalshop. While the woodshop was characteristically stolid, inartistic, very British, with a talent for self-government, the metalshop was always on the verge of some explosion. This was partly because the men were ill-assorted, but mainly the fault of the foreman, W. A. White. White was one of the oldest members of the Guild, having joined Ashbee's Ruskin class in 1888, and it was, Ashbee admitted, solely on ground of seniority that he was now a foreman. Although he had some sterling qualities, including a natural feeling for design, he had no more tact, complained Ashbee, than a seal or a whale. In fact, he was known as THE WHALE in the workshop, and he was the target for innumerable jokes about his big flat feet and the boots that had no bend in them. His tactlessness, as Ashbee frequently lamented, militated against his management of men, and so did his bad temper: 'Ask him a question when he is in a bearish mood, and he will snort at you negatively, blowing the words up at you through a great black bristly moustache, so that though you cannot hear what the words are, you know them not to be sweet.' To make matters worse, though he was not too bad an actor, his singing voice was terrible to listen to, and he had to be kept well in the background at all the Guild's musical festivities. He totally lacked the 'homogenic touch' in which Ashbee put such faith, the sympathy for men and power to handle them which was so central to the theory of the Guild. All in all, White was an obvious liability as foreman. But what, in a humane and democratic set-up, do you do with White and others like him, men too good to cast off and yet not good enough to fill the places set for them? It was a crucial problem. Ashbee's attitude was generous. As he put it in the Journal: 'Modern competition says: "Sack them", and that is the method of business employed by the great philanthropists of our day, the Samuel Morleys, the Sidney Waterlows, and Andrew Carnegies, but I cannot get myself to regard it as in any sense moral, honourable, or loyal; and when a man has put at your service the 14 best years of his life he is entitled to more recognition'.[12]

Wherever the Guild was, in Gloucestershire or Whitechapel, W. A. White would still have been a problem. But there were other difficulties looming which were more peculiar to Campden. Early in the year, much to the dismay of Ashbee, George Colverd, a particularly promising apprentice silversmith, announced that he was leaving to become a footballer. He had, in fact, been restless since he first arrived in Campden, finding the rural life no compensation for the prospect of a place in the Millwall Reserves: but his final defection was very sad for Ashbee, who had had great hopes for George, one of his 'own pet Cockneys'.[13]

One of the best of the jewellers, Fred Partridge, also left the Guild, but for quite a different reason, a reason which made Janet burn with indignation: 'the way of a man with a maid'. Fred Partridge was a chemist's son from Barnstaple, a large fine rather Nordic figure with a rugged face and shaggy hair and a mouth described by Janet as 'too curved and unstable to be quite safe'.[14] He was more middle-class in background, more flamboyant in appearance, than most of the Guild

(11) She had previously worked with Douglas Cockerell in London.

(12) In fact Fred Partridge and May were later reconciled and married. But May committed suicide in 1917.

(13) i.e.
I do not love thee Dr Fell.
The reason why I cannot tell,
But this I know I know full well,
I do not love thee, Dr Fell.

craftsmen, addicted to what the boys called the 'Jolly Art Style' of dress, complete from flannel shirt to sandals. Partridge was engaged to the daughter of a doctor in Birmingham, demure, polite May Hart, and this match had had the Ashbees' blessing; but with the arrival of Statia Power in Campden, it appears that he rather lost his head. Statia Power, an Essex House Press binder (11), was a big statuesque girl who, as Janet later saw it, 'played fast and gloriously' in her years in Campden.[15] When Janet first took her to tea at the Guest House, Fred Partridge had obviously been impressed:

'I say isn't she FINE?' Partridge said to me next morning; 'but we'll have to break her of that long skirt.' And that was the beginning . . . then she was lonely in her lodgings and he was lonely at the Guest House; and she desired to make a silver ring with garnets and he wanted to show her how to solder; and she tried to illuminate on vellum, and he burned to display his skill in manuscript writing; and that was the continuation.[16]

With poor May Hart so obviously jilted, there was nothing for it but for Partridge to leave Campden (12). He took it very badly, and wrote bitterly to Ashbee, 'You are a peculiar man and I don't like you', to which Ashbee replied amiably, quoting Dr Fell (13). Janet, ever-rational, saw the whole episode as the inevitable consequence of introducing female labour to the Guild.

On the top of all this, the Skipper lost his temper. The Skipper, alias the Steward of the Guest House, was Will Hart, the wood-carver. He and his brother George Hart, the silversmith, had been enlisted for the Guild by Ashbee at a craft exhibition at Hitchin, and soon became two of its most highly favoured members. Although he rarely read a book, George was made the Guild Librarian, and Will had the boys of Braithwaite House put in his care. This particular fracas – the ejection of Sid Cotton, the Mad Hatter, for truculence and rudeness, a decision which in his heart Ashbee agreed with – shows how a minor issue, easily ignored in London, in the atmosphere of Campden could quickly cause a drama. This was something which Ashbee had not perhaps foreseen.

The Skipper's equanimity, it seems, quite soon recovered, and Ashbee's faith in him was certainly not shaken. For Ashbee, whose enthusiasms sometimes ran away with him, Will Hart was a curious kind of idol. He saw him as one of the born leaders of men, one of those rare people who were truly homogenic without being aware of it:

To me – it is a man's view of a man – the skipper is very beautiful, – for his strength, his chivalry, his manliness. The soul that is form here, 'doth the body make'. No stranger could pass the skipper in the street without looking twice – the fine carriage, the lissom body of the seaman, the strong square head, the impenetrable blue eyes, – their tenderness and loyalty. When he bowls at cricket it is the Greek discobolus. For myself, I admit to a sense of wistfulness, often at getting so much more of the loyalty than the tenderness. Will he never have done holding himself in?[17]

Perhaps the most striking thing in Ashbee's view of Hart was not its amazingly intense romanticism so much as its underlying seriousness of attitude. It was, to say the least, unusual in those days for someone of Ashbee's education and background to treat working men as he did, as people of importance and considerable interest. He gave an impression, which was on the whole sincere, of enjoying a conversation with his Guildsmen just as much as he thrived on a discussion with Goldsworthy Lowes Dickinson or Sidney Webb. He was paternal to his craftsmen, but never patronizing (14). He took immense trouble with

(14) Ashbee's attitude was very close to William Morris's ideal of Socialism: 'How will you sail a ship in a socialist condition? How? Why with a captain and mates and sailing master and engineer (if it be a steamer) and ABs and stokers and so on and so on. *Only* there will be no 1st, 2nd and 3rd class among the passengers: the sailors and stokers will be as well-fed and lodged as the captain or passengers; and the captain and the stoker will have the same pay.' (*Communism: a lecture.* Fabian Tracts, 1903)

(15) Alec Miller told the story of how, in the early days in Whitechapel, one of the pillars of the Guild, the cabinet-maker C. V. Adams, had come in unexpectedly when a life-class was in progress. '*Mr* Ashbee', he cried out, '*you* call that a "nude model" – I call it a naked woman!' In the heat of the moment, he had quite forgotten he was meant to call Mr Ashbee 'C.R.A.'

(16) Ashbee's tale of Archie Ramage's

recruitment is revealing: 'He had been a week at Campden on a visit, he had said never a word the whole 7 days though he had taken everything in. We had been out on a day's excursion, some six of us, and there was a hot discussion on conscience and instinct and how to choose the right. One of us said something that upset his Scotch equanimity, he lifted up his voice and spake – "It appears to me" he said with the utmost caution, "that what is right will always commend itself to the understanding of a man who has not been spoilt by an artifeecial life".

'This determined me that on the earliest possible occasion we must have Archie in the Guild – a method of selection that would hardly recommend itself to the understanding of any reasonable employer of Labour unless Scotch – but that likewise I have never regretted.' (*Ashbee Journal*, October 1903). Archie Ramage eventually became a Presbyterian minister, and Ashbee sometimes used to speak from his pulpit in Gravesend.

the members of the Guild, in working hours and out; he put unending energy into developing their special interests and talents. So much so that the older men would sometimes grumble at it: Old Dick Read had always called the farm at Poynetts, where the Guild boys went for weekends, 'bread and jam junction'. (Things had not been so easy in Old Dick Read's Chartist days.) Some of them still baulked at calling their director 'C.R.A.' instead of 'Mr Ashbee', as he had stipulated (15). To some of them it simply seemed unnatural. But in this, as in his other democratic schemes, he persevered.

The Guildsmen saw Ashbee in several different roles. First of all, as the architect with his London office to attend to as well as the office which he now ran in Campden. Then as the designer. In spite of his ideas about releasing the creative instincts of the craftsman, in practice Ashbee kept a quite tight overall control on the products of the Guild, and by the time the Guild arrived in Campden he was apparently designing almost all the furniture, silverwork, jewellery and ironwork made at the Guild. For his design work, Ashbee had another small office, in the Silk Mill. 'There', wrote Alec Miller, 'we knew him as the Guild Director, settling problems of workshop administration, placating difficult customers or Guildsmen, always busy, always with paper and pencil in hand, always approachable and friendly, asking one's opinion on this or that design, about which he knew much more than we did! Then suddenly the "Director" would disappear, and with an engaging smile he would say, "Come and swim tonight" or "Let's have a walk around Dover's Hill".'[18]

Alec Miller and his boon companion, Archie Ramage, a pair so inseparable that they were usually referred to as 'the Scotch boys', were frequently invited on these tramps across the Cotswolds. They were particular favourites of Ashbee's, and ideal Guild material. Archie, too, had come from Glasgow. He arrived the previous August for a holiday with Alec, and after observing what seemed to him 'the miracle of the Guild' (in contrast to the newspaper office where he worked as a compositor) and falling in love with the Gloucestershire countryside, he made up his mind to move to Campden permanently (16). Ashbee saw the great potential of his Scotch boys, and worked on it assiduously, mixing education with pleasure. He describes in a letter to Janet one especially idyllic Sunday spent walking with Alec and Archie in the sunshine, up hills and through woods listening to skylarks, discussing man's relation to the universe and reading a selection of Elizabethan lyrics which they carried in their pockets. They also took Keats' 'Belle Dame Sans Merci', which the Scotch boys enjoyed more than Ashbee had expected: 'We read the poem', he told Janet, 'up on top of the wolds, and voted that Heaven was in it.'[19]

Ashbee had a good many reasons to be cheerful in the spring of 1903. There were, admittedly, some minor troubles in the background: the Essex House Press, partly perhaps because of the growing obscurity of its titles, was having difficulty selling its books to the Americans, a market it very much relied on; the Guild jewellers, faced with increasing competition from highly-capitalized companies like Liberty's, were feeling commercially rather insecure. On top of this, news came that a faithful Guild customer, the Hungarian Count Ervin Batthyany, had been put in a lunatic asylum, not because he was necessarily insane but because he had been preaching Tolstoyism to his peasants. But these minor disasters seemed at the time no more than temporary hitches. The main thing was the Guild had been a year in Campden. From the social point of view, the experiment was working. A Whit Monday Fête was held in Campden, the proceeds of which were to go towards the swimming pool, and the local paper commented: 'The townspeople and the members of the Guild of Handicraft (who may by this time be looked upon as townspeople rather than strangers) worked together with a will and arranged a round of amusements such as one would have to go many miles to surpass.'[20] The town was decked out with

(17) Lionel Curtis (1872–1955), public servant par excellence. Some of his colleagues compared him with Isaiah because of his burning zeal, and called him 'the prophet'. As a young man, he had been so determined to gain practical experience of the working of the Poor Law that he disguised himself as a tramp, begging for bread along the road and spending his nights in workhouses.

His friendship with Ashbee dated back to Chelsea days, when Ashbee had restored the house which Turner had once lived in for Curtis and Max Balfour, the painter. He was a great favourite of Ashbee's mother, to the extent of being known as 'the little Mother's sunbeam'. He went out to South Africa, to fight in the war, and in 1899 became secretary to Lord Milner and then Town Clerk of Johannesburg. At the time of Ashbee's visit, at the age of 31, he was assistant Colonial Secretary organizing municipal government throughout the Transvaal.

Later in life, he founded The Round Table and devoted himself to the cause of Commonwealth.

(18) Other people, too, found Ashbee's politics perplexing. A few years later, in the unexpected setting of Reid's Hotel in Madeira, he came upon a local Gloucestershire MP, the Liberal, Sir Walter Essex: 'What I can't understand in you', Essex said to Ashbee, 'is that you go so much further than I do in many things and yet you're such a tory.' (Ashbee Memoirs, March 1909)

bunting, flags and garlands, and the round of amusements included sports and dancing, a tug of war, and a procession of decorative chariots, one of which, a wagonful of children representing 'Summer', adorned with wild flowers from the fields around Campden, was attributed to Mrs Ashbee and Miss Power. The festivities ended with a grand tattoo.

In the summer, the Ashbees spent two months in South Africa, sailing on the RMS *Briton*. (They travelled First Saloon.) The expedition seems to have been partly a holiday and partly a sales mission for the Guild of Handicraft. They had many friends and contacts in South Africa. It was the era of 'Milner's Kindergarten', the collection of astonishingly able young administrators gathered together by the High Commissioner, Sir Alfred Milner, to reconstruct the country after the Boer War. The Kindergarten men were of Ashbee's generation. Many of them, like him, had been involved in the East London settlement movement in the 1880s and in the early days at Toynbee Hall. Lionel Curtis (17), one of Milner's main aides, was one of Ashbee's oldest and closest friends, so the Ashbees straight away felt on familiar territory. Soon Ashbee was involved in discussing such comfortable topics as the Winchester School Colony, the School of Architecture and the Applied Arts and the prospects for a branch of the Guild of Handicraft in the Transvaal.

Ashbee was in many ways enchanted with South Africa, finding everyone delightfully young and optimistic, and largely agreeing with their élitist policy of keeping out the riff-raff and allowing only the best men in as emigrants. His attitude seems to have slightly shocked the Guildsmen back at Campden. 'Your letter was read at the dinner table yesterday, and caused great amusement', reported Alec Miller. 'You are really becoming a Tory Imperialist (18), and of a rank kind.'[21] But Ashbee was wholly unrepentant. He realized the irony of his position. He strongly believed the Morris-Ruskin dictum that the real wealth of a community consists not in its material assets but in its sound men and women. But he simply could not see how to apply it to South Africa, where 75 per cent of the community seemed to him not merely to be living in a state of barbarism, but also to be physically unable through centuries of mental and moral backwardness to form part of the community's civilized life. He recognized the dilemma: 'Are we to give equal opportunity to all, the Socialist faith – and order life and labour on that hypothesis? are we to wait until the higher race has drawn the lower up to it? Or is the other terrible thing to happen; — a fusion that would imply the loss and ruin of everything we hold sacred, good or beautiful?' This he could not bear to contemplate. Even stronger than Ashbee's democratic urges were his highly emotional patriotic instincts, his obsession with standard, his colonialist ideas for planting out in Africa the very best of England (19). He agreed with Lionel Curtis in their discussions for the South African branch of the Guild of Handicraft (which did not in fact materialize) that the work must always be done by white labour and highest skill. 'It is interesting', wrote Ashbee in his Journal while staying in Pretoria, 'to note how completely the English Socialist changes when brought into direct touch with the native question. His universalism goes.'[22]

Life in Campden went on evenly in the Ashbees' absence. Chris Corbin, metalworker, got married; the village pump was accidentally knocked down; but otherwise there seems to have been little news to greet them when they returned to their City of the Sun. They had come back with a few commissions from South Africa – Ashbee had been asked to design a coat of arms for the city of Johannesburg, and the architect Herbert Baker (20) had ordered some furniture and woodwork from the Guild – and, with their usual delight at seeing the quiet

(19) His faith in Britain's might and his admiration for Elizabethan England, the puissant days of Frobisher and Drake, had perhaps originally been stimulated by his Cambridge history tutor, Mandell Creighton, who had specialised in the age of Queen Elizabeth and was much concerned with the analysis of power.

(20) Herbert Baker (1862–1946, later Sir Herbert). The great Colonialist architect. He went to South Africa in 1892 to make his career in the 'land of promise', and became Architect-in-Chief to Milner's Kindergarten, evolving a style of building which, while unmistakably English, had traditional Afrikaaner overtones. Ashbee, on his visit, had admired it greatly, writing: 'I wipe out of my mind all the foolish preconceptions as to the ugliness or vulgarity of upstart Johannesburg for I have seen today

Baker's buildings, the red sandstone crag sites, the fir and cypress, and the rolling purple hills of the rand.

Baker's own house, which he shares with Curtis, Hitchens and Balfour, springing like a jewel castle from out of the rock, its arcades, and stoeps, its red cedar shingled roof, the open court, the white columns, the pergola with the circular garden below, and the wonderful veiled view into the sunset light is one of the most exquisite pieces of architecture I have ever seen.' (*Ashbee Memoirs*, 7 July 1903). The furniture which Baker commissioned from the Guild was made in hardwoods – rosewood, ebony etc. – specifically for his Afrikaaner buildings. Baker later returned to England and collaborated with Lutyens on New Delhi. He also redesigned the Bank of England, incorporating Soane's original Banking Halls.

streets of Campden after a few weeks' absence, they quickly settled back into their countrified routine.

Ashbee at that time spent part of the week in London, in his Cheyne Walk office. He tended to travel up on Tuesday and return on Friday. But one gets the impression from his Journals that he was increasingly less interested in London, and that Campden was the place he most wanted to be. This impression is confirmed by Laurence Housman's description of Ashbee on a London visit, in a letter to Janet in summer 1903:

Your husband came and piled a suggestion of debts and broken promises and false hopes upon my conscience, which I have since then been trying to shake off. My memory of his conversation is vague and I was chiefly concerned with the way he buttons his cuffs: — *how* I can't tell you, there was a sort of 'il n'y a pas de quoi' air about them – like a 'swiss roll' coming undone. He also wore a napkin ring instead of a scarf pin: so he manages altogether to look as if he had come to luncheon bringing his sheaves with him.[23]

Further along Cheyne Walk, in the Ashbees' old home, the house with the copper door, Whistler was slowly dying. The tenancy had not been a success. Apart from the fact that the house was decorated in a style so alien to his tastes that his friends could never understand why he had taken it, the noise of the construction work next door, where another building of Ashbee's was in progress, disturbed and infuriated him so much that it became a terrible obsession. The commotion of the building work, the hammering and knocking, threw him into dreadful rages and, according to Joseph Pennell, his biographer, it had a great deal to do with shortening his life. Whistler's fury took the form of a ferocious personal vendetta against Ashbee, whom he accused of tricking him. He drummed up all possible support against him, and did his best, without success, to have him hounded out of the Art Workers' Guild. It was a sad affair. Ashbee was not apparently very sympathetic to the plight of Whistler, arguing that since he was not paying his rent, any ordinary landlord would by now have turned him out. But contemporary accounts of aged Whistler, moved downstairs at the insistence of the doctor to a little room beside the studio, lying on an Empire bed in his silk nightshirt with a little knitted shawl over his shoulders, are certainly pathetic. Whistler died in Ashbee's house on 17 July.

In Campden, through the late summer and the autumn, catching up perhaps on opportunities lost while the Ashbees were abroad, the visitors were coming in thick and fast: 'so thick', as Ashbee put it, 'that one has to hold oneself in fairly tight if one is not to let one's work be interfered with.' The solution they attempted was to congregate their visitors at weekends, in the country-house manner, so that they entertained each other. But this plan does not seem to have been totally successful, as there are frequent accounts in Ashbee's Journal of visitors who stayed a week or longer. Ashbee's policy of open house and open mind attracted a most curious assortment of arrivals. One week it was Mr and Mrs Eckhard, from Manchester, a violently free-trading German Jew and his wife. Both were immensely interesting, rich and sympathetic, but, according to Ashbee, hard as nails. A week or two before, it had been a charming young American professor from Kansas (or was it Oklahoma? in the flurry of visits, Ashbee could not quite remember) who came to investigate the working of the Guild. Around the same time, Laurence Housman, 'in pursuit of that will-o'-the-wisp the simple life', en route on foot from Hereford to London in protest against railways, sent his luggage on ahead of him. To Ashbee's great amusement, it arrived by train.

In the early years, Campden and the Guild also attracted visitors from quite a different literary tradition. Its East End associations, the whole symbolic story of the flight of the Guild from the city to the country, made it something of a Mecca for the radical-realist authors of the period, writers in the Arthur Morrison tradition, intent on portraying life among the poor in London at its least hopeful and most squalid. Their chosen setting was very often Whitechapel, and some of these writers no doubt came to Campden with the romantic notion (which the Guildsmen would have treated with good-natured cynicism) that here were people who had just escaped from outcast London.

One of these visitors was Richard Whiteing, whose novel of the slums, *No. 5 John Street* had been a notorious success. The famous American writer Jack London also arrived to see the Guild at Campden (21). Ashbee, it appears, had met him first in San Francisco on his National Trust lecture tour in 1900, and when Jack London came to England three years later, first to report on Edward VII's coronation and then (by way of contrast) to collect material for an exposé of

(21) Americans were usually particularly welcome at Campden, with the exception of one who spat out of the window at Braithwaite. The Guild had its standards, and he was asked to leave.

poverty in Whitechapel, he lived for a few weeks in Ashbee's house in Chelsea.

Disguised as a tramp, apparently convincingly, Jack London would close the Ashbees' copper door behind him to make forays into the worst of the East End slums and doss-houses. His experiences in Whitechapel were to form the basis of his powerful reportage on *The People of the Abyss*. In the midst of his research, he went to Campden for the weekend. By this time he was clearly addicted to disguises since he travelled with the pseudonym of Mr Egan, appearing at Woolstaplers' Hall one evening respectably dressed in a dinner jacket. Alec Miller described him as a large good-looking youngish man, a vivid, interesting talker, pungent and racy, but seldom sustaining his subjects of discussion. He drank Ashbee's whisky rather hard and launched into a violent diatribe on poverty and ILP.

Those more temperate Socialists Sidney and Beatrice Webb were in Gloucestershire again, on their annual working holiday. They spent their mornings labouring on their magnum opus on local government. Beatrice concentrated on the immediate scheme; Sidney's task was the compilation of the details and final revision of the total masterplan. Progress was excellent, better than in London, since the Webbs were undisturbed in their Aston Magna cottage. When the weather was bad (as it seems to have been often in summer 1903), Sidney would carry on working after lunch while Beatrice went out to brood over the current chapters, trudging in the rain along the dripping lanes. Whenever the rain stopped, the Webbs got out their bicycles. 'Some delightful rides we had together in the few fine days', wrote Beatrice, looking back on their idyllic weeks in Gloucester, 'happy hours of light-hearted companionship, arguing about our book or plotting our little plans.'[24]

The Webbs often made an expedition to Campden, and would also take their visitors to see 'the Ashbees' works'. The Guild workshops had by now a fixed role in local life as a good place for an outing on a summer afternoon. Indeed eventually the incursions of the sightseers threatened such disruption to the routine of the craftsmen that, for self-preservation, a fixed charge of one shilling was levied for visits to the workshops which, on weekdays, had to take place between the hours of 2 and 4.[25] (It seems these regulations were waived for serious customers.) Probably the niceties of Guild theory and structure were lost on the innumerable parties which descended to be taken round the Silk Mill. But the visitors enjoyed their little tour, and came again.

A fairly frequent visitor was Lady Elcho, leading lady of 'the Souls', that elegant, intense little group of aristocratic intellectuals. Vague, charming, clever, eccentric Lady Elcho was one of the most scintillating women of her day, who seems to have captivated men of all conditions, from Arthur Balfour, the Prime Minister, to H. G. Wells. With her characteristic impetuosity, she took up the Guild of Handicraft, enthralling even Ashbee. ('I swear by her', he wrote, 'but then she's a Celt and properly educated and she has "empfindung" and that's why all the other Countesses think her mad and strange.'[26]) She would come over to Campden, sometimes bringing throngs of friends, and she invited the Guild boys back to Stanway. They, too, appear to have succumbed to her legendary charms. In the course of their first visit she, rather typically, slipped on a path and tore one of the flounces of her violet dress (22). She ripped it off and flung it in the rose beds. For months afterwards, apparently, the flounce was to be seen hanging up in Braithwaite House amongst the boys' most precious trophies.

The famous actress Mrs Patrick Campbell was a friend of Lady Elcho's and often stayed at Stanway. They were a striking pair as they travelled round the country. In this Cotswold setting, their appearance and their manner was, to say the least, unusual. One day in September, they arrived in Chipping Campden, and the resulting scene, in which the Webbs, acknowledged leaders of the intellectual Socialists, were outmanœuvred by the great but silly actress, was brilliantly described by Janet, who (unlike her husband) was never overawed by a celebrity.

Another Mad Hatter's Tea Party, and this time in the isolated Cotswold Hills. The Sidney Webbs invited us to see them in their summer quarters at Aston Magna, the beautiful little village rapidly being spoiled by Lord Redesdale's brick-fields hard by. – As we were on the point of starting, I saw two wonderful ladies, evidently not indigenous, rustle up to our threshold; one of them gave an appreciative poke with her sunshade to the 1840 bay window, and said in a stage voice; 'Look, darling, isn't this too exquisite? *Quite* the most beautiful thing I have ever seen', and with that Minnie opened the door and showed in Lady Elcho, AND Mrs. Patrick Campbell. They both wore that air of coming to see a curiosity which always annoys me; but I was swept into my own drawing room with their skirts, and simulated an easy cordiality. I was just warming up to my subject and trying to

(22) Lady Elcho was always inclined to be clumsy. As Margot Asquith described her in her memoirs: 'She was always a great joy, but she was physically and mentally badly equipped for the little things of life.'

(23) George Loosely, an artist recently arrived in Campden.

choke off their fulsome admiration, when Mrs. Pat crackled her black 'glacé' train into a chair, and leaning forward with the tragedy of a Mélisande, said hoarsely: 'Tell me what it feels like to be as strong as that!' – This nearly did for my gravity, but replying that it felt like a cow who feels nothing at all, I resumed the showman, and soon got them into the High Street, the Guild being their real objective. Every familiar face was a question mark, and 'Loosely' (23) coming out of the Post Office beat a hasty retreat as he caught my eye.

'I suppose you've had a lot of Monks and that here, haven't you?' asked Mrs. Pat, pointing to the Market Hall which in some dim way, I suppose, suggested cloisters – when with a sudden scream, she hurled herself, Paris opera cloak and all, in front of the historic Station bus; her aim was to rescue from death a horrible little dog called I believe a gryphon, into the details of whose breeding it is not good to enquire too closely. She clutched the little beast up out of the dust, and hid it in her neck with a kiss.

'Isn't he too adorable?' she said, 'he has Mary Elcho's eyes, he has, and Arthur Balfour's nose, and Wemyss's whiskers!'

The likeness was indisputable, but one loathed the way it was said. We hurried through the works, pleading our engagement. 'Oh that's all right,' said Mrs. Pat, 'we're going there too' – and she caught up a great green enamel chain which matched her glass ornaments to perfection, and flung it over her head with a finished gesture.

The really delicious point of the afternoon was the juxtaposition of the Sidney Webbs, our four selves, Lord Redesdale's two sedate daughters, and Miss Beatrice Chamberlain.

The little room was strewn almost ostentatiously with blue books; for the tea tray a scanty space was cleared among sheaves of MSS Statistics, and the Webbs received us with their delightful air of conscious seriousness, an unbending from habitual toil, as it were, a concession to the frivolous neighbourliness of their friends. With all a dubious glance was reserved for Mrs. Pat, who with her clothes and her gryphon took up one-third of the available space. Clearly, she was not expected in the train of the aristocrat. But even kings have had jesters, and, as Lady Gainsborough says 'Mary Elcho always likes to have these outré people about her, you know!'

However, she had to be put up with. Sidney Webb sat on the edge of his chair, and tried to let himself down to her conversational level. His wife chose the simpler way of ignoring her altogether. But Mrs. Pat was not going to be ignored. She was being snubbed, so she would play to the gallery. The fiscal policy did not interest her – nor the educational status of Campden – nor the beauties of the Batsford Gardens – what SHE wanted was to talk about herself.

And gradually, as by a magnetism, we found we were the gallery to which she was playing, and that do what we would, she swayed us to her mood, and we laughed at her extravagant clownery. She rocked herself on the window seat, having secured her audience.

'Yes,' she drawled, 'it's really very delightful to be a complete lunatic – you see nobody expects anything of you – you have no standard' – with a meaning glance at Mrs. Webb – 'to live up to, and you can have a real good time.'

Mrs. Webb drew herself up and flushed pink – this was too close to home to be passed without challenge. She glanced at her notes about the room and remarked in her most Webby manner: 'Well of course if you are writing the history of Local Government you can't exactly be a lunatic.'

Mrs. Pat laughed, having the best of the situation. 'Can't you?' she jeered – 'why I should have thought that was just what you would be under those circumstances!' (24)[27]

In spite of all the visitors, diversions and travels, Ashbee was still intent on his current Campden project: the building of the bathing pool for the Guild and for the village. The plan was for a pool 153 feet long, 105 feet wide, with depth graduating from 3 feet 6 inches to 7 feet 6 inches. It was intended to be used for mixed bathing: another decision guaranteed to shock the vicarage. Originally, though the

(24) Beatrice Webb always said her husband hated silly women: 'How he detested Mrs Pat Campbell when she was brought to see us by Lady Elcho! G.B.S.'s subsequent infatuation he regarded as a clear case of sexual senility!' (Beatrice Webb: *Our Partnership*). But perhaps there was a bit of wishful thinking in this view.

(25) The manifestation of this could be alarming. Phoebe Haydon, Ashbee's loyal secretary, recollected her arrival for her original interview at Ashbee's office, 37 Cheyne Walk: 'The house looked "freakish" and imposing, and the doorknocker, which we discovered was not a doorknocker at all, but an ornament in the shape of a naked boy with every detail shown to perfection, rather scared me. I felt as though I was being enticed into an immoral house and was glad there was another girl to keep me company'. (Phoebe Haydon:

Memoirs of a Faithful Secretary, unpublished MS in Felicity Ashbee's possession.)

(26) Even in 1912, when John Rothenstein arrived at Bedales, this fresh-air fanaticism lingered. There were still a few convinced 'Early Christians' at the school, easily distinguished by certain outward signs: 'they affected sandals, and coats that looked as though they had been made at home or else in some remote fishing village, and they showed a predilection for cold baths, a vegetable diet, for brown bread, and in season and out of it for fresh air, the colder the better. The outlook expressed by these outward signs was in politics liberal or Socialist, but Socialist according to Morris rather than to Marx'. (John Rothenstein, *Summer's Lease,* Hamish Hamilton 1965)

scheme was later on abandoned as impractical, Ashbee had also planned to stock the pool with fish.

The pool opened in August, and in September the first Campden Aquatic Sports were held. Guild members, according to the local paper, won every single race: they had no doubt had more practice than contenders from the village. A silver challenge cup, designed by W. A. White and made by Jack Baily, was presented by a suitable friend of the Ashbee's, Lieutenant R. Montague Glossop from Hull.

The bathing pool, like most of Ashbee's enterprises, had both a symbolic and a practical attraction. It expressed his belief that fresh air made better people, that contact with nature much improved the moral fibre. It also reflected his appreciation of the purity and beauty of the naked human form (25). These ideas were not, of course, peculiar to Ashbee: they were central to the whole high-flown philosophy of comradeship, promoted with such ardour by the friends of Edward Carpenter and aficionados of Walt Whitman, and an important element in the foundation of Abbotsholme and Bedales, the new progressive schools.

The poems of Walt Whitman, with their robust emphasis on the glories of the elements and unaffected splendour of the masculine physique, had been a great source of inspiration to Ashbee's Cambridge generation. Abbotsholme had opened in 1889, to educate the new and reformed Directing Classes, with the guiding principle, which owed a lot to Whitman, that 'to render the body strong, clear and lovely is a religious duty'. J. H. Badley, who founded Bedales four years later, always praised the life-giving power of Whitman's writing, to which he too had responded with alacrity when he was an undergraduate at King's. As Badley wrote later, Whitman 'seemed to throw open the windows of stuffy rooms, and to call one out into the open to face every kind of weather rejoicing in a world of comradeship and freedom.'[28] In the new progressive schools, at which the members of the future ruling classes learned not only Greek and Latin but also carpentry and bee-keeping, emerging trained not just in book-work but in useful manual labour, this rugged camaraderie was everywhere in evidence. Abbotsholme and Bedales and their various successors were set up in an uncompromising open air tradition, with unrelenting emphasis on exercise and hygiene: the boys slept between blankets with the windows left wide open. Instead of playing football, they went out to dig potatoes. In the pioneering days of Abbotsholme and Bedales, the idea of *mens sana in corpore sano* was taken to its absolute extremes (26).

Through his friendship with Carpenter, a co-founder of Abbotsholme, Ashbee had himself been very much involved in the New Education in its infancy, when an outpost of the Guild had been established at the school. He was thoroughly in sympathy with the new schools' ethos, and New Educational attitudes had obviously influenced his plans for Campden pool. But there was another motive, a case of parish politics. One of the great preoccupations, since the Guild came out to Gloucestershire, was the need to fuse the Guild life with the life of Chipping Campden, and the Ashbees clearly saw the diplomatic possibilities of putting up a pool in which the townspeople could share (27).

'The coming of Christmas', wrote Ashbee late in 1903, 'and the rehearsing of the "School for Scandal" induces a desire to review one's neighbours.' He had by now had 18 months to sum them up, and he appreciated all their oddities and quirks. He enjoyed, and understood, the structure of the old community, the relationship of landlord and tenant, man and master, even though he soon began to fight to have it altered. Affectionately, he listed the familiar village figures: Louis Dease, the Landlord's agent: aged Stanley Ulric, Chairman of the Parish Council, an admirable speaker but an unsuccessful farmer; the three ecclesiastics, Anglican, Roman Catholic and Nonconformist, 'a sort of Trinity of Institution in themselves'.

The Rectory set contained the mad Mrs. Morris, the group of elderly ladies who live in what the Campden children call 'Old Maids' Row'; the lignous Grammar School Master, a man very badly carved and painted; and the ancient spinster, very masculine, hawk-like with a blond moustache whom Charley Downer in one of his moments of improvisation hit off as 'Old Buck Freeman', which name she will probably keep.

There are two delightful old farmer ladies (everybody in Campden is old) Mrs. Izod of Westington, whose family if not actually herself, has been in Campden since the time of Harold – and Mrs. Manton her sister who came over with the Hugenot silk spinners, and still has bobbins and reels from the hand looms of the 17th century in her back lumber room.

Then there is old 'Farmer Big-shilling' and old 'Farmer Nibblecrust'; the one because he makes the coin spread over so much, the other because he wastes so little.

(27) The idea continued to attract him. Much later, in the 1930s, when he had retired to Godden Green in Kent, he built a second swimming pool. This again he encouraged local villagers to use.

The one looking like a Normandy pippin, scarlet and wholesome, the other like Father Christmas, with a smile of intricate benevolence. I met this dear old man once on a Committee where we had to pour facts into his deaf ear; but that's another story.

Last and most picturesque of institutions is old Dolphin the postman–poet, the pensioner, who keeps the childrens' window and has about 15 hats that he wreathes around with flowers. He walks along the street with a kitten on his shoulder. Old Dolphin has a sense of beauty and we love him for it.[29]

The Ashbees' favourite neighbour was Mrs Martha Dunn, their invaluable ally, whose house in the village was used as a kind of annexe to the Guild of Handicraft. She was a sharp-tongued woman, but extremely tender-hearted to anybody obviously in need of help. 'Look here', she said, for instance, to George Loosely the painter, who was lodging with her and was struggling with his darning, 'I want you to let me do for you; it is a waste of time for you to mend your socks. The likes of you has got to do the painting, the likes of us the mending. Now you – you be the better for my mending your socks, and we shall all be the happier for your paintings.'

Mrs Dunn had a husband but he was not much in evidence. He was simply treated as Mrs Dunn's accessory though in fact a half-obliterated sign over his door, saying 'Richard Dunn, licensed Maltster', proved that he had once had a trade and an identity. Ashbee liked to tell Richard Dunn's sad story, which in some ways was depressingly typical of Campden, a place where time moved slowly and enterprise was sluggish:

Once, during the ten years that we have been at Campden, a week's malting came his way, and Richard Dunn thought that trade had revived, and the world was going to go on as of old. But the world did nothing of the sort, there are too many big brewers in it, and so he settled down again to his customary vocation of looking at the weather between 8 and 10 in the morning and chatting to the various people that pass along the street. For the rest, he has a few rents to collect and acts as a sort of handyman in his wife's establishment. She knows exactly what he can do, and what not, and her injunctions are swift and pronounced. Janet asked her once whether he would put up the Maypole in the Orchard for her. 'Richard put up the maypole? What next?' said she 'certainly not – Richard's the greatest muff on a ladder you ever seen'. Richard knows his place, and his place for the most part is to sit in the ingle of her big cosy kitchen in bewildered admiration of Martha Dunn.[30]

Mrs Dunn was one of the citizens of Campden whose life changed most completely when the Guild arrived in Gloucestershire. The Guild, from then on, was her main focus of attention. But although Martha Dunn's total involvement was exceptional, many other villagers were drawn into Guild activities and some were actually found employment by the Guild. For instance, a good group of local workmen – masons, carpenters, hurdle and gate-makers and so on, who continued the traditions of village craftmanship – worked on the restoration of houses for the Guildsmen. In many different ways, in a surprisingly short time, the life of the two communities was interweaving.

The Londoners soon seemed to adapt to life in Campden. Perhaps it took the women longer than the men; the wives were more prone to surges of nostalgia for the minutiae of life in Whitechapel, and travellers to London were apparently commissioned to bring back certain brands of fish-and-chips from Mile End Road. But many of the men, far from feeling at a loss so many miles away from their familiar London setting, seem to have found a corresponding role in Campden with remarkable rapidity and ease. The Whitechapel wit, the blacksmith Charlie Downer, whose jokes and mimicry had convulsed the Guild in London, was soon re-established as the Gloucestershire comedian. Charley Plunkett, the french polisher, Secularist and Bradlaughite, a bit of a fanatic whose language was apparently habitually lurid and verging on the blasphemous (although underneath it he was very kind and friendly), was soon in his element as scourge of Chipping Campden (28). Even old Tom Jellife, the solemn, stern trade unionist who had been so doubtful about moving out of London, soon found his own niche in local politics and pothouses. He now seemed all set to end his days in the *Lygon Arms*, where he had taken up his quarters.

For many people, the Great Move had gone well. Better, perhaps, than might have been expected. But there were underlying local problems which increased in their acuteness as the Guild got settled in. As Ashbee came to realize, Arcadia had its difficulties, and there was certainly a seamy side to it. Lionel Curtis, the South African administrator, using a convenient phrase from the Boer War, described it as an

---

(28) Gloucestershire, in fact, gave him a new lease of life. Ashbee later recalled how Charley Plunkett, then already a grandfather, had married for the second time. His wife was local and much younger. 'They tried it first without the sanction of a wedding ring, to see if a love child would come, which it did –

a delightful boy, the apple of his father's eye. And old Plunkett, asked the other day whether it was a success, or he regretted what he had done, answered laconically: "Best bloody thing I ever did in my life".' (*Ashbee Memoirs*, 1921)

'outlander problem', and the analogy was accurate. The East London emigrants wanted all sorts of amenities – proper housing and sanitation, running water, milk for the children, better education – which the Campden ruling classes were not able, or not inclined, to give them. Concessions made to the emigrants from London could only lead to trouble from the local population, whose standards of living were very low indeed. With local agricultural labourers earning as little as 12*s* a week, as against the Guild Craftsmen, who were making between 30*s* and £4, the situation was potentially explosive. Even Guild apprentices were then earning 10*s*. The inequality was dangerously obvious. Not even a free cottage on the Gainsborough estate, admittedly picturesque although dilapidated, or the occasional landlord's rabbit, could compensate the local labourers for such conditions.

A confrontation came in the Guild's second year in Campden. A labourer's child had died, and at the inquest it emerged that the child had starved because there was no milk for it. This led to a considerable Gloucestershire controversy, in which Ashbee and the more politically-minded of the Guildsmen involved themselves with energy, over proposals to alter the terms of the Ebrington Cow Charity. This ancient foundation of Ebrington, the parish next to Campden, compelled a local landowner to maintain a cow to provide milk for the poor of the parish, as selected by the charity trustees. Because of the obvious impracticalities of administering such a cumbersome charity in the early years of the twentieth century, it was now suggested to the Charity Commissioners that the landlord's obligation to provide milk for charitable purposes should be redeemed for a money payment, which would be invested to form a secure endowment for the charity. This proposal Ashbee – whose romantic view of life in the country inclined more towards the concept of milk from the cow than dividends from Consols – opposed vehemently, seeing himself as the champion of the honest agricultural labourer against the machinations of local landowners.

The arguments pro and con the Ebrington Cow Charity were hideously complex, and it is perfectly feasible to argue that Ashbee in fact fought on the side of the reactionaries. However, the episode, whichever way one looked at it, marked a new and more politically active phase in the life of the Guild at Chipping Campden. It was not in the nature of the Guild, or of its leader, to let sleeping dogs lie or injustices continue (even if they sometimes misunderstood the issues). It was not just the life of the Guild which concerned them but the life of the whole community in which they found themselves. Ashbee loved the country-

4

The Jolly Craftsmen's Chorus 1904

The Guild play for 1904 was *School for Scandal*. Three performances were given in mid-January in the village hall, to enthusiastic audiences. The profits, once again, went to Campden Bathing Lake. Almost all the actors were Guild members or associates, assiduously schooled by C. R. Ashbee. Alec Miller, the young wood-carver and Campden man of letters, was cast as Charles Surface, despite his Glasgow accent. Statia Power, the Junoesque Guild bookbinder, took the part of Lady Sneerwell, a perceptive piece of casting. Ashbee himself was, of course, Sir Peter Teazle, shaving off his moustache and small imperial for the purpose, a sacrifice which added to his oddness of appearance and dismayed his wife and friends. (So much so he was prevailed upon to go abroad the following summer to regrow it.)

Because the Guild of Handicraft was mainly a man's world, and wives of Guildsmen evidently lacked dramatic talent, the leading female actresses in Guild plays were imported. This year Gwendolen Bishop was brought in as Lady Teazle. Mrs Bishop, wife of Gerald, strong supporter of the Guild, the conscientious Fabian who appears in Ashbee's Journals, was a semi-professional actress, used to audiences a good deal more sophisticated than the farmers in corduroys in Campden village hall. She had been the Virgin in Housman's controversial Nativity Play, with Gordon Craig settings, and had also acted at the Court (1). Gwendolen Bishop, with her enigmatic beauty, her soft tawny hair and strange green eyes, fashionably dressed in shapeless sludge-brown robes from Jaeger, was a glittering example of one of Shaw's New Women. Her private life was packed, perhaps inevitably, with dramatic incident. While Gerald worked somewhat prosaically in

(1) Now the Royal Court Theatre in Sloane Square and then, as now, committed to progressive British drama.

a photographic business in Soho, spurred on, said Janet Ashbee, by the hope of a future life with Gwendolen in a garden or a 'Garden City', Gwendolen herself had more flamboyant aspirations. At the time of *School for Scandal*, she had recently returned from Florence where she had been – without her husband – 'seeing LIFE!' (She later married Clifford Bax, the playwright, but it seems she proved too much for him as well.) Needless to say, Gwendolen was not the style of person the average apprentice-craftsman of the early nineteen-hundreds would be likely to encounter, let alone act opposite. But this meeting of extremes, this expansion of experience, was something which gave Ashbee's Guild its special character and was indeed one of its major raisons d'être.

The years of the Guild of Handicraft in Chipping Campden were something unique in the life of England. There had been experimental communities before but very few as large and as coherent as this one. It was an episode of unusual conviction, in its emphasis on aesthetic excellence and in its creation of a special kind of life-style, and in many ways it was a swan-song: such extraordinary optimism never came again.

The life of the Guild, as it became established in its peaceful rural setting, formed the most thoroughgoing expression of the radical beliefs of the Arts and Crafts movement. Although many craftsmen (and artists) of the period put forward these same theories and, to a greater or lesser extent, practised them, no one but Ashbee had attempted to develop the ideas of William Morris on so many fronts and in so ambitious a manner. No one else had had the courage (and is it so surprising?) to push forward to its logical conclusion the idea that men are responsible for what they make and that workers should all, if possible, be artists; the idea that work and leisure should be almost interchangeable, and both should be enjoyed; the theory that everyone should do his share of manual labour, that the workers should be thinking and the thinkers should be working; the idea that the best work is done in natural surroundings; the fundamental precept that good work will make good men.

It is important to realize that, as far as the Arts and Crafts movement was concerned, Ashbee belonged to the second generation. His attitude in some respects was different from that of the contemporaries and friends of William Morris. In those early days, it seemed to Ashbee, the great masters of painting, architecture and sculpture – Morris himself, the 'Master Craftsman'; the painters G. F. Watts, Ford Madox Brown, Burne-Jones; the architects Bodley, Philip Webb and T. G. Jackson;

the sculptors Hamo Thorneycroft and Stirling Lee; the potter William De Morgan; and many others who set up their own workshops, admired the Middle Ages and talked Socialism – were emphatically individuals first, not Guildsmen. Perhaps, at the time, suggested Ashbee, this individualism was inevitable: 'They and their generation were adventurers in the uncharted sea of Victorian commercialism. Most of the crafts had been destroyed, or so helplessly crippled by the Industrial Revolution that the first job of the mid-nineteenth century was to learn again what they once were. Tapestry, Pottery, Cabinet-making, the Building Crafts, Silverware, Glassware, Earthenware, even Painting, had all to be rediscovered. That discovery, and its meaning, was the work of the protagonists. Workshop tradition and its continuity came later. That was the work of the next generation, and the Guild.'[1]

Ashbee saw his task not just as the revival of neglected handicrafts. To a great extent the groundwork had been done already. By 1900, the phase of technical experimentation was over. The time had now come, as Ashbee saw it, for the craftsmen to be 'more real and more direct in their hold on life'. They must find a way of making the crafts more self-supporting. This would mean that craftsmen must now also get involved in life's 'elemental processes': work on the land, cooking and baking, husbandry and housework. Ashbee (although one must admit he did not practice what he preached and was very rarely seen with a sweeping brush or shovel) argued with great conviction that craftsmen must be ready to take a hand in life's direct, essential activities: 'things that show what it is well to have and what it is better to do without, all those things that imply a simpler living of life.'[2] Though more perhaps than Ashbee himself realized or admitted, these ideas were strongly influenced by Morris – still more Ruskin – they had moved on far beyond the technical preoccupations of the more narrow-minded of the Arts and Crafts practitioners. His ideas were close to those of the Garden City prophets, with their mission of restoring the People to the Land.

In fact, the handicrafts of the Guild in Chipping Campden were, by Arts and Crafts standards, eminently respectable. They were, so to speak, at the top end of the market. Guild furniture and jewellery and, in particular, Guild silver were highly regarded in the best Arts and Crafts circles and respectfully reviewed in the artistic magazines. The Essex House Press, in that great age of private presses, seems to have had a comparable reputation; partly perhaps because of its connection with Kelmscott, but also because the decorative qualities of Essex House

Press books, with their drawings and their woodcuts and their fanciful initials, gave them their own character, wayward and romantic, very much in keeping with advanced Edwardian taste (2).

If the crafts of the Guild, in the final analysis, lacked the ultimate finesse, the absolute consistency one finds in the work of, say, Gimson and the Barnsleys (3), who had moved out to the Cotswolds a few years before Ashbee, one has to remember that Ashbee's aims were broader, one has to see the Guild work in its context, as the product of eight different workshops and fifty different craftsmen. The work of the Guild was the work of a community. For Ashbee and the Guildsmen (or anyway those Guildsmen who were properly converted) the work of the Guild was the product of good fellowship. At its most ideal, life was work and work was life.

The Simple Life, as lived by the Guild at Chipping Campden in its early years, was a good life and a full life. It was a working life, revolving round the Silk Mill. But it could not have been further from the drudgery of normal industry in London or in Birmingham. Repose, margin, leisure, reserve, restraint and colour in life – the things which for years Ashbee had wanted for his Guildsmen – were all within reach, in the green fields of Gloucestershire. The early Socialist dream of escaping from the city and re-establishing the dignity of craftsmanship in some ancient, lovely, very English rural setting could almost be said to have materialized.

An ecstatic account of those early days in Campden was given by Charles Rowley. The title he chose, *A Workshop Paradise,* shows how close he felt that Ashbee had come towards creating Socialist perfection. He wrote with admiration of the ease with which the craftsmen had settled into the Silk Mill as if born to it:

One could readily imagine that they were native to the place. An old mill with ground and upper stories lends itself to handicraft workshops of this nature. Every window looks out onto a lovely common garden, every bench has a posy on it. Nothing could be more delightful than doing rationally good work in such surroundings.'[3]

Rational work in a natural environment: this was the summit of Arts and Crafts ambition.

The Arts and Crafts movement, and Ashbee in particular, had strong views on leisure. They could not abide a loafer. Rich loafers, spending idle weekends in country houses, or poorer loafers, lounging around music halls and taverns, were equally distasteful to Ashbee, who believed in creative recreation, pleasures which improved community relations, leisure which was inextricably linked with life. In his view – which admittedly was somewhat biased – the move to Chipping Campden had proved the total falseness of the common belief that the townsman loves the music halls and gas lamps. 'He does nothing of the sort' – as Ashbee maintained firmly in *Craftsmanship in Competitive Industry*, his own account of the years in Chipping Campden – 'he hates them if he can get something better or more genuine.'[4] And, certainly, the range of home-grown Campden entertainments was impressive. As well as the Guild plays, at the beginning of each year, there were summer Swimming Sports. There was football, hockey, cricket; there was bicycling and gardening. For musical Guildsmen, there was the village band, a flagging institution revived by Jim Pyment, the foreman of the woodshop. It had special uniform, with peaked cap and gold frogging. Townspeople and Guildsmen played in it together. It must have seemed a fine example of the proper use of leisure as it marched down Campden High Street, with Jim Pyment at its head.

The style of life for the Guild in Chipping Campden was to some extent set by the ménage of the Ashbees in Woolstaplers' Hall, in the main street of the small town. Although you could not call them committed Simple Lifers – they were not, for instance, trying to make £100 a year out of an acre, as other people were in that first age of self-sufficiency, and their diet by no means mainly curdled milk – the Ashbees, like many of their intellectual friends, were mildly obsessed with getting back to basics (4). This was the spirit which encouraged Mrs Ashbee to address her husband in her letters as 'Dear Lad'.

Their clothes were Simple Clothes. Janet, a sure sign of an emancipated woman, had dispensed with stays, having left them on the beach

(2) Later on, however, the Endeavour typeface, designed by C. R. Ashbee for the Press in 1901, was harshly criticized by Stanley Morison, who stated that the Arts and Crafts movement has produced 'no more inglorious achievement . . . truly "a vain thing fondly invented "'. (*Type Designs of Past and Present*, 1926)

(3) Ernest Gimson (1864–1919) and the Barnsley brothers, Ernest (1863–1926) and Sidney (1865–1926), architects and craftsmen, who moved

to the Cotswolds in 1893, settling in Sapperton in 1903. Although Gimson, too, from time to time considered setting up a village craft community in Gloucestershire, these plans never developed and their workshops remained relatively individual and small-scale.

(4) Not that this was always as easy as it seemed: for instance, Goldsworthy Lowes Dickinson, on the farm at Tilford, failed ignominiously to learn to milk a cow.

before her first bathe with her husband, soon after she got married, and never again worn them. Although she did not favour such extremes of fashion – or non-fashion – as the mud-brown Jaeger shifts worn by her friend Gwendolen Bishop, and indeed she hardly had the figure for them, her own tastes in clothes were recognizably Aesthetic, and her Ruskin-serge jackets and her peasant smocks and sunhats and her fishermen's jerseys must have seemed a bit eccentric to her Chipping Campden neighbours, whether grand or lowly. Ashbee, too, dressed true to type, as if he were for ever playing Praed, Bernard Shaw's artistic anarchist. He wore the Norfolk jacket (5), almost ad infinitum, with knickerbockers, woollen socks and good stout boots.

The Ashbees' régime at Woolstaplers', in contrast to the formal bourgeois households both had known as children, was characterized by a studied spontaneity. Their food was Simple Food. Meals were plain and wholesome: little omelettes, fruit pies with cream, and good strong coffee. Their life was full of Simple Pleasures: rambling in the summer, singing catches in the winter. Ashbee, whenever he could gather in an audience, was particularly fond of reading poetry aloud (6).

Woolstaplers' Hall was, by all accounts, a cheerful, friendly house. The decor was in the true Arts and Crafts tradition, that curious amalgam of the austere and the fanciful common in Morris circles from the 1860s onwards: a style which encompassed bare boards strewn with Eastern carpets; oak furniture, some plain and some elaborately painted; rush-seated country chairs; William Morris curtains; ornate tapestries and hangings; a profusion of knick-knacks (though one did not call them knick-knacks, for knick-knacks were disapproved of in such Socialist households). Many of the ornaments, the lustre jugs and pewter platters, the beaten copper clocks and the hammered silver dishes, were inscribed with little mottoes or a line or two of poetry. ('INSCRIPTION MANIA', as *Studio* magazine once called it.) Ashbee was himself in the forefront of this fashion, which appealed to his

(5) The Norfolk Jacket, a grey tweed coat with four outer pockets, a belt and high lapels, was more or less the uniform at Abbotsholme and Bedales, both for boys and staff. For Cecil Reddie, first headmaster of Abbotsholme, the Norfolk Jacket had great symbolic meaning: it made no compromise with the hated raiment of rich and idle people and those who delighted in the 'fleshpots'.

(6) This passion continued. His daughter Felicity maintains she must be the only person left in England who has listened to *The Earthly Paradise* from end to end.

somewhat mediaeval sense of humour. The CRAFT OF THE GUILD
had never been forgotten, and indeed the original painted plaster panel
of the ship in full sail was now hanging in the Silk Mill. With the
same triumphant ingenuity, Ashbee's own family book-plate showed a
bee and tree.

Woolstaplers', though idiosyncratic in its decor, was very welcoming
and homely. It was an artist's house, but it was not overpoweringly
Artistic in appearance: 'It glowed with colour like a plum', as Janet
described it later.[5] It was a focus for Guild social activity. Friday night
sing-songs became an institution. The particular atmosphere of those
convivial evenings at Woolstaplers' Hall made a good impression on
Alec Miller, who later described a specially memorable gathering:

We trooped into C.R.A's library, perhaps a dozen or fifteen of us and found the
Ashbees and two friends, a quick-eyed observant woman, and a quiet dark man
with a pointed beard. Presently, the boys being all seated on the floors, C.R.A.
pointed a minatory forefinger at the lady and, in a singularly sweet tenor voice,
began the song, 'Mrs Webb, will you lend me thy grey mare?' and so for the first
time I heard that splendid song, *Widdecombe Fair*, with the refrain sung as 'and old
Uncle Ashbee and all'. Gradually it dawned on me that the visitors were Mr and
Mrs Sidney Webb, of whom I knew little but that they were busy writing a history
of Trade Unionism. These 'sing-songs' were always a joy to me. Again it was the
group sense, the presence of, and contact with, interesting people. Any visitors of
C.R.A's or of the Guild were there. The room was unique and beautiful; the
books, perhaps six or seven thousand of them, were to me a constant source of
delight.[6]

Of all the young Guildsmen, Alec Miller was the most receptive to
Ashbee's ideas and most grateful for his influence. He was one of the
small party selected to go sketching in France with Ashbee in summer
1904. Will Hart, 'the Skipper', Ashbee's idol, was invited, with
George Chettle, a pupil in the architectural office, and the four of them
set off to Chartres via Rouen, Evreux and Dreux. This tour of French
cathedrals was a very great success. 'It was a quite unclouded party',
wrote Ashbee in his Journal: 'it could scarcely fail to be with such
travelling companions, for "the Skipper" is so strong and fair and free,
and Alec Miller improves the more I know him, having great power
and thoughtfulness, and he is surely a most lovable person'.[7] In the
intervals from sketching, they swam and lazed and read. The authors
they took with them for the journey had been chosen with Ashbee's
usual catholicity: Sterne, William Morris, Meredith, a Wilkie Collins,
a Dickens and the Golden Treasury. However, it turned out that Alec

knew such quantities of poetry by heart they hardly needed an anthology.

Ashbee was at his best on this sort of expedition, happy and relaxed, helpful and informative without being pedagogic. He was naturally disposed to enjoy being with young men, and especially the boys whom he considered *his* boys, whose talents he encouraged and whose development he cared about intensely. Alec Miller, who had never been abroad before, found the experience enormously exciting, and explained how he and the other boys absorbed ideas of history, art and literature almost unconsciously, simply through Ashbee's companionship and mental stimulus. 'Indeed', he wrote later, 'looking back on it, this and the association with C.R.A's friends was the vital cultural influence in many young lives which were thereby transformed.'[8]

Ashbee, of course, had hopes of spreading culture, ideas of art and literature, not to mention history, far beyond his own young Guild apprentices. He was much preoccupied with plans for the expansion of local education, a policy the Campden ruling classes regarded with suspicion. But since Ashbee tended to thrive on controversy, and saw and deprecated the self-interest of his enemies, mounting local opposition did nothing to deter him from his schemes for new and larger buildings for the Technical School in Chipping Campden, scheduled to open in the autumn. In fact it only spurred him on.

Relations with the local landed gentry, problematic ever since the Guild arrived in Campden, showed no signs of improvement. Early in 1904, Janet narrowly avoided what might have been a monumental row with Lady Gainsborough. Only the diplomatic intervention of Rob Holland, constant friend and adviser of the Ashbees and the Guild, prevented her from sending a strongly-worded letter on the subject of support for the Bathing Lake at Campden. Rob Holland put forward a good case for discretion: 'such a letter as you have written', he told Janet, 'would declare war to the knife.'[9]

The clash with the Gainsboroughs was successfully averted. But later, in the summer, the other leading landlord of the neighbourhood, Lord Harrowby, launched an attack on Archie Ramage, Guild com-

(7) Frances Mitford was daughter of the 1st Baron Redesdale (memorable as the nobleman who in 1906 accompanied Prince Arthur of Connaught to Japan to invest the Mikado with the Order of the Garter). Frances was therefore aunt to Nancy and her sisters. Although Janet had foreseen a solitary future for her, she married Alexander Horace Cyril Kearsey, a distinguished soldier, three years later.

1. (*Previous page*). C. R. Ashbee photographed by his friend Frank Lloyd Wright in 1900. He was then in his late thirties.

2. Janet Ashbee photographed by Hollyer late 1899, soon after her marriage.

3. Janet Ashbee in the garden of Woolstaplers' Hall, Chipping Campden.

4. View down Campden High Street past the Market Hall, famous scene of antique beauty which enraptured Algernon Gissing and other Cotswold visitors.

5. Arthur Cameron, Guild metalworker, and family by their cottage in Watery Lane, Gloucestershire. The scene is captioned 'Picture of reformed Cockneys in Arcadia'.

6. Edward Carpenter at Millthorpe, dressed for simple living. His sandals were almost certainly home-made.

7. View of the Silk Mill from the garden. At the time of the Great Move, wrote Ashbee, there could still be seen 'the green twinkle of the lattice windows of the old silk weavers'.

8. The old Silk Mill, Chipping Campden, used by the Guild of Handicraft from 1902 onwards as its main workshops and offices.

Overleaf:

9. Gardening class at the Campden School of Arts and Crafts, c. 1905.

10. Cookery class at the Campden School of Arts and Crafts.

11. The Swimming Sports in Campden Bathing Lake.

12. Charley Downer, Guild blacksmith, as Touchstone in the Guild production of *As You Like It*. His attendants are two boys from the village.

13. Decorative initials drawn by C. R. Ashbee for *The Prayer Book of King Edward VII*, published by the Essex House Press in 1903. Art Workers' Guild collection.

14. C. R. Ashbee in 1903. Drawing by William Strang. Art Workers' Guild collection.

15. The Guild of Handicraft, group photograph probably taken in 1906 or
1907.

1 Arthur Cameron, metalworker. 2 Unknown. 3 George Hart, silversmith.
4 Unknown. 5 George Vickery, secretary. 6 Walter Curtis, cabinet-maker.
7 Will Hart, carver. 8 Tom Jellife, cabinet-maker. 9 Wally Curtis, cabinet-
maker. 10 Alf Smith, gardener. 11 William Wall, cabinet-maker. 12 John
Angus, clerk. 13 Keyte. 14 Herbert Osborn, cabinet-maker. 15 Unknown.
16 Fleetwood Varley, enameller. 17 Bill Mark, enameller. 18 Unknown.
19 Jim Pyment, cabinet-maker. 20 Bill Thornton, blacksmith. 21 Edward Toy,
silversmith. 22 Bill Scurr, jeweller. 23 Webster. 24 J. T. Webster, manager.
25 Arthur Naylor. 26 Unknown. 27 Bill Wride, cabinet-maker. 28 Charlie
Daniels, jeweller. 29 Walter Edwards, silversmith. 30 Alec Miller, carver and
modeller. 31 Bert Humphries, silversmith. 32 Micky Moran, jeweller.
33 Arthur Bunten, cabinet-maker. 34 Jack Cameron, metalworker.
35 Mark Merriman, enameller. 36 Stanley Keeley, metalworker.
37 Golden Keeley.

16. The carvers at work at the Guild of Handicraft. The carving at the back is 'The Spirit of Modern Hungary' for the de Szasz house in Budapest, c. 1905–6.

17. The woodshop on the second floor of the old Silk Mill. This was the most consistently busy of Guild workshops.

18. The Guild blacksmiths. The forge was set up in an outhouse near the old
Silk Mill. After the demise of the Guild, Charley Downer and Bill Thornton ran
the smithy independently.

19. The machine shop. Like the smithy, this was in a building set apart from the old Silk Mill. Ashbee argued that the use of basic minimum machinery freed the craftsmen from unnecessary drudgery, conserving their energy for the more creative tasks.

20. Roughcast cottages at Catbrook designed by C. R. Ashbee and built for the Guild craftsmen, 1903.

21. Piano by Broadwood with decorated case by C. R. Ashbee, executed by Walter Taylor, late 1900. Now at Toynbee Hall.

22. Houses in Cheyne Walk, Chelsea, by C. R. Ashbee. No. 74, with beaten copper door, was built for the Ashbees on their marriage.

23. Double-handled silver dish designed by C. R. Ashbee and made by the Guild of Handicraft, 1902. Worshipful Company of Goldsmiths' collection.

24. Silver dish with looped handle designed by C. R. Ashbee and made by the Guild of Handicraft, 1900. Victoria and Albert Museum.

25. Jewelled finial for comb designed by C. R. Ashbee and made by the Guild of Handicraft, c. 1903. In a private collection, New York.

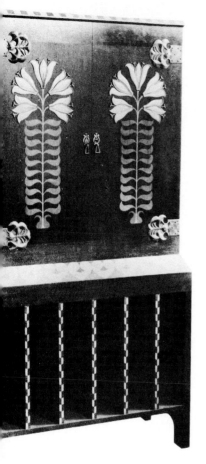

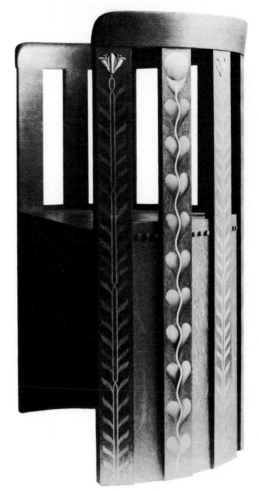

26. Pendant jewel in the form of a peacock designed by C. R. Ashbee and made by the Guild of Handicraft, c. 1903. Victoria and Albert Museum.

27 and 28. Painted music cabinet and curved seat made by the Guild of Handicraft for the Grand Duke of Hesse's Palace at Darmstadt, about 1898. The design is by M. H. Baillie Scott.

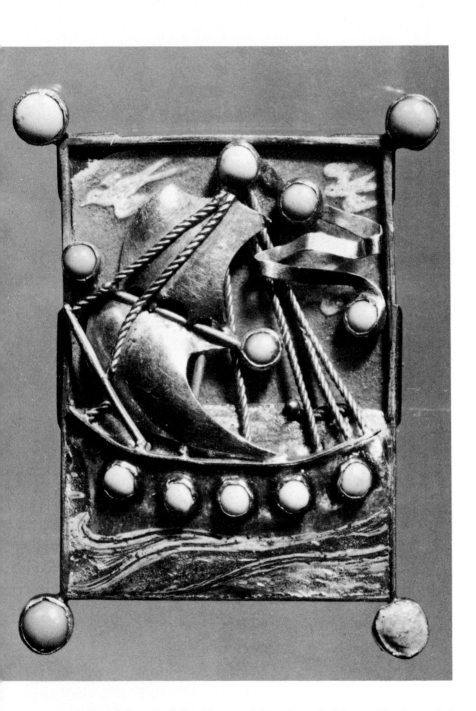

29. Brooch in enamelled gold, exemplifying the craft of the Guild. The applied decoration is set with turquoises. Part of a larger necklace designed by C. R. Ashbee, c. 1903. Victoria and Albert Museum.

positor and serious young Socialist. Harrowby – hardly a favourite with Ashbee who described him as the sort of man Holbein would have drawn as the shark-like, mean, sharp-nosed, short-chinned incipiently puritanical bounder of the day – got up on the platform at a public meeting at Mickleton, fished out a Fabian Tract and blamed its distribution on the revolutionary element in Campden. Ashbee enjoyed the scene: 'The best of the joke was that all the time Archie the founder of the little Labour Union was in the audience watching, with his large earnest blue eyes, his Lordship lashing himself into an imaginary fury . . . It is not in men of this calibre to see what a young Scottish idealist is driving at, or to understand how a workman comes to think the distribution of Fabian tracts is a good thing for Hodge, poor, dumb, down trodden fellow that he is. Better housing for the people, better schooling, common lands and sweeter conditions of life and independent life, are all things we need, and need very badly here in Campden, but we shall get none of them if men like Lord Harrowby, or the crew that applaud him on a public platform can help it. Meantime go ahead Archie!'[10]

Summer was, once again, a time for expeditions. The Ashbees were not by any means at loggerheads with all the country gentry, and with an avidity which may have dismayed the Campden Labour Union, visited some of the great houses in the area. They were on good terms, for instance, with the Redesdales at Batsford, and Lord Redesdale's eldest daughter, the somewhat unfathomable Frances (7), whose hair was going white before she had turned thirty, became a close friend of Janet Ashbee's. ('We sat long in the great drawing room alone', Janet recounted later in her Journal, 'and talked broad and deep.'[11])

They went to see the Dillons at Ditchley Park, the great Gibbs mansion near Oxford, where they were given an exhaustive tour, beginning on the lawns, among the cedars, and proceeding through the state rooms, past the portraits and the treasures, with innumerable anecdotes along the way. Lord Dillon 'played guide to his treasures and pictures with a delicate and shadowy flippancy', wrote Janet, 'and he wanders from his own quaint notions, to scraps of 18th Century gossip, and daintily scandalous stories.'[12] Some of his anecdotes were rather gruesome. Lord Dillon, then Warden of the Tower of London and a formidable expert on armour and weapons, was obsessed with the histories of famous executions, and his conversation was full of macabre references to blocks, swords, axes, silken rope, and so on, memories of the demise of Thomas More and Anne Boleyn.

For Ashbee, as for many of the followers of Morris, the great houses of England had immense significance. They were important not just as stone and timber, bricks and mortar, but as monuments of national life, a part of England's heritage. The campaign for conservation, which had started in a small way, with the foundation of Morris's Society for the Protection of Ancient Buildings (familiarly known as 'Anti-Scrape'), had now, nearly thirty years later, much expanded. With his Survey of London and his National Trust connections, Ashbee had been right at the heart of this development. Although he was no longer active in the National Trust, having had a final rupture with Octavia Hill, 'the little lady in the mushroom hat' as he described her, with whom his relations had always been uncertain (8), he supported the aims and the ideals of the movement. Architecture was the Index of Communal Greatness (the phrase has a grandiloquence typical of Ashbee). Dytchley Park may not in fact have been exactly Ashbee's period – his ideal was really Montacute – but he could still appreciate intensely its romantic aura, its historic connotations, its place in British life and British landscape, and maybe above all its importance as a sample of building in England as it used to be.

Ashbee's romantic view of architecture was very much an Art Workers' Guild attitude. It was the view of Philip Webb, Lethaby and Gimson and other architect-craftsmen of the period, who managed to combine (with a breadth of vision which future generations of architects found breathtaking) a grandiose and mystic approach to architecture, the concept of buildings which had *hearts* in them, with the commonsense idea that an architect was nothing but a workman of a rather special species. As Lethaby once so succinctly put it, 'A work of art is a well-made boot'.

In practice, Ashbee may not have taken up the building crafts with such enthusiasm as some of his contemporaries, building walls out of cob, as Ernest Gimson did in Devon, or performing his own decorative plasterwork. In fact, surprisingly for someone whose great life-work was promoting craftsmanship, his manual dexterity was only very

(8) When she died, however, he paid a tribute to her as one of the Great Women of her time, women he admired although they rather disconcerted him : 'I have now met or come across in life most of the great women of Octavia Hill's type – Mrs Fawcett, Emily Davis, Mrs Garrett Anderson, Miss Beale, Miss Buss, Miss Cons, Jane Addams. Life is a fuller and larger thing for having done so.' (*Ashbee Memoirs,* August 1912)

(9) And indeed in his old age, according to his daughter, he took great pride in teaching himself simple garden bricklaying.

average (except when it came to decorating letter capitals). Perhaps he had too volatile a temperament to make a good hand-worker. He was easily distracted. All the same, he believed strongly in the old Arts and Crafts theory that the architect's place was not sitting at his drawing board but out on the site inspiriting the builders (9). The contemporary practice of handing out the contract to the lowest tenderer, regardless of the likely standard of the craftsmanship, seemed to him alarmingly wrong-headed, resulting in bad buildings and discontented workmen. In his architectural work in and around Campden, his methods were as mediaeval as they could be. His builders, a combination of Guild and village craftsmen, were told to take their time and do the job as well as possible, an idyllic situation for the craftsmen and the architect, although, as Ashbee later shamelessly admitted, involving his clients in considerable expense.

The driving force of Ashbee's life, as he frequently reminded anyone who seemed in danger of forgetting, was primarily an aesthetic one. The Standard of Beauty, revealed to him at Cambridge, was with him all his life. This was, after all, why he had chosen Chipping Campden, a small town of quite exceptional visual quality, even by Cotswold standards, for his Guild community and why, having arrived there, he went to such great lengths, with a fervour which almost reached fanaticism, to conserve it and improve it. His attitude at first seems to have mystified the locals, whose standards of beauty may have lacked sophistication and for many of whom Campden was just the place they lived in. But gradually, as Gordon Russell recollected, people began accepting Ashbee's viewpoint and local building standards improved greatly. Tactless he may have been (an unfortunate affliction for someone so concerned with community relations), but he did the town a lasting service, pointing out to Campden how good Campden really was.[13]

It was Ashbee's great preoccupation with aesthetics which distinguished the Guild of Handicraft so fundamentally from many of the other experiments in communal living at that time. There was Simple Life and Simple Life, and the more extreme communities, the anarchists and communists, regarded aesthetics (perhaps rightly) with suspicion: in such circles, as Ashbee remarked sadly after a visit to the Moorhay community of Early Christians, 'beauty seems ever to have the mark of Cain upon it'.[14] This struck him again when he and Alec Miller and the blacksmith, Fred Brown, set off on a summer outing on their bicycles to the Whiteway Community at Miserden, near Stroud. This was a Tolstoyan agricultural settlement, founded by a group of idealists from Croydon and thoroughly uncompromising in both aims and atmosphere. Its members, in violent reaction against the suburban life they had escaped from, were not only anti-property and anti-marriage but also evidently opposed to bourgeois comforts. As Ashbee described Whiteway in his Journal, it made a bleak contrast to the cosy life of Campden:

We found here people who seem to be 'back to the land' in grim earnest. I had long talks with some of them. They hold the other end of the stick we are ourselves shaping at Campden, but their problem, could they work it out, is a much more important one than ours. How to live by its produce on a given piece of English land. Treating their agriculture not as exchange but for the purpose of produce only, and paying their rates, for the 90 acres of land they farm, out of a common pasturage and grass crop. They have little home-built cabins of wood and brick dotted about among their allotment patches. 'Tis all very uncouth and experimental. In the cabins are pianos, books, machine made chairs and tables and other of the unearned incrementa of civilisation, protesting as it were against this half-hearted return to barbarism.[15]

The many little ironies of life at Whiteway – and indeed of life at Campden – were obvious to Ashbee. Malcolm Muggeridge, too, who had connections with Whiteway through his family in Croydon and who went there as a boy, was fascinated by its tragi-comic history: the saga of disasters, quarrels, jealousies, departures; the problems and upheavals besetting those attempting to build Utopia among the wooden huts at Miserden. One could not help admiring a venture so intrepid. Ashbee wished it success, noting that the children looked happy and healthy and that their varied accents, Austrian, Russian, Cockney, Scottish and Yorkshire, were gradually getting tinged with Gloucestershire.

Ashbee and his party left the Colony in time for luncheon up the hill, at the sumptuous sanatorium for consumptives run by Dr Etlinger. Footmen were in attendance. Here, they heard the opposite view of Whiteway and a cautionary tale which much appealed to Ashbee: the Colonists naturally tended towards nudity (10); the Doctor's patients, having been ordered to wear less clothes and walk barefoot in the interests of recovery, found they were being mistaken for the Colonists; Dr Etlinger's patients were now back in socks and boots.

(10) It was apparently the sight of two young nudists from the Colony, named (with the usual defiant non-conformity) Elfie and Doddles, bathing in the pool at Whiteway, which gave Malcolm Muggeridge his first intimation of sex. (Malcolm Muggeridge: *The Green Stick,* 1972)

In Campden, the visitors kept on arriving. They were time-consuming, but made good material for the Journal.

There was, for instance, the famous Lady Elcho:

Lady Elcho the wonderful, the nonchalant, the strangely fascinating, the man's woman (Janet does not like her!) whirled over to Campden on Friday in her motor. She brought old Mr Raper and some of her house guests to tea at Woolstaplers. Campden has become a sort of show place for the neighbouring Country houses and we now dress in white moirée and Niger leather when we drive for a short 30 miles – so as to be conveniently home for dinner.[16]

A few weeks later, there was the joke Professor:

A Titanic Teuton has descended upon us. One Prof. Waentig of Munster – or as Carlyle might have called him Teufelsdruck Waentig. He is writing a book – çela va sans dire – on Handicraft in the modern social scheme of things, and having a holiday he came in a Bee line from Munster to Campden. The skipper took him in charge, Archie Ramage and Alec Miller talked Socialism to him, and he – My word how he talked! – German or English indifferently, amazingly, wonderfully! Het set up his verb in the remote distance and then stalked it, so to speak, through mountains of nouns, adjectives, participles, relatives and grammatic compounds. The verb was always there right enough, it tried to escape, poor thing, to creep confused into the sand and hide itself, but it could not, it was fettered, fascinated.[17]

The indefatigable Professor spent ten hours cross-examining Ashbee, who felt he was being treated as a document on search. He took a morning reading the Guild Articles and Rules, the fruits of fifteen years' slow democratic labour, and to Ashbee's faintly dismayed amazement, had them memorized and tabulated in the afternoon.

One day when Lady Elcho came to see the Ashbees, she found them packing up to go to Hamburg. 'But why Hamburg?' she asked, in her usual grand manner. 'What a funny place to go.'[18] Ashbee, who made all possible excuses for Lady Elcho, described this comment later as 'the deliciously inconsequential question of the British aristocratic', and he admitted that for once he was inclined to share her point of view.

As it happened, he and Janet were on their way to Hamburg for Ashbee's cousin's wedding. It was not an event he was greatly looking forward to. Although when he was younger, when the Guild was in its very early days in Whitechapel, he had had much closer ties with his mother's Hamburg family, connections had lapsed and he had not been to Germany for nearly sixteen years. His grandfather, the archetypal Hamburg-Jewish merchant, solidly respectable, gentlemanly in his dealings, unostentatious and formal in his way of life, had died some years before, and Ashbee suspected, rightly, that the new generation had a very different outlook.

The visit turned out as badly as he had anticipated. Maybe even worse. To someone with Ashbee's very well-tuned social conscience, with his highly cultivated taste for simple pleasures, the lavish vulgarity of his cousin's wedding came close to agony. He was appalled by the whole succession of events: the 'polter abend' the night before the wedding, when elaborate verses were read to bride and bridegroom; the grand display of tawdry silver wedding presents; the pompous ceremony in the Lutheran Church, with the wedding guests decked out in their most ostentatious jewels; finally, the massive banquet for the clan and its connections at the bride's mother's house, where 85 people sat down and ate 10 courses, while an orchestra played in the garden and from time to time a tucket announced yet another musical toast.

Ashbee disliked the wedding feast so much that he compared it to the worse excesses of the Italian Renaissance, the time they threw Pope Leo's golden dishes into the Tiber. He found the display of extravagant materialism not just wholly uncongenial but also faintly ominous: 'I don't think this sort of thing can last, I'm quite certain that it ought not to', he wrote in his Journal in late summer 1904, a comment he must surely have looked back to ten years later. Hamburg had undergone an alarming transformation: 'The riches come pouring into the great merchant city, now the chief outlet of imperial Germany, and Military discipline gives it a somewhat coarse unspiritual finish'.[19] Whereas his old grandfather had saved the tips he cut off his cigars, the cigars they smoked in Hamburg were now 9 inches long, which meant that at least half was always thrown away unsmoked.

To Ashbee, with his views on the dignity of labour, the ruthlessness of modern Hamburg attitudes seemed shocking. It was certainly ironic that while Ashbee, in the Cotswolds, was fighting for the rights of local agricultural labourers, his cousin, chatelaine of an estate in Schleswig, was no longer employing German workers for the harvest but importing Poles, since they were cheaper. The men were paid 9d a day, the women 6d. When Ashbee remonstrated, he was told the Polish labourers were better off in Germany than back home in Silesia where men got only 6d and women $2\frac{1}{2}d$ (plus a few potatoes and a ration of skimmed milk).

(11) By the mid-1970s, De Morgan pots were reaching £300–£400 each at Sotheby's and Christie's.

The right rate for the job; the true rewards of labour; the economic problems of idealistic enterprise. These complicated questions, with their tortuous solutions, at that time were very much on Ashbee's mind. Stopping off in London on their way to Germany, he and Janet had had dinner with William De Morgan who gave them the news that, after many years of alarums and excursions, his pottery-making had been finally abandoned. The men had been discharged and the works closed. De Morgan took it well and tried to make a joke of it. ' "My potting days are over" he said ruefully, waving his dear funny flattened forehead above a soup plate. "It costs me so much money every year to make pots that I can't make pots any more" '.[20] But Ashbee saw the sadness of the situation, blaming the folly of the world for throwing away the skill and great originality of an artist-craftsman like De Morgan. 'There has been nothing like De Morgan's work I think', wrote Ashbee in the Journal, 'since the work of Gubbio and the Hispano moresque ware but we will not let him work at it.' He added perceptively: 'After his death we shall for great sums collect it into cabinets' (11).

The idea had been broached that De Morgan's pottery should be resurrected by the Guild at Chipping Campden. As the Guild of Handicraft had earlier absorbed William Morris's Kelmscott Press, with its men and its equipment, the proposal now was that De Morgan's foreman Ewbank, with his store of technical expertise and knowledge of De Morgan's traditions, should bring some of his craftsmen to join the Guild in Gloucestershire. But Ashbee, with uncharacteristic caution, had vetoed the scheme. The problems of building kilns at Campden seemed to daunt him. Perhaps, now the Guild had had two years away from London, he was starting to feel that he had taken on too much. 'We ourselves', he wrote wanly, having refused De Morgan, 'have as much sail as we can carry, and times are bad.'[21]

It was just beginning to dawn upon the Guild and its supporters that Guild finances were definitely shaky. This was of as much concern to the Guildsmen as to Ashbee, for it was essentially a co-operative enterprise. The finances of the Guild had, right from the beginning, been based on the idea that the men should have a stake in it. Although in 1888 the pooled resources of the first of the Guildsmen came to less than £50, by 1898 – when the Guild of Handicraft, on Rob Holland's advice, was reconstituted as a limited company – the men's share holdings amounted to between £700 and £800. In the years of expansion, as Guild profits rose from £362 in 1898 to £994 in 1901, the Guildsmen's own dividends had increased correspondingly. There

were signs of euphoria in the Shareholders' Report for the year ending
1901, the year in which the Guild received the Royal Warrant as
Jewellers and Silversmiths to H.M. Queen Alexandra and the year in
which the exodus to Campden was decided, a time of optimism when
anything seemed possible and when the vistas of democracy looked
practically endless. The 1901 report even confidently stated that the
Guild of Handicraft was to be the *property* of its Guildsmen 'in no
distant future'.

Since then, the Reports had been progressively less cheerful. Profits
in 1902 were down to £545 (though this was explained by the expenses
of the move). Profits in 1903 were only £410 (though this time the
decrease was attributed to the cost of opening a Gallery in Dering Yard
in Bond Street to show and sell Guild furniture from Campden).
However convincingly-worded the excuses, and however heartening
the proposals for the future, the Guildsmen were becoming dimly aware
of economic pressures. It was only a hint. They were most of them quite
busy. They were also much absorbed by Guild activities in Campden.
But, as Alec Miller comments in his memoirs on this period, 'there was
an ominous note recurring at the quarterly Guild meetings, and we
realised that there was a certain insecurity about Guild finances!'[22]

The idea of profit-sharing – which as the Guildsmen were beginning
to find out had its snares and its delusions as well as all its virtues – was,
one might imagine, part of the whole logic of the Arts and Crafts
movement, part of the whole concept of self-determination. Workmen
should have a say in what they made and how they made it. But profit-
sharing schemes, as has been proved before and since, are less simple

(12) Katharine Adams was one of the
great binders of her day. She trained
with Sarah Prideaux and set up the
Eadburgha Bindery in Broadway a
year or two after the Guild arrived in
Campden. She did a good deal of
work for St John Hornby's Ashendene
Press and for Sidney Cockerell, a
life-long friend. (Indeed at one time,
she and Cockerell seemed on the verge
of marriage: 'I would have married
her', Cockerell reflected later, 'but she
was five years older than I and by the
time I could afford to marry we could
not have had a family'.)

Katharine Adams eventually
married Edmund Webb and gave up
the Bindery. (It is now a gift shop.)
When she died in 1952, aged 88,
Gordon Russell, who had known her
as a boy in Broadway, wrote her *Times*
obituary: 'The absolute integrity
which she applied as a matter of course
to every detail of her work, coupled
with her fine sense of design and
intuitive skill in handling material,
have inspired me ever since.'

than they sound to actually implement, and for one reason or another, profit-sharing was a fairly rare phenomenon, even in the workshops of the most committed Arts and Crafts men.

William Morris, for instance, most fervent of spokesmen for individual liberty and the dignity of craftsmanship, had never quite managed to free his own workers from the capitalist practice he so much denigrated. Some of his chief technicians had a formal share in profits, but many of the others were day-workers or on piece-work. He was the employer and they were the employed, a state of affairs which evidently rather worried him, for in a letter on the subject to Georgiana Burne-Jones,[23] he attempts a defence of his position, arguing (a little lamely) that if he were to keep only a nominal proportion of his last year's profits, say £4 a week or £200 a year, and distribute the remaining £1600 among the 100 people he employed, no one would in fact be any better off. They would still be members of the working class, with all the disadvantages of that position. Anyway, he added, could he really expect Janey, his wife, and his two daughters, one of them an invalid, to manage on a mere £4 a week?

Ashbee's own persistence in working out a formula both morally acceptable and (far more difficult) practically functional seems all the more remarkable because so rare. Of the Arts and Crafts workshops near Ashbee in the Cotswolds only the Guild of Handicraft was in any sense self-governing. Katharine Adams (12), bookbinder, in Broadway, had two or three assistants, artistically-dressed ladies organized and paid in the conventional way. Ernest Gimson, in Sapperton, employed eight or ten men, four good woodworkers from London plus a variable number of craftsmen he trained locally, but though Gimson's working methods meant that he worked closely with his craftsmen, relying on their skill and their experience, the relationship was still the old one of man and master. Sidney Barnsley, the furniture maker, employed no one, not just to avoid the inevitable pitfalls of labour relations but because he enjoyed the making more than the designing. He was the ultimate Arts and Crafts perfectionist, even chopping up his logs of wood himself.

It was in Birmingham, surprisingly enough, that Ashbee's Guild had its closest parallel. What Ashbee was now coming to grips with in the country, the Birmingham Guild of Handicraft had been attempting in the centre of a highly industrialized town. The Guild had been founded around 1890 by a group of fairly prominent citizens of Birmingham, in conscious imitation of Ashbee's Guild of Handicraft. Ashbee had himself given the main address at the inaugural meeting, and Arthur

Dixon (13), leading figure in the Guild and responsible for much of the design work, had worked at Ashbee's School of Handicraft in Whitechapel from 1892 to 1893. The structure of the Birmingham Guild was close to Ashbee's, with teaching being carried on alongside making, and the aims were similarly idealistic. The Guild was run as a co-operative workshop, with predictable emphasis on corporate life. The soul of the workman was considered all-important. In theory at least, the needs of the craftsman came before those of the merchant. The machine must stay subservient: this was basic Guild philosophy. The Birmingham Guild motto was 'By Hammer and Hand.'

(13) Arthur Dixon (1856–1929), architect as well as designer. His most impressive building seems to have been the pro-cathedral in Seoul, Korea.

The Ashbees liked the Dixons, but were always rather scathing about the Guild in Birmingham, criticizing its social life, which was evidently a pale shadow of Guild life with the Ashbees.

(14) Like the closely-knit group of artists and designers working in Glasgow at this same period, the Birmingham Group was very localized. The central figure (equivalent to Fra Newbery in Glasgow) was the headmaster of the Art School, Edward R. Taylor. The group, whose work was mainly illustration and printmaking, tempera and gesso, stained glass, embroidery and metalwork, included Henry Payne, Joseph Southall, E. H. New, Bernard Sleigh, Mary Newill and Arthur and Georgie Gaskin, the jewellers, who eventually went to live in Chipping Campden.

(15) Gilbert Murray (1866–1957, named after his mother's cousin, W. S. Gilbert of Gilbert and Sullivan). Popular champion of Greek culture. His readings from his own translations from the Greek had at that time become

a kind of cult. 'They came into our dramatic literature', Bernard Shaw wrote in 1905, 'with all the impulsive power of an original work', to shouts of 'Author !' Murray had to explain that the author was long dead.

(16) Sir Oliver Lodge (1851–1940), first principal of Birmingham University, the earliest of the provincial universities to receive a charter. He was a physicist and his experiments on the relative motion of matter and ether were described in his obituary as heroic. He was also immersed in the study of psychic phenomena. His pioneer experiments in thought-transference and in particular his investigations of the famous mediums Mrs Piper and Eusapia Palladino had satisfactorily convinced him that the mind *survives* the dissolution of the body.

Birmingham at that time, although sharing all the problems of the big industrial cities, seems to have had an unusually vivacious cultural life. Besides the Guild of Handicraft, there was a Bromsgrove Guild of Applied Art, founded about 1897, and also a considerable nucleus of artists and designers, later known as the Birmingham Group (14), which centred round the School of Art. The intellectual life was evidently very stimulating. According to Janet, on a visit to the Dixons in November 1904, Birmingham had more charms than might have been imagined:

This is a wonderful place: a curious mixture of bourgeoisie and romance, dullness and intellectual activity; materialism and spirituality. On Thursday we went to a meeting of the Socratic Society — Gilbert Murray (15) on his newly translated *Troades*. We have all been agog lately over the revelations in Euripidean tragedy that Murray has been giving to the world – the *Bacchae*, that horrible and most majestic play – and the *Hippolytus* that Granville Barker has been staging in town so admirably. The man Murray is just what you would imagine from the tender and illumined handling he gives to the Greek. A clear cut squarish face, wide brows, and a beautiful restraint and dignity in all the features. Long bony hands which he used simply and with ineffectual naiveté – during the reading. This new play is so distressful a tragedy, unrelieved except by darker or lighter veins of suffering, as to be quite unfit for acting. But it was a wonderful thing to hear it read in that poignant and yet almost bare manner; the audience listened, keyed up to snapping point, with a tangible intensity – the thing was so dreadfully alive after these 2400 years.[24]

Janet was in her element. The intellectual climate of Birmingham agreed with her, and – although she would have been reluctant to admit it – she was at her very best without her husband at her side. With Ashbee, she was always a bit on the defensive, always ready to smooth over the tricky situations frequently created by his legendary tactlessness. Alone with other people of her intellectual calibre, where her quiet beauty and her easy friendliness made her the centre of attention, Janet came into her own.

The social event of the visit was a party arranged by Mrs Dixon in Janet's honour. The Principal of Birmingham University, Sir Oliver Lodge (16), and his wife were there to meet her. Lady Lodge, mother of twelve, appears in Janet's journal as 'a large and pleasant person with no special outline'. Her husband, however, apparently considered her the most beautiful woman in the world.

Sir Oliver sat at one end of the dinner table, with Janet opposite. (She had particularly asked to face Sir Oliver so that she could catch his splendid look.) Lady Lodge was at the other end, and in between, described with great enjoyment by Janet in her diary, were the lesser luminaries of the Birmingham scene:

On the other side of poor Arthur Dixon, whose green eyes twinkled sadly at me from behind a mound of conscientious salad (17), sat Mrs Catterson Smith. Her principles and her temperament alike are against the wearing of evening dress; and an enveloping garment of black, without form and void, – a rudimentary opening at the throat, and large baskets of grapes fashioned in seed pearls and hung round the shoulders, represented to her the limits of decorum. She has the terrible effect of a suction pump; – approach her, and every idea will leave you, you forget the English language – and the power of laughter. The whole company felt it, and struggled – Mrs Pinsent's crimson velvet and my crimson damask on either side of the table acted however as non conductors, and preserved the life of the remainder.

Catterson Smith (18) himself, who is so beautiful that one forgives him much, even his wife, talked quietly of old time Socialism, of methods of teaching drawing (he is now head of the Bm. School of Art) and of Fabianism. He feels a little traitorous in leaving the proletariat neighbourhood of Mosely (sic) for the rarified air of Edgbaston – 'A great gulf is fixed,' he said plaintively, 'between the two' – no wonder with that cinder spewing steam tramway as the only tie.

After dinner Mrs Pinsent (19) and I settled down in the back drawing room and talked Workhouses, Special Schools, Lunacy, Physical Deterioration etc. She is an eminent novelist, and I understand her 'No Place for Repentance' made quite a stir some years ago. She has brought up three children in a thoroughly

(17) Poor Arthur Dixon was eating salad because he was religious and this was Friday.

(18) The Catterson Smiths were familiar figures in Birmingham artistic circles. Robert Catterson Smith, who came from Dublin, was originally a painter and illustrator and as a young man worked as an assistant to William Morris, preparing drawings for printing at the Kelmscott Press. (He worked on the Burne-Jones illustrations for Chaucer.) He later took to silversmithing and became Headmaster of the Vittoria Street School for Jewellers and Silversmiths. Then, in 1903, he succeeded Edward Taylor as

headmaster of the Birmingham School of Art.

(19) Mrs (later Dame) Ellen Frances Pinsent (1866–1949). She and her husband Hume, a solicitor, were respected citizens of Birmingham. She was the first woman on the City Council, and was especially concerned with mental health.

(20) Louis Dease, Lord Gainsborough's agent, had recently left Campden, to the regret of Ashbee: 'what shall we do without the fantastic Celtic lie?' (*Ashbee Memoirs*, September 1904)

rationalistic and material manner – no place for Religion – and is now on the Royal Commission for enquiry into the provision for the feebleminded and crippled. Her negation of the Spiritual is almost amusing in the light of such splendid work as she does, constantly, voluntarily, and among the most hopeless and despairing section of the community.

Dan Leno in crimson velvet with yellow herring bone stitch represents her appearance – but there is fine and human capability in her face.

We were soon joined by Sir Oliver who settled himself down for the evening between us, and was ready to discuss anything, from Dionysus and the Parallel with Christ, the double birth and the sacrificial blood, to Bentley's Cathedral and the Campden children's carols. His Herculean simplicity is astounding; some time ago he discovered Religion and wrote and told the papers; now he has discovered Greek classics and is wild with amazement and delight. He himself had no public school education, and has risen in a certain measure quite from the ranks. The philosophers say he is *pre-eminent in Science*; and the Scientists that his philosophy is *wide and admirable*; but you feel in face of a great elemental spirit, a gentle Titan who has not yet got far enough from childhood not to feel very vividly the easy joys, and quick disappointments of humanity. This gives to his manner and conversation an indescribable freshness and piquancy of outlook – you are prepared for anything. He thinks aloud, and writes to the papers as he thinks, with a kind of naive pride...[25]

Going home on the train to Chipping Campden, Janet seems to have suffered some sort of a reaction to the pleasures of Birmingham. Prospects for the winter seemed suddenly alarming, and she realized she had to put some pressure on her husband to re-let the London house, which had been standing empty since Whistler had died in it the previous summer. 'Please', she wrote to Charley who was at his Chelsea office, as soon as she reached Campden, 'I feel very strongly on this.'[26]

She was also very anxious about Ashbee's state of health. He was suffering from some mysterious form of rheumatism. Because of this rheumatism – 'if it *is* rheumatism' – Janet wrote suggesting they should move from Woolstaplers' to the Dease's empty house in Campden AT ONCE before the winter (20). 'Anything is worth doing to get well', entreated Janet: 'I can move in two days easily and gladly.'[27] She added quite severely that Arthur Dixon, who had had the same affliction the year before, had been completely cured by *steadfastly obeying* a good doctor on questions of *diet*.

It seems from the diary that Janet's gloom soon lifted. She was always disposed to get vicarious satisfaction from the successful love-affairs of others – this was partly sheer generosity of nature and partly a reflection on her own strange situation in her marriage – and the romance of Statia Power and George Loosely seems to have much improved her spirits and provided the Guild with a good talking-point for months.

The affair had begun slowly. Their first meeting, two years earlier, had not been in the least propitious. Although George, like all the others, had been impressed with Statia when Ashbee first took him to see her in the Binding Shop ('My word', he said to Charley outside in the street afterwards, 'what a magnificent animal'), Statia for many months had poured scorn on poor George Loosely, complaining about his bright red beard, his eyes, his spectacles, the loose-limbed way he walked. 'I do like a *manly* man', she said to Janet, and asked her not to ask them to Woolstaplers' together.

But George was persevering. The winter before, he had been worried about Statia, who was looking ill and drawn. Being (conveniently) psychic, he had used the 'suggestive method' to improve her state of mind, sending uplifting psychic messages 500 yards down Campden High Street, from his studio to her Binding Shop.

The method worked well. George hinted that perhaps it worked a bit *too* well. ('The idea was terrifying' comments Janet.) But although his psychic waves had paved the way to greater intimacy and he had taken lessons in bookbinding from Statia, and had indeed sewed up all his old Kipling stories, she still could not bear his beard, his glasses or his voice.

George then took a desperate step. 'When I came from Birmingham on Saturday', as Janet told the story, 'he met me without a beard. What is more he lied so shamelessly about it that I knew all.'

He asked Janet to go straight round to his studio. The atmosphere was suitably dramatic. 'The studio was dusk, and red lights worthy of a Maeterlinck interior were playing from the doors of his stove.' Statia came in, came up to Janet and kissed her. This true Arts and Crafts romance – Ashbee would surely have called it 'noble' – had reached a happy ending: 'They had taken hands and stood like Adam and Eve for beauty, and with an extraordinary elemental light in their eyes.'[28]

After all this, one may well wonder how normal life went on in Chipping Campden. But the routine in the workshops was by then

(21) Guild silver made in Campden has the London hall-mark, G of H Ld. Earlier pieces (made before the Guild became a limited company) are generally hall-marked CRA.

(22) Though he suffered off and on from lumbago all his life.

too well-established to be at all disrupted by extraneous events. The jewellers in the Silk Mill went on producing jewellery (though by autumn 1904, the economic pressures had led to a certain lowering in quality). The silversmiths were still fairly busy with commissions for important City cups, as well as table and church silver (21). At this period, the woodworkers were continuously occupied with work for Lord Beauchamp at Madresfield Court, Malvern. The designs for the new library included two large carved panels 11 feet high, depicting – with typical Arts and Crafts allusiveness – the Tree of Knowledge and the Tree of Life. The Essex House Press had just announced the publication of a new Bible to be used in churches, a large-scale project (though by no means as ambitious as the Prayer Book produced the year before), and was also planning an edition of Ashbee's own poems, *Echoes from the City of the Sun*. Even Statia Power, despite the elemental light, was back working in her Bindery; her books were described in a contemporary prospectus as being 'in various leathers, and also in ebony, rose and hollywood, and in silver with enamels'.[29]

In all the activity of winter 1904, Ashbee's own afflictions appear to have receded. Maybe he took advice on diet from Arthur Dixon or maybe the salt hose operations (referred to in a letter of solicitude from Alec Miller) had worked at least a temporary cure (22). In any case, proposals for the evacuation of Woolstaplers' Hall were apparently pursued no further and everybody's energies and interests directed to the newly-opened Campden School of Arts and Crafts.

Village schools of arts and crafts were not, of course, entirely novel. The first cottage-art classes, influenced by Ruskin, were a typical phenomenon of the 1880s, and more recently the Home Art and Industries Association and the Rural Industries Co-operation Society had encouraged the proliferation of rural craft schools and even set up depots for the sale of work produced. The founders of these classes were, like Ashbee, concerned with keeping country people in the country in contentment, instead of allowing them to crowd into the cities, and intent on reviving the traditional village industries and restoring the workman's pride in his productions. All these aims Ashbee agreed with, but as usual he went further. He insisted that country people needed much more 'culture'. And culture, to him, implied a broader education. Every citizen of England, Ashbee argued passionately, needed training not just in the three Rs but also the three Hs: Hand, Heart and Head.

'To discover local wants', as he wrote a little later in a paper on the subject, 'we must examine closely what are the actual social conditions.

What do people live on? What do they earn? What land have they that they can till? What is the family budget? What social ramifications are there with other grades of life? Is there a carpenter cousin, a sailor brother, a colonist away? We must look at the boys standing at the street corners and ask why they stand there and what we can do to stop it. We must ask at the same time why so many fields are covered with thistles, and why the roofs of so many cottages are falling in. Any conscientious examination of local wants will quickly reveal what they are.'[30]

In Gloucestershire around 1900, it was obvious that one of the most urgent of local needs was simply the means of subsistence. For a labourer trying to support his family on twelve shillings a week, classes in Freehand Drawing and Instrumental Music may have seemed beside the point (23). But this is not how Ashbee saw it. He saw it as his role to fulfil a local need which the locals themselves were hardly yet aware of. A School of Arts and Crafts should awaken possibilities, make some attempt to fill the kind of spiritual vacuum left by the irrelevance in present-day conditions of the old rural hierarchy of local squire and parson, and to counteract the depression of the villages emptied and decayed by the drift into the town.

With optimistic trust in the efficacy of drafting the labourer's lad into physical drill classes and lectures on the 'Heroes of Civilisation', and giving the village plumber's apprentice courses in gardening, lead glazing and music, Ashbee had been working hard since he first arrived in Campden to put rural education on a proper footing. Right from the beginning, the Guild craftsmen had been acting as instructors at the Technical School in Campden, and by 1904, the educational programme had very much expanded. Ashbee then took the big step of buying new school premises, with various donations from his family and friends and a modest contribution from Gloucester County Council. The school building, Elm Tree House in Campden High Street, backed on to an old malt barn, conveniently convertible into a lecture hall.

The plans moved on so fast that the 'bucolic party', as Ashbee rudely called them, the landowners and farmers, traditionally opposed to education of the masses, were taken by surprise.

(23) As one of them once said: 'The wurst of eddicated people is that they be so demmed ignorant'.

(24) i.e. Lord Gainsborough.

'Dear Ashbee', wrote Lord Gainsborough, evidently startled by the way things were progressing:

I have been away from here so much lately, that I have not heard anything in detail as to how the Technical School question was progressing.

I did not know you had decided to rebuild or equip the old building you told me you had bought, for the purpose. Though not averse to a great deal of what you have done in the direction of Technical Education, I feel that as Chairman of the Grammar School Governors, I must side with them, and not throw myself hurriedly into anything that would appear to be opposed to their wishes and views.[31]

Ashbee replied, with his usual high-handedness, that the School of Arts and Crafts was now a fait accompli and denied any ill-will, at least on his side. (If the Grammar School faction was a little irritated, this was surely only jealousy at his success.) He went on to suggest that the Earl could himself pour oil on potentially troubled waters by taking the Chair at the opening ceremony. Perhaps to his surprise, Lord Gainsborough agreed.

The ceremony was a very grand affair. Ashbee described it in his journal with rather shamefaced pride:

We have had a function – galore! With all the County in carriages and motors, an address from Lord Redesdale and the little White King (24) in the Chair. It was at the opening of our new Technical School buildings – the Campden School of Arts and Crafts we now call it – or rather the Board of Education desires to call it to the bewilderment of the bucolic mind. There were County Officials, H.M.School Inspectors, Trustees etc., on the platform and I felt like a sort of aesthetic Punch and Judy man who was beating the big drum and pulling the strings to make the puppets work and dance. The little White King danced beautifully. A year ago he had told me that he was not interested in higher education (that is what they call it officially), didn't believe in it, didn't want to have anything to do with it, and here he was, on a public platform, the centre of all eyes, talking the well known shibboleths of handicraft, the need for better education, the desirability etc, etc . . . Dear little man, it was all so conscientious and studied and artificial, one felt like stroking him and – 'Well' said Alice – 'it wasn't so alarming after all . . . now take breath and try again!'

Peers are very much like bell-wethers, and the flock follow them about from one social gathering to another.[32]

After this remarkable inauguration, Campden School of Arts and Crafts settled into its first term. Recruitment was high. There were 205 students for the period 1904–5, 90 of them men, 65 of them women and 50 elementary school children. Some were local people, some were

Guildsmen and their families: although by this time distinctions were getting blurred.

They came to the School to study drawing, design, carving; for advanced students, there was a life class (a class which Gordon Russell was later on to join). There were courses in carpentry and classes in gardening; Elm Tree House garden was divided into plots ten yards long and three yards wide where pupils were instructed in sowing parsnips, turnips, onions, carrots and potatoes. A good deal of emphasis was put on music and much attention given to physical fitness, with drill and swimming classes. Ashbee, always a devotee of self-sufficiency (at least for other people), gave the domestic crafts a special place in the curriculum. Cookery classes were very well subscribed, and a laundry class was introduced.

The laundry class was an example of a subject brought in to meet a local need: 'It seems extraordinarily foolish', wrote Ashbee in the Annual Report on the School of Arts and Crafts, 'that so rudimentary a craft as starching should have practically disappeared in a place of 1500 inhabitants, and that when the folk of Campden want their shirts and collars starched they have to send them by carrier to Evesham.' It was the same instinct to encourage local skills which led Ashbee to set up a class in lead glazing, a craft which had once been relatively commonplace but which had by this time more or less died out.

Of all the School of Arts and Crafts' activities, the programme of lectures was perhaps the most impressive. The list for 1904–5, redolent of almost all of Ashbee's chief obsessions, from the quaintest details of country lore and customs to the broadest theories of architectural planning, shows how good he was at getting speakers of distinction, even people with an international reputation, to the old Malt House in Chipping Campden High Street. There were fifteen lectures, from October to March:

October 28. Wentworth Huyshe.
The Dayspring of English Art and Letters.

November 4. Rev. R. M. Nason.
How Campden and the Wold came by their Saints' names.

November 11. Walter Crane.
Design in relation to the Crafts.

November 18. W. A. White.
Hammered Brass Ware.

November 25. C. R. Ashbee.
The Romantic Movement and the Work of the Pre-Raphaelites in England in the 19th century.

December 2. J. R. Barlow.
The Bournville Village Trust.

December 9. Lawrence Hodson.
William Morris's Sigurd the Volsung.

February 3. Mr Adams.
The Garden City Movement, or the City of the Future.

February 10. Owen Fleming.
The First Principles of Building as illustrated in Campden and the Cotswolds.

February 17. Mrs C. R. Ashbee.
The Growth and Influence of Music. (No. 1) The earliest music and the music of monks and minstrels.

February 24. Alec Miller.
Notes on Craftsmanship from the writing of John Ruskin.

March 3. Mrs C. R. Ashbee.
The Growth and Influence of Music. (No. 2) The Elizabethans to Purcell and the Germans up to Beethoven.

March 10. Gerald M. Bishop.
Holidays and Holidaymakers from before Paganism to after Lubbock.

March 17. Mrs C. R. Ashbee.
The Growth and Influence of Music. (No. 3) From Beethoven to our own time, with the music of the Anglican hymn, the opera and music hall.

March 24. Edward Carpenter.
Small Holdings and Life on the land.

In this atmosphere of unremitting intellectual stimulus, towards the end of 1904, the Guild of Handicraft settled down to study Shakespeare's *As You Like It*, for performance after Christmas. The choice was popular. It was a play of the locality. The rustic characters still had their counterparts in Gloucestershire. And, for the first time, some native actors were included, among them a real shepherd complete with his own crook.

The Song of Giles Cockbill 1905

As You Like It, third of the plays which the Guild performed in Campden, was the most successful yet. This was partly because of the Gloucestershire connection, emphasized by Ashbee in the Play Bill:

As You Like It is essentially a local play. The Forest of Arden is not far away, Corin and Silvius were as likely as not Cotswold Shepherds, Audrey must have come from the Wolds; and Shakespeare might have seen, probably did see, Charles the Wrestler challenge the lads of Campden, Weston, Aston, and Willersey at the games on Dover's Hill.[1]

Another reason for the play's success was no doubt its inspired casting. Ashbee himself was Jaques, the sort of part which suited his peculiar sense of fantasy; the blacksmith Charley Downer was a comic Cockney Touchstone; Alec Miller was Orlando; Will Hart was Charles the Wrestler; and W. A. White, the foreman of the woodshop, was a suitably dignified Duke. Gwendolen Bishop, last year's Lady Teazle, the Guild's favourite leading lady, came to take the part of Rosalind. So apt was the casting that not only was Ashbee's secretary Hilda persuaded to keep her Shakespearian name Phoebe, she also later married the shepherd she played opposite. The other shepherd, Corin, was acted by a newcomer to Campden, F. L. Griggs (1).

The attempt of the Managers of the Church Schools, urged on by Ashbee's sworn enemy the Parson, to sabotage the play by preventing the village children from attending it was foiled in time, and the highlight of the evening was the little Pages' song, sung by two small boys from Campden, which was tumultuously applauded. The music in the play was especially distinguished. The Ashbees' neighbour, Joseph Moorat, had contributed a special setting of 'Blow, Blow, Thou Winter Wind'.

After the production, Janet, clearly quite exhausted, went away to Kent for a few days with her parents: 'I sort of felt I *had* to get away after playing box office to *As You Like It*', she wrote rather apologetically to Charley. But Ashbee himself, in spite of a bad cold, was evidently buoyed up by his managerial triumphs, not just because *As You Like It* made a profit but because it advanced so many causes he believed in: not only providing both instruction and pleasure for the Guildsmen, culminating in the traditional end-of-production party in full costume, but also giving the townspeople a valuable lesson in community traditions and enhancing their awareness of their place in local life.

This was of course a great time for the revival of local traditions. There had been a recent surge of interest in country myth and legend, local song and dance. Rural traditions fascinated Ashbee, and Campden itself, he soon discovered, was a gold-mine. In this relatively remote part of the countryside, many of the old traditions still persisted (2). He became an avid collector of reminiscences and records of Gloucestershire May Games, May Queens, Jack-in-the-Greens, Whitsun festivities and Christmas wakes. He revelled in local legends, like the famous backsword fight between Spyres of Mickleton and Prestage of Campden, a one-handed contest fought with the left hand tied to the hocks. One champion lost an eye; the other got so badly bruised that he died a fortnight later. But no one really worried since the Campden man had won.

(1) F. L. Griggs (1876–1938), the illustrator and print-maker. He first came to Campden in 1903 when he was working on the illustrations for the Oxfordshire and Cotswolds volume of the *Highways and Byways* guides, arriving (most uncharacteristically) on a Rex motor tricycle. The town totally enthralled him, and he came back in 1904 to settle, remaining in Campden all his life.

(2) In fact it was not far off, at Headington near Oxford, that the sight of Morris dancing, a tradition still continuing in 1899, inspired Cecil Sharp to start on his great life-work of recording and reviving folk song.

In Sapperton, as well, which Cecil Sharp visited several times on his investigative travels, old country customs lingered. There were people who remembered the Harvest Home dances and the ancient Mummer's Play, and encouraged by Sharp, Ernest Gimson and his wife led the folk revival in the village. Every Saturday evening Gimson joined the class of boys and girls at the village hall learning the old dances, while Mrs Gimson played the piano. The idea of the revival of traditional merriments appealed strongly to the rural wing of the Arts and Crafts movement, and Gimson was a tireless enthusiast: 'In all the village pastimes he was the leader, and the youngest; no merry-making or dance went half so well without him; when he led the Twenty-Ninth of May there were no idle feet.' (F. L. Griggs in *Ernest Gimson, His Life and Work*, Shakespeare Head Press, 1924)

Amongst the old folk tales and rural legends of the area, a district particularly rich in country fable, Campden had its own pièce de résistance: the famous Cotswold Games on Kingcombe Plain. These first took place in 1611, the invention of Robert Dover, a local lawyer and estate agent with many literary-academic friends in London. He had seen the ancient Whitsun Ales, the games which had been held for several centuries at Kingcombe, and with a spirit of enterprise comparable to Ashbee's and indeed a somewhat similar ambition to revive the best of life in mediaeval England, he determined to transform the rather rough-and-tumble Ales into an annual gathering of great sophistication.

As well as the basic country sports of wrestling, vaulting, leap-frogging, shin-kicking and so on, Dover's Games, which were held on the Thursday and Friday after Whitsun, included more elegant forms of entertainment, such as handling the pike and archery. Card games and games of chess were played in special tents set up for the festivities. Visitors from London brought choirs to sing new songs and demonstrated new dances from the city. The traditional centrepiece of Dover's Games was a realistic model of Dover Castle built of board and armed with guns which fired from time to time, alarming the spectators who were massed on the sweeping hill above the plain at Kingcombe. This hill was originally called the Cotswold Hill, but was renamed Dover's Hill (3) in Robert Dover's honour.

In their day, the Cotswold Games had had a national reputation. Some of Dover's London friends – among them Michael Drayton, Thomas Heywood and Ben Jonson – went so far as to write poems in praise of Dover and the Games at Chipping Campden. This effusive collection, *Annalia Dubrensia,* was published in 1636. However, by the time the Guild arrived in Campden, the Cotswold Games had long since lost their glowing reputation. By the mid-nineteenth century, they were ruined by an influx of rowdy spectators from the big industrial cities and, in the interests of law and order, the Games were discontinued in the 1850s. Ashbee, needless to say, when he arrived in Campden, saw it as his mission to re-revive them, and eagerly included the *Annalia Dubrensia* in his repertoire of Cotswold readings.

(3) Dover's Hill, which in 1926 was under threat of being sold as the site for a hotel, was bought by F. L. Griggs, great devotee of Campden, who then raised funds to give it to the National Trust.

(4) In the thirties, Masefield did in fact settle for a while at Pinbury Park near Sapperton.

In its romantic setting, with its picturesque traditions and its vaguely literary associations, Campden was well set, in the early nineteen-hundreds, to become a kind of intellectual cult. At a time when the Open Road philosophy was strong among writers and artists of a certain rugged type, Campden seemed an ideal centre for excursions into rural England. John Masefield, in particular, dreamed constantly of Campden as the antidote to hateful life in London. Masefield had by now acquired a wife and baby ('an elderly wife and a very modern baby', as Janet described them with her usual candour[2]), and looked forward to the day when they would go and live in Campden, he making his poems, and his wife – whose special interests, said Janet, ranged from ancient Greek and modern English literature to speculative philosophy and the search for the Infinite – teaching in the secondary schools (4).

In the spring of 1905, the Masefields were in Campden, and on their return home John (or Jan, as he then liked to be called) wrote a letter to his hostess:

1, Diamond Terrace.
Greenwich.
April 4th. 1905.

We wish to thank you very much for our delightful holiday at Campden, and for the jolly hours we had with you, and for the jolly tunes you played. I was so home-sick for Campden, on the journey, I could do nothing but string rhymes: viz :–

When I from Campden town depart
I leave my wits, I lose my Art,
A melancholy clouds my face
I feel as though I fell from grace.
 With morals sapped and manners gone
Sing willow willow willow

But when I come to Campden town
I've adjectives for every Noun
I tire pretty patient Con
With brilliant conversa-ti-on
My virtues beam from every pore
I feel myself a man and more
Sing all a green palm bough shall be my garland.

Then last night I wrote some words to the tune of a topsail halliard chanty called *Whiskey Johnny*, it is a jolly tune, perhaps you have it in your book.

There's many a road for folk to roam
 Eastward, Westward
But the best is the road that leads men home
 To Campden on the Cotswolds.

There's many a Township fair and sweet
 Northward, Southward
But the best is the one grey lovely street
 Of Campden on the Cotswolds.

There's many a market filled with men
 Eastward, Westward
But none that you long to walk again
 Like Campden on the Cotswolds.

Ah many a mile shall I tramp and drift
 Northward, Southward,
Ere I see the golden wind-vanes shift
 At Campden on the Cotswolds.

Ere I see the plum boom dust the ground
 Eastward, Westward,
And the May wind blowing the wind-vanes round
 At Campden on the Cotswolds.

And the soft green grass and the daisies white
 Northward, Southward
And Dover's Hill in the golden light
 And Campden on the Cotswolds.

On many a road, and many a track
 Eastward, Westward
Shall I trudge in the rain till I wander back
 To Campden on the Cotswolds.

I shall sleep neath many an Elm and Oak
 Northward, Southward,
Ere I see the blest blue chimney smoke
 Of Campden on the Cotswolds.

Ere I see the street lie pale in the moon
  Eastward, Westward
Or hear the Church bells chime a tune
  At Campden on the Cotswolds.

But I trust when the tramp is done and past
  Northward, Southward
The Saints may send us safe at last
  To Campden on the Cotswolds.[3]

One of the things Masefield found inspiring about Gloucestershire was its suggestion of mystery and tragedy. Campden was by no means only buttercups and skylarks. He sensed, and responded to, an underlying aura of the strange and the macabre (5). The following year he wrote a play, *The Campden Wonder,* based on a notorious local story. (The original account was written, not long after the event in 1660, by Sir Thomas Overbury who was then living close to Campden, at Weston-sub-Edge.) It is an odd and complex tale concerning William Harrison, respectable old steward to Juliana, Lady Campden, who disappeared collecting rents a few miles outside the town; John Perry, Harrison's servant, and his mother and his brother were then hanged for the murder; a year and a half later, Harrison reappeared suddenly, saying he had been sold into slavery in Turkey, and shortly afterwards, his wife committed suicide. This unfathomable mystery, full of dramatic incident and inexplicably tortuous relationships, fascinated Masefield, and was taken up by other writers of the period: Hugh Ross Williamson used it as the basis for his novel *The Silver Bowl* and Andrew Lang included it in his *Historical Mysteries.* The Masefield version, a somewhat cavalier interpretation of the course of events in Overbury's narrative, was produced by Granville-Barker (6) who like Masefield soon became a fairly frequent visitor to Gloucestershire.

(5) This feeling was general. The Rothenstein family, who came to live in Gloucestershire a few years later, took it almost as a matter of course to find their sheepdog shot in the face at the bottom of a well. 'In our part of the Cotswolds', John Rothenstein recalled, 'there was an undercurrent of madness and violence: we knew the daughter of a man hanged for murder: his father ill-treated his mother and he threatened to kill him unless he left her alone and he carried out his threat. People, even children, used to jump down wells. So the murder of a dog would have seemed no great wonder to certain of our neighbours' (John Rothenstein: *Summer's Lease,* Hamish Hamilton, 1965)

Soon after the Guild arrived in Campden, it in effect became a kind of rural outpost for New English Drama. William Poel came to give advice on Guild productions. Granville-Barker came to lecture to the School of Arts and Crafts. It was in fact at one of Granville-Barker's Campden lectures, on the Shakespearian theatre, that Laurence Housman, sitting in the audience, received his 'call' (as he described it in his autobiography) to begin writing seriously for the stage.

Housman particularly loved to be in Campden, and on his frequent visits would always lodge at Braithwaite, where the young Guildsmen and apprentices enjoyed his endless stories and spent many worthwhile hours sitting round the table discussing politics, religion and art. Alec Miller, who was living at Braithwaite at this period, recalled that in 1904 or 1905 Housman and Granville-Barker stayed for two whole weeks in Campden. 'They were writing a play together – "Prunella, or Love in a Dutch Garden" (7) – and they seemed exceedingly happy about it.'[4] (As it happened *Prunella*, an updated pierrot story, did not do well in London, but in America it proved comparatively popular, particularly on the touring circuit.)

Absorbed as they were by the English masque tradition and the long history of country ceremonial, Campden had a great deal to offer the

(6) Harley Granville-Barker (1877–1946), actor, producer, dramatist and critic, one of the leading theatrical Fabians and friend of Bernard Shaw. At the time he came to Campden, he had just embarked on his famous three-year season at the Court where, in partnership with John Vedrenne, he produced 32 plays by 17 authors, including Masefield, Galsworthy, St John Hankin, Ibsen, Maeterlinck, Euripides (in the Gilbert Murray version) and 11 works by Shaw. He was also much involved with plans for a National Theatre and in 1904, with William Archer, had drawn up the first detailed *Scheme and Estimates*.

(7) The Dutch Garden was in fact Joseph Moorat's Campden garden, later owned by the dramatist St John Hankin.

(8) Paul Woodroffe (1875–1945), illustrator, heraldic artist and stained-glass designer. A little after Ashbee, he too came to live in Campden.

(9) The Song Book was also no doubt meant as a discouragement to Guildsmen who got carried away in the excitement of the moment and started singing songs which the Ashbees disapproved of. Janet had complained, for instance, that at the Birthday Feast in 1901, Charlie Daniel's performance of *The Shipwreck* was appalling: 'It was almost worse than Lodder's rendering of *High-tiddleti-i-ti*, which represents the depths of public house vulgarity'. (*Ashbee Memoirs*, June 1901)

new writers. They seem to have found the Guild atmosphere rewarding. Both Housman and Masefield were involved in a Guild project which came to fruition in 1905. This was the publication of the Essex House Song Book, a collection of the lyrics and catches, hymns and psalms, marching songs and choruses and comic verses which the Guild used at their sing-songs. The Song Book, decoratively printed in Ashbee's Endeavour type, in red and black, with the music drawn by Paul Woodroffe (8), included Laurence Housman's *Campden Maypole Song,* and *London Town* and *Honest Dover's Fancy* by John Masefield.

The Song Book could be bought as two bound volumes or else sheet by sheet (at 1*s* for paper, 5*s* for vellum). It was a characteristic Guild of Handicraft production, both in its style and its sense of moral purpose. 'The collection', Ashbee wrote in the prospectus, 'is one with a motive; it is a collection, too, that seeks to be essentially English in the greater sense of the word' (9).

The songs had been collected together gradually, since the very early days of the Guild in Whitechapel, and in a sense the Essex House Song Book was itself a history of the Guild. It revived old memories of workshop days in London, weekends at Long Crendon, the first few months in Campden. Some of the songs were written specially by Ashbee to mark particular events in the Guild calendar; some were revivals of songs sung in past Guild plays. Great emphasis was put on the community of Guildsmen, the life of jovial fellowship and high ideals of craftsmanship. Ashbee's song *Joan's Ale at the Guild of Handicraft* ends with the toast 'Good luck to the Guild'.

The Essex House Song Book was edited by Janet, who herself wrote many of the airs and lyrics. Another contributor was Gerald Bishop, who often came to Campden at weekends and for holidays, and shared the Ashbees' passion for the folklore of the Cotswolds. In contrast to his work for the Stage Society, which involved demanding roles in plays by Bernard Shaw, he enjoyed rehearsing the Campden village children in a May Day play he wrote for them. The play, *A May Day Interlude,* first performed at Whitsuntide in 1904 in the open market place in Campden High Street, under the direction of Mrs C. R. Ashbee, was later published by the Essex House Press.

Gerald Bishop, with Masefield and Housman, was to feature in a book of Cotswold Ballads which the Ashbees were then planning. This collection, they decided, should be called *Giles Cockbill,* in honour of a famous local character, an early Victorian agricultural labourer, who makes his first appearance in the Weston-sub-Edge minutes as a boy scaring the birds off common fields, before the enclosure of the land round Dover's Hill. Ashbee had an ancient photograph of Cockbill much much later, as an aged man in corduroys and stove-pipe hat.

From then on, Cotswold Ballads started flying to and fro. The Ashbees' own letters were full of experimental Campden airs and choruses. Janet submitted some verses to John Masefield, who wrote back with great enthusiasm (10), saying, 'You have a great gift of poetry, and a feeling for country life, which I honestly thought was dead in England', and suggesting she might possibly amend her final stanza.[5] Masefield then sent Janet a poem of his own for inclusion in *Giles Cockbill*. It was a particularly good one, suffused with the spirit of the Guild in Chipping Campden:

On Campden Wold the skylark sings,
In Campden Town the traveller finds
The inward peace which beauty brings
To bless and heal tormented minds.

O still it is in Campden Town
Man lives and works, and hates and likes,
The beech leaves drop and rustle down
The bells chime when the Church Clock strikes.

The plough teams jangle to the field,
By rick and stack the straying kine
Munch wisps of the fat acres yield,
The golden wind-vanes swing and shine.

And there is beauty everywhere,
In that grey curving English Street,
The man who goes a-wandering there
I think his blood doth quicker beat,

And no man walks her lovely ways,
And marks the shifty wind-vanes gleam
But thinks of noble deeds and days,
And builds a town of Troy in dream.

For there those elemental fires,
Set hearts aflame like glowing coal,
To build and gild the carven spires,
To crown the city of the soul.

As well as Cotswold history and local balladeering, the Ashbees
were much occupied, around this period, with the contemporary
realities of local politics. Early in 1905, the Guildsmen, who by then
controlled a large proportion of the votes on the Rural District Council,
made a bid to have Mrs Ashbee elected. Janet stood as an a-political
candidate, upholding women's interests. She was not a violent feminist,
and never active in the women's suffrage movement, but she had a strong
conviction, explained in her manifesto, that women should be represented on local government committees, 'so many of their duties having
to do with health, sanitation, the relief and treatment of the poor, including old people and children, in short, with just those subjects
which a woman needs to know and understand.'[6] It was a brave fight.
But the prospect of a woman on the Rural District Council was too
much for the Gloucestershire traditionalists to swallow. Janet was
defeated by the combined forces of Agriculture and the Church (both
Catholic and C. of E.).

Soon after her defeat, Janet went away, and Ashbee sent her a news-
letter from Campden:

Things go on in your absence with that intellectual dash and activity so well
understood in our little City of the Sun, the Children of Braithwaite are disporting
themselves on the hockey field, George Chettle and Alec are going home together
at Easter, 'the Skipper' is having his walls painted maroon – he says a change is
needed and he is sick of green – Syd Cotton has got over the blow of your defeat on
the district Council but is still rather aggressively chivalrous and would like to
make it hot for reactionary parsons and farmers, Mrs. Dunn, dear soul, looks in
occasionally to see that the world is treating me properly (I found her screwing on
the handle of the library door last night) and the boys' gardening class is a success.[7]

Not only was the Skipper altering his colour-scheme, Woolstaplers'

(10) When, later in the year, Ashbee
sent Masefield his own new book of
poems, *Echoes from the City of the Sun,*
the reaction seems somehow less
whole-hearted: 'Now about your brave
book of poems which I have read, and
so has Con. I like best your lyrics, and
the lyrics I like best the most intense.'
On the whole, he seems to have found
the collection too intellectual and too
studied, but he approved of Ashbee's
poem *The Clock of St Mary's in*
Whitechapel more than most because, he
explained in a letter to Ashbee, 'it has
in it more of your own distinctive
utterance, more of your personality,
more of your own imaginative energy.
I like poetry that rings of the writer's
self, that is not his fancy, or his
literature, or his sentiment, or any
other quality or accomplishment, but
his entire nature giving voice.'
(Quoted *Ashbee Journals,* 22 November
1905)

Hall itself was getting a spring-cleaning. (Ashbee complained of total upheaval in the Library, having discovered his beloved *Phaedo* head downwards among the French novels.) The feeling of imminent change was fairly general. Summer 1905 was in many ways a turning-point. In spite of the setback of the Rural District Council, life in Campden, and the Guild, was developing quite rapidly. The town now had its first piped water supply as well as its first motor car: a tiller-steered Stanley steam car, owned by the local doctor. In 1905, the doctor also brought in the first telephone (though this was just a private line through to his partner: there was no public telephone till 1923). The little town of Campden, since the day when Gissing saw it, had been modernized considerably, and two years later, in spite of inevitable local disapproval, girls were to be admitted to the local Grammar School.

The character of Campden, much altered by the influx of the Guild and Guildsmen's families, was further changed by the arrival of two artists, F. L. Griggs and Paul Woodroffe, who, although associated with the Guild, were never Guildsmen and who, both being people of an innate independence, set up spheres of influence almost in rivalry to Ashbee's.

When he came to live in Campden, Griggs was 28. He was smooth-haired and large-nosed, youthful-looking, very serious and reticent in manner, though always eager, given the occasion, to sit down at the harpsichord and burst into a folk-song. His career was by this time reasonably well-advanced, sustained by an important commission to illustrate the *Highways and Byways Guides* for Macmillan (11). He had also by this time tentatively begun etching, although his famous series of fantasy landscapes did not start till 1912. He knew Emery Walker,

(11) This was in fact a life-long commission. Griggs was still working on Essex when he died.

(12) This intense mediaevalism evidently made him inconvenient to live with. There is a legend still extant in Chipping Campden that it was only after his death his wife felt able to go out and buy herself an electric iron.

(13) Joseph Nuttgens, artist-craftsman in stained glass, who went to work with Woodroffe in Campden in 1923, recalls that he obviously, perhaps too

obviously, came from a good family, ex-Stonyhurst College, and that his wife was a Lynch-Staunton, and related to Lady Bellingham. 'It was all', comments Nuttgens, 'very much that sort of set up.'

But in spite of his aloofness of manner, maintains Nuttgens, Paul Woodroffe was really a well-intentioned man who could never bring himself to reprimand his craftsmen and who privately lamented the fact that his own workshops lacked the easy camaraderie of those in Ashbee's Guild. (Letter to the author, 1978)

who was always a great friend, and had met Sidney Cockerell. Already, he had his own connections with the Arts and Crafts movement. Ironically enough, his early introductions were in fact to the men who had been closest to the Master Craftsman, William Morris. This inner sanctum Ashbee never really penetrated.

By the time he got to Campden, Griggs's tastes and inclinations were set into a pattern of convivial masculinity which did not quite accord with the intellectual fervour of the régime at the Ashbees. (The sexual ambiguity also, perhaps, upset him. He was more at home with simple-hearted men like Norman Jewson, and Gimson and the Barnsleys, who became devoted friends.) Although at first Griggs lodged at Braithwaite House, and always got on well with many of the Guildsmen, he soon took a long lease on Dover's House in Campden High Street, a dignified and rather gloomy eighteenth-century stone building which he furnished with well-chosen Georgian pieces and fine water-colours.

As it developed, Griggs's mania for Campden exceeded even Ashbee's. 'Campden, to Griggs, was a passion', as his friend Russell Alexander later on explained it, 'not merely for what it was, as he knew it at its best, in its beauty and its charm, but for what it represented, in his mind, as a survival, in its tenacious hold of what seemed to him to be older and better things than many of the things of today.'[8] He saw Campden, and fought almost with frenzy to preserve it, as one of the last survivals of a glorious and fast-vanishing England (12). He loved its old festivals and holidays and merry-makings, its songs and its bell-ringing. (He even instituted an annual feast for bell-ringers, held at the Lygon Arms: roast beef, apple pie and cream and a ripe old Cheddar or Double Gloucester cheese, with best draught ale from Stratford.) He looked on Campden as the epitome of much that was best in England, land of Shakespeare, Drayton, Milton, and he revelled in small details of country life: the twittering of swallows and the first sound of the cuckoo; the sudden sight of cranesbills by the roadside; the rhythm of the seasons; the quiet and the peace.

Compared with F. L. Griggs, Paul Woodroffe, a tall austere-looking young man with a high-bridged nose and rather beady eyes, an exemplary Catholic who had cold baths every morning, was a very much more rarefied citizen of Campden (13). He had illustrated several Essex House Press publications, and it may have been Ashbee who encouraged him to settle in the Cotswolds, although he and the Ashbees were by no means bosom friends. He had fairly recently embarked on stained-glass making – 'I find your bête noire Woodroffe doing really good glass', said Laurence Housman in a letter to Janet late in 1903 –

and when Ashbee reconstructed a house at Westington for Woodroffe (14), he designed a stained-glass studio beside it in the garden.

Woodroffe had moved in in late autumn 1904. His style of life was altogether different from the Ashbees'. He was no democrat, either in theory or in practice, and regarded Guild community activities with panic. 'I think strictly entre nous', Housman was soon reporting, 'that the Guild's manners or morals have rather frightened poor old bête grise',[9] (as Woodroffe was by that time being called in Ashbee circles.) His own establishment, rather precious, very formal, almost fin de siècle in atmosphere, and quite unique in Campden – indeed, one might guess, quite unique in Gloucestershire – was well described by Janet in a letter to her husband dated 28 June 1905:

Yesterday I had tea with Bête Grise on his little terrace. The tea had a bachelorish readymade-in-the-shop-outside flavour but the setting was perfect; blue larkspurs, lilac Campanulas, orange lilies, white roses, a real lawn, and an orchard, and b.g. himself in a fascinating purple tie and with his two sattelites (15) Binns and Pippet, nice youths, but all three suffering from awe-inspiring calm and silence.[10]

Alongside these incursions of new residents for Campden, connected with the Guild yet not quite of it, the life of the Guild itself was changing subtly. In a way it had become more independent of the Ashbees. It had developed, gradually, its own momentum. The Guild had by then been three years in Chipping Campden, and its work and its festivities, its weddings and its christenings, were by now a commonplace of the life of the small town.

Among the newly married, Statia Power, the bookbinder, now Mrs George Loosely, had set up house in Campden in considerable style, complete with the Encyclopedia Britannica, most remarkable of all the Loosely wedding presents, in a revolving bookcase. Statia had turned over a new leaf so completely that Janet was soon complaining that the bourgeoisie, the conventionality, the desire to stand well with the powers that be, the assertiveness and the touch of vulgarity which had

---

(14) Now known as Woodroffe House.

(15) *Sic.* Janet had a fluent style but her spelling was erratic.

(16) Benjamin Martin Chandler, an enthusiastic amateur craftsman, an American, who spent some time working at the Guild. He later lived at Hidcote House and was joint-purchaser of one of Ashbee's Kelmscott presses. He had plans to set up a private press in Campden, but this never in fact materialized.

combined to set her against Statia at their first meeting, were now showing through again. What was more, she appeared to be swamping her poor husband who was turning rapidly into a comfortable, solid, well-groomed, docile, almost fatuous Englishman, with no ideas or conversation. Statia and George, much to Janet's disapproval, tended to embarrass callers by sitting locked in an immoveable embrace.

The most significant of Mrs Ashbee's strictures, which in tone are so venomous they rather make one wonder if in fact she slightly envied this bourgeois domesticity, is her comment that the Looselys seemed determined to sever connection with the Guild and the freedom which it stood for. This desire for independence Janet could not understand.

But the point was that Guild freedom, like most other kinds of freedom, was freedom for some and constriction to others. The structure of the Guild, and the running of each workshop, allowed great latitude to individual craftsmen. But, though free to an extent almost unknown in other workshops, the Guild was also strongly paternalistic, and the degree of loyalty and deep involvement which Ashbee expected from the Guildsmen could well, to those who did not sympathize with it, seem irksome. The Guild Idea was so much biased towards men rather than women that it did not always accord well with married life.

Nor was Guild freedom, by mid-1905, by any means freedom from financial worries. 'Rob Holland was here Saturday and Sunday', wrote Ashbee in June, in a letter to Janet, 'but he was very down about things. Finance mainly. We are not marking time, we are losing money. One bad half year seems to follow another, and there appears but little chance of pulling round this half.'[11] The prospects seemed depressing. 'But why grizzle when the sun shines?', asked Ashbee, one of nature's rapid recoverers. The Cotswolds were still full of unexpected pleasures, like the strange and delightful American wearing a blue shirt and black silk bow tie who turned up the day before from Montague, Massachussets, on a bicycle and put in an order for *Giles Cockbill,* and the rich neighbour (16) who drove over in his motor-car from Stow in sixteen and a half minutes and carried off George Chettle and Alec back to Oxford in three-quarters of an hour. Although Ashbee disapproved, on a dozen different grounds, of motorists and motors, he was also half-admiring of these early Cotswold feats of skill and daring. 'As Oscar Wilde would say', wrote Ashbee, ' "Time is waste of money".'

The Ashbees had also been cheered up by the discovery of the little church close by at Saintbury. This gave a new focus to their weekends in the country. Their religious orthodoxy was certainly questionable – indeed Lawrence Hodson once described Ashbee's Prayer Book as 'the

E

most hopelessly uncatholic production' he had ever come across[12] – but having a great weakness for ritual, they definitely liked to go to Church on Sunday. They were more or less ostracized from the church at Campden, on suspicion of Bohemianism, socialism, anarchism, not to mention atheism, and they had been rather at a loss until they lit on Parson Nason.

Janet described their meeting in her Journal:

We were making a tour of the neighbouring Churches, more architecturally than devotionally, when we found Saintbury nestled on the side of the hill, over-looking Bredon and Malvern, and just below a clump of stone pines. As we admired the Norman body, and Gothic spire of the building, a queer little man bustled up, with gray close cropped head, big bony nose, and sparkling eyes, and began showing us the details with evident love and enthusiasm. He bubbled over with fun and good humoured kindliness, and finally, whipping his cassock over his arm, asked us to have a glass of milk at the Rectory.[13]

This was the first of many visits to the Nasons. The following Sunday the Ashbees walked the three and a half miles across the hill to Saintbury for matins, and this became the regular routine. Many of the Guildsmen and their friends would join the party, and after the service they would picnic in the garden, with the Nasons' numerous and boisterous children joining in.

Saintbury was a convenient distance for an outing. The Ashbees fairly frequently went over to have supper with the Nasons and their family, and one of the Nasons' daughters has vivid recollections of her Uncle Charley (who was not the most reliable of horsemen) riding over to see them on a real milk-white steed.

Quickly, the Nasons became the most intimate of the Ashbees'

(17) Nevill Forbes (1883–1929), Reader and later Professor of Russian at Oxford. He was six years younger than Janet, unusually musical and always very delicate. As a boy he suffered from tuberculosis and was sent to a sanatorium in Russia, a hutted encampment on the steppes at Orenburg, for a course of koumiss treatment, a somewhat drastic remedy involving the drinking of fermented mares' milk which his uncle, George Carrick, a doctor specializing in the treatment of tuberculosis, had perfected. (For an account of Nevill's years at 'Dzhanetovka', the Russian sanatorium named after Janet, see an article by Felicity Ashbee in *Oxford Slavonic Papers*, Vol. IX, 1976.) After his traumatic childhood, it is not perhaps surprising that Nevill always tended towards hypochondria. Though his academic career had been successful, he committed suicide at the age of 45.

friends in Campden. They had many points of contact. They too had only recently moved into the Cotswolds: they had come from a busy northern parish. And they too found the intellectual and spiritual climate of Gloucestershire at times rather oppressive. Their parish of 120 souls was anything but lively, and the timber transept screen they had commissioned from Gimson was generally considered 'a blot on the Church'. Having met such like-minded people as the Ashbees, they were not tempted to cross-examine them too rigorously about their exact religious antecedents. They seemed to know their places in the Prayer-book; they discussed the sermons after lunch; they had the hall-mark of communicants. Why enquire further? They were glad to have the Guild to swell the congregation. Ashbee read the lessons for them in his well-known tenor voice.

The Nasons' seven children (eight born and one buried) were a source of great delight to Janet and also a reason for intermittent anguish. Janet was by this time 27, and though her maternal instincts were unusually active, she was still childless. The sight of children in such glorious profusion was sometimes, in her worst moods of depression, almost more than she could bear.

Perhaps, paradoxically, the quiet of country life, the very tranquillity which brought the Guild to Campden, tended to exacerbate her inner restlessness. Janet spent more time in Campden than her husband did, and she was beginning to feel her isolation. She saw very little of her immediate family. She particularly missed her only brother Nevill (17), on whom as a child she had lavished much devotion. Nevill, it appears, did not get on with Ashbee who clearly despised his nervous effeminacy. This instinctive dislike between the two men closest to her was a constant source of sadness, an additional disturbance.

Certainly at this period Janet was in a state of considerable emotional turmoil, and there were few people in the Cotswolds she could turn to. Her marriage had always been in many ways an odd one. Sexually, it was particularly inconclusive. Ashbee had little or no sexual feeling for women – 'To me', he once said, 'a beautiful woman is always a work of art, the mechanism of which I appreciate but the sentiment of which I am out of sympathy with'[14] – and her own almost total ignorance of sexual practice left the situation at something of an impasse. Ashbee never really recognized the feminine in Janet. He had always tended to treat her as an extra, though particularly charming, Guild apprentice. But although her role as comrade, Ashbee's helpmate and companion, seemed to her at one time, in her early years of marriage, when every-thing was strange and new, wholly exhilarating, it had more recently, as she herself became maturer, given rise to recurring unhappiness and doubt.

In point of fact, compared with the marriages of many of Ashbee's contemporary architects and craftsmen, Janet's role was in some ways enviably independent. Even in enlightened Socialist-artistic circles, to treat a wife so much as an equal was unusual. Arts and Crafts wives were very often relegated to embroidering cushion covers and illuminating manuscripts. Women of the Simple Life were almost always in the background. Janet's own position as an almost equal partner, whose judgment was relied on and respected by her husband, should perhaps, one might have thought, have been enough to satisfy her. But this is to ignore the Ethel M. Dell instinct: Janet, who had been almost too young for serious suitors and whose state of innocence when she married was remarkable, had a reprehensibly bourgeois yearning, unsatisfied by Ashbee, for true romantic love.

An autobiographical novel, *Rachel,* which Janet wrote a few years later, gives an extraordinary insight into the oddnesses and strains of Ashbee's marriage. It is a highly evocative tale of Arts and Crafts life, love, honour, sacrifice, redemption. The chief protagonists are Arnold Keane and his wife Rachel, realistic portraits of the Ashbees, and the sober conscientious Socialist, David Northwind alias Gerald Bishop, whose relationship with Janet – with its strange, disturbing mixture of sexual restraint and spiritual recklessness, for Janet refused doggedly ever to be his mistress – was to dominate her life for the next six or seven years.

The novel tells the story, very candidly and touchingly, of Rachel's early memories of Arnold's visits to her parents' house in Surrey (as a child of 10, she had found his uncouth arrogance embarrassing); the unexpected present, a bracelet in chrysoprase and blue enamel made in the Guild workshop, which Arnold had sent her before she went to Germany, at the age of 15, to study music; her first visit to his mother, the formidable mistress of a disconcertingly artistic house in Chelsea; Arnold's formally-worded passionless proposal which, without quite knowing why, she had accepted; their marriage and the wedding night at Essex House, when Arnold comes in in his nightshirt with a candle, smiles at Rachel reassuringly, tucks himself up in a matter-of-fact way, and blows out the light.

The antipathy between Janet and Mrs Ashbee, not referred to in the Journals, comes out clearly in the novel. In the book, old Mrs Keane is a considerable tartar, proud of her house and her own unceasing industry (she is endlessly knitting useful granular grey garments), proud of her well-educated daughters and proudest of all of her devoted son. Mirroring a journey which Ashbee and Janet and old Mrs Ashbee took to America in 1900, the novel described the disastrous clash of temperament of two strong-minded women. 'Only a visionary', comments Rachel as narrator, 'could have planned such a mad combination of natures and hoped it might succeed.'[15] The simultaneous proximity of wife and mother proved too much for Arnold's nerves; when the three were together, a shutter went down over his eyes, his brow contracted, his spirits fell and signs of actual physical malaise appeared.

Soon after they returned from this nightmare of a voyage (the reality was surely no less painful than the fiction), the Ashbees moved to Campden. Campden, in the novel, is Littledean, a city of enchantment, perfect setting for a tale of high romance and chivalry. 'Who can describe the charm, the magic of Littledean?' asks Rachel, 'that perfect grey curving street, gable after gable, each house with its own particular set of mullioned windows, rough grey slate roofs, ashlar chimneys, and moulded with the cunning of the mediaeval and renaissance mason's skill. Little porches, pent houses, pillars, a few Jacobean pilasters flanking the later, almost the latest, houses...'[16]

David makes his appearance fairly early in the story. But less as the hero, more as the appendage, almost the vassal, of his forceful wife Olivia. Janet's portrait of Gwendolen Bishop, the flamboyantly unconventional Olivia Northwind, is, even with hindsight, tinged with admiration. Slender, shapely, green-eyed, walking like a willow tree in motion: this was just the kind of woman Janet would have loved to be.

Rachel and Olivia, in the early days in London, met often at the swimming bath, where Rachel is encouraged to pursue her passion for nakedness, and revels in the warm clear green water. Olivia rarely mentions her marriage but Rachel gathers (with some surprise) that she has a husband somewhere in an office. She also learns that Olivia is a connoisseur of cats.

Then Olivia asks the Keanes to dinner. Another of Rachel's illusions is shattered when she finds Olivia lives in a flat, like other people. But it is an evening of some significance, described with Janet's usual perception and lucidity:

The chief features of the evening that stuck in Rachel's memory were that they sat at an immensely long narrow black table, that the room was stencilled with blue lotuses, and that a tall jonquil grew out of a brown Cornish crock. That cats kept getting up into the backs of their chairs, and that, remote at the end of the table sat Mr Northwind, a legal looking man in gold spectacles who had been coerced into wearing a brown velvet coat. The only thing that really seemed to belong to Olivia were the jonquil and the cats, and possibly the coat. She was dressed in a long spare white frock, her soft straight tawny hair slipped half down from its combs and yet did not look untidy; her feet were bare, in sandals, and long and slim like the feet of a mediaeval French saint, and she wore unusual Eastern rings and gems. Rachel thought her 'wonderful', and Arnold too felt her power, and liked her clean boyishness. She was not a good talker, but her enthusiasms, and the phrases she had picked up from her Bohemian circle, stood her in place of intellect.

Her husband hardly spoke, and seemed a little worried by the cats; the whole evening he sat, looking rather tired, and watched his wife with worship in his eyes.

Rachel dismissed him as a nonentity, and their paths did not cross again for several years.[17]

The events which follow, covering the period from 1900 to 1903, corroborated by more matter-of-fact entries in the Ashbees' journals, lead on from headstrong Olivia's increasing restlessness and flight to Italy in search of self-fulfilment to David's depression and loneliness and Rachel's attempts to comfort him. They culminate, predictably, in 'that fateful evening' (described by Mrs Ashbee, natural romantic novelist) 'when he had prayed for her help and she had leaned to him over the abyss'.[18]

The scene of recognition, in which Rachel and David acknowledge their love, takes place two years later in the little church at Crossbury (the synonym for Saintbury). Rachel is to be godmother to the parson's latest child, a child called Katherine (in real life as in fiction). She had negotiated for David to be godfather, a scheme which had required all her powers of diplomacy, since David (like Gerald) is a forthright non-believer. David and Rachel, joining hands over the baby, dream of strange unlikelihoods, perhaps impossibilities. Both are childless, both are isolated in their marriages: they seem to make believe the child is theirs.

The elation of the time, the power of sexual attraction, the new abundant love that Rachel felt for David, is graphically described by Mrs Ashbee in her novel. It was an idyllic summer of rambles through the country, visits to lost churches, cycle rides, Edwardian pleasures, permeated through for the hero and the heroine with a sense both of discovery and new-found inner peace.

The spirit of that summer 1905, with its high-minded joys, is beautifully captured in the description of Rachel and David in the Fens:

They laid their cycles against a hedge and together sought a place to rest. A white-yellow cornfield stretched for miles by the side of the road, and at the corner was a little tangled glade, briony and dogrose-hips embroidering the edge of a pinewood.

Rachel sat on a little mound, her feet in a dry ditch, every thing was bone-dry, and glittering with heat – and pulled out a couple of MS fairytales by a well-known writer, an intimate friend of both. David lay propped on one elbow: the cloudy veiled sun-light of a baking August day washed everything in a haze of silver.

She read 'Peace be with you', and 'peace is', he replied thro' the darkness . . . She looked at David . . . and his eyes replied.

'Peace is,' he said, 'that is for us, isn't it; after many days.'

His head was level with her shoulder, and obeying an impulse she dared not justify, she put her left hand on his hair.[19]

The intensity of Janet's fictional reconstruction of her love-affair with Gerald Bishop (written in 1908 when the affair was over) can be explained not only by her own depth of emotion, unassuaged by the physical love which she so longed for, since the idea of sexual unfaithfulness appalled her, but also by the fact that the affair was so clandestine. In a little town like Campden, where the gossip spread like wildfire and the Guild was particularly vulnerable, Janet realized that discretion was essential. But for someone whose nature was so honest and so open, this need for secrecy was a considerable strain.

She did not try to keep it a secret from her husband. An unflinching candour was part of Ashbee's creed, and he was too unpossessive to be jealous. His attitude to Janet was curiously avuncular. He was concerned about her, but he gave her complete latitude. He had always encouraged her, right from the beginning, to go her own way and, if necessary, to make her own mistakes. And in a sense it was this total trust and freedom, this unconventional view of wifely dues and duties, which had slowly but surely propelled Janet into the arms of Gerald Bishop, stalwart Fabian. Unlike Ashbee, he called her 'Little One' and often laughed at her. Unlike Ashbee again, he did not expect too much of her. In fact, he took charge of her, in a decisive manner which Janet, unused to it, found positively thrilling. Perhaps, in the end, she was more ideally suited to the Garden City than the City of the Sun.

Ashbee quite approved of Gerald. Even though he may have lacked the homogenic spark, and was clearly not a suitable candidate for comradeship, he had much to recommend him. He was a staunch idealist: in his way, as staunch as Ashbee. He loved the Cotswolds and he cared about the Guild. If he loved Ashbee's wife too, well, this was further proof of his good sense and powers of discernment. Indeed, it sometimes seemed to Janet that her husband was glad to shelve some of the responsibilities of marriage, almost relieved that Gerald had taken over aspects of his role.

Besides, he himself had other dreams, other diversions. On 6 June 1905, he wrote to Janet:

'Tis a great mistake (as the poets always say but nobody believes them), to suppose that romance is dead. On Saturday I was bored to death by a party of 85 Birmingham Ruskinites to whom I had to smile and smile and act as cicerone with a 'pass to the left please' for 3 mortal hours and a speech in between, when – I had my reward. Swift and sudden like a sunflash out of the sky came my reward!

I fled from the 85 Birmingham Ruskinites to the lake and there I saw – there was no doubt about it – a young Greek God disporting himself in the sunlight. I'm not sure which God – I think a Hermes, but am not quite certain. There was a slight impediment in his speech, which is not customary in a Hermes, but his eyes were lovely, and a beautiful mouth! You should have seen how he played ball too. The ubiquitous Moran, with his fine sportsman's instinct had seized upon him at once for polo, and begged him in his most winsome way to strip a second time and show his swimming – then he introduced him to me as a naked Irishman of 25 who was wandering on a holiday through England. It is evident he was a Greek God or he would not have made plumb for Campden bathing lake on a bicycle flight from Yorkshire to Connemara. Nor would he have knocked for shelter at Dover's House – mark the humanism of it! – and then stayed for a week in Campden for its sheer beauty! Whether Hermes or not we have not as I say yet discovered. The Skipper who also has an instinct that way clinched matters by insisting upon his coming to Braithwaite. That's where the shade of Dover has gone for the nonce; and Hermes is to help us beat the Oxford team next week at Water Polo. With such a slip from Ilyssus we shall win – we must win![20]

A week or two later, Ashbee went to Budapest. This was a working holiday, which he described later as one of the most delicious fortnights of his life. He was greeted as a kind of culture hero. Ashbee's reputation as a designer (like that of Charles Rennie Mackintosh) was considerably higher in the intellectual salons of mid-Europe than it was in Britain. The Vienna Secession Exhibition of 1900, in which Ashbee and the Guild had 52 exhibits, had focused attention on his work (18),

(18) 'Ashbee's furniture', wrote an admiring critic, 'seems like a bite of black bread after a Lucullan feast.' (Quoted Georg Eisler 'Achievements of the Vienna Secession', *Apollo* 1971, pp.44–51)

(19) Ashbee's Budapest building was destroyed, though whether in World War I or II remains uncertain. De Szasz himself died in the siege of 1944.

and three years later the Wiener Werkstätten, founded by Josef Hoff-
mann, had been deliberately modelled on the Guild. In Hungary,
Ashbee had a particularly loyal nucleus of admirers, and he had now
been commissioned to design a house in Budapest for Zombor de
Szasz and his wife Elsa. De Szasz, a Hungarian politician, 'an
aristocrat playing with the ideals of democracy',[21] had the right
qualifications to be Ashbee's perfect client.

Ashbee worked on the plans for the de Szasz house in the early
mornings and late afternoons, avoiding the heat of the day. At noon, he
regularly went swimming in the Danube, basking in the sun, watching
the boys bathing, trying to discover the ideal Magyar type. This was a
great period of Hungarian nationalism, a time of patriotic fervour with
which Ashbee was in sympathy. He and Alec, he decided, would
design a large carved figure of the spirit of Modern Hungary, coloured
and gilded, to be the centrepiece of de Szasz's hall (19).

Excited as he was by the atmosphere of Hungary, the fantastic,
poetical, colourful life of modern Budapest with its artistic aspirations,
his natural sense of irony kept surfacing. 'What in the world am I
doing here?' he asked himself. It seemed odd that Campden, Gloucestershire, should be doing work for Hungarian noblemen, and equally
unlikely that he should be employed as a sort of interpreter for their
aesthetic ideals. He could not help laughing at the way The Studio and
the artistic magazines of so many nationalities were littered among his
host's rooms amongst the Guild furniture. However, he managed to
settle his mind to it; 'English work alone will he have, unless it be
Hungarian, and as the work of Hungary, in her present psychological
and economic development means only the German commercial
article, L'Art nouveau and so forth, is it for me to blame him? Rather
do I commend his taste as well as his patriotism.'[22]

Ashbee immersed himself in the detail of the building work, planning
and drawing, mastering the complexities of cubing up in two arith-
metical systems and three languages, weighing bricks and gauging tiles,
instructing builders and supervising workmen. He made the comment
that Hungarian builders, both the men and women, worked amazingly
long hours in a terrific heat, and got through a lot more work than any
labourers in Britain.

He got back to Campden, reinvigorated, in time for the Swimming
Sports, the highlight of the season, resulting in a brilliant victory for
Campden against Ledbury, 1 goal to 0. Twenty-five swimmers went in
for the duck race, and the prize was a genuine duck from George
Haines's farm. Old Farmer Tucker did the judging on his crutches,

and three farmers' girls entered for the ladies' race. Here was the final fusion between Art and Agriculture, and Ashbee was in a mood for self-congratulation.

Only the Church was still holding out against him. In contrast to the colour and drama of the Bathing Lake, with the Skipper's team in scarlet caps looking like youths in a painting by Masaccio, a more humdrum procession was heading down the High Street towards the annual school treat and sale of work. Parson Carrington had made the tactical error of hiring Pyment's band (who charged 2 guineas), and had to suffer the indignity of walking in a cavalcade led by Charley Downer, blacksmith, and Arthur Bunten, cabinet-maker, while the watching Guildsmen almost split their sides with laughing. Pyment himself, who by now had the band so well under control he could entrust it to his minions, spent the afternoon quietly chuckling in his workshop, and later wandered down to the Sports to smoke his pipe.

6

The Guild's Three 'Prentices 1906

Early in 1906 Janet was writing in the Journal:

Nearly 4 years in this little grey City – it seems more like 40! The weather-worn dove coloured stone has a way of catching and fixing one's affections; and even the opposition, the Vicar, the pig-headed farmers, the stupid politicians (and we have elections next week!) are all part of it – and seem as necessary as the mist and the rain and the rheumatism and the muddy roads – yes and the Sundays over Dover's Hill to Saintbury, the hockey matches, the swimming lake and the Xmas Play. Campden is still very Elizabethan and it seems natural that *The Knight of the Burning Pestle* should be welcomed and given four full houses . . .[1]

The Guild had now been in Campden long enough to have become part of the fabric of the town, and the Guild plays produced each New Year by Ashbee were a permanent fixture in the local social calendar. The play for 1906, Beaumont and Fletcher's comedy of London City life, with its cast of masters and apprentices, was a natural choice for Guild performance and had in fact been acted by the Guild before, in 1899, before the move to Campden, when William Poel himself had coached the actors, aiming to recreate the rough-and-ready spontaneity of a scratch production by any random group of half-trained apprentices in the City of London in the reign of James I.

For the Campden production, the Ashbees had hoped that Gwendolen Bishop would play the hero, Jasper, repeating her success as Lady Teazle in 1904 and Rosalind in 1905. On the face of it, considering Gerald's romance with Janet, this may seem untimely casting. But the sexual mores of the Arts and Crafts movement, though by no means outré, were on the whole unusually tolerant and sensible. Perhaps there was a notion that art should rise above emotional entanglements. At any rate, the liaison between Mrs Ashbee and the estranged husband of the actress did not apparently in theory preclude her from taking leading roles in Guild of Handicraft productions. The reason she did not appear in 1906 was purely technical: she was already busy with *Electra* at the Court.

Ashbee himself was especially attached to Beaumont and Fletcher's comedy of workshop manners. The idea of the apprentice-hero was almost an obsession, occurring frequently in his own literary works. The apprentice is the central figure in his early workshop tale *From White-chapel to Camelot* and appears again in *The Building of Thelema*, on which Ashbee was working throughout his Campden era. This long prose romance, which was finally published in 1910, features Ralfe, an East London joiner's apprentice who, in his search for the ideal working city of Thelema, symbolizes the English Industrial Democracy. Around his questing hero, Ashbee gradually assembles a cast of hundreds: ranging from Ralfe's four workshop friends, Charley, Jacko, Syd and Cyril, to John Bunyan, Walt Whitman, Socrates and Jesus Christ (1).

It may have been the camaraderie of the apprentices in Beaumont and Fletcher which encouraged Ashbee, early on in 1906, to take stock of his own Guild boys past and present, to review what they had done and to see how they were shaping. He had focused his main hopes on the young men of the Guild, influenced both by his own romantic view of English boyhood and also by the practical consideration that the young men were more malleable, more receptive, than the majority of the middle-aged Guild craftsmen. But by now even a perennial optimist like Ashbee had to admit to some major disappointments, which he attributed to the malevolence of providence. There had been many changes since the early hopeful days when the idea of the move to the country was first mooted, and several of Ashbee's favourite apprentices had left the Guild for other occupations. Some had already gone before the Guild arrived in Campden: Cyril Kelsey, 'the Professor', an apprentice metal worker, had given up the craft and was now working as a clerk in a London shippers' office; Lewis Hughes, after an altercation with the manager, had recklessly got himself a job in a trade

---

(1) Goldsworthy Lowes Dickinson, when sent it, did not like it. 'Why! I don't know', he wrote back apologetically, 'some ultimate question of taste, I suppose.' (Quoted *Ashbee Journals*, 1910)

(2) He made a notable appearance in the Essex House Alphabet:
H stands for Hardiman, great Benfleet Squire,
Who never gets lower and never gets higher,
But shambles along at a nondescript gait,
With his little grey eyes and his little bald pate,
But Bill's the best natured old fellow in Bow,
He never shows fight and he never says NO;
And he makes such fine brooches and beautiful rings,
Besides oyster boats, girdles and other odd things.

workshop; Alf Pilkington, the joiner, had left to join the army, and had since then emigrated to Canada where Ashbee had recently heard that he was prospering. Ned West (or Jimmy Green) had been removed from Campden, after his illness, by his terrifying mother, the 'cockatrice-in-velvet', and had never reappeared. George Colverd, who went back to London to play football for Millwall, was a boy whose loss Ashbee especially regretted. He still kept in touch with George and wrote in the Journal wistfully: 'Of him I hear that he is one of the best young silversmiths in the Craft and a leading footballer. I wish I could see him again.'[2]

Illnesses were also depleting the Guild workshops. Poor Syd Cotton, the cabinet-maker, had been struck down by consumption the previous summer and, helped by the Guild, had now set sail for Canada. (Ashbee was not sure he did not miss Syd Cotton, his 'wild, silly, affectionate mad hatter' whom nobody would take to, more than any of them, except for Lewis Hughes.) Ernest Godman, chief assistant in Ashbee's architectural office in London, an invaluable technician, a methodical scholarly young man zealously devoted to his master, had also fallen a victim to consumption, and in February 1906 he died.

Almost simultaneously, the news reached the Guild in Campden of the death of Bill Hardiman, the silversmith and modeller, reputedly rescued from the cats' meat barrow in Whitechapel by Ashbee and one of the earliest members of the Guild (2). For some years now, he had been going gradually crazy. First of all, his madness took a harmless form, but recently he had been prone to fantasies of persecution, at the height of which he had travelled down to Campden brandishing a stick at his old foreman, W. A. White and Mrs White, his wife, accusing them of setting the detectives on to him. His death must have been greeted with relief as well as sadness. Ashbee used the occasion to draw a useful moral: 'His little life is an object lesson', he wrote, 'in the conditions of modern labour. He was one of the unfit, but he had exquisite skill and taste.'[3] The way his natural talent had been nurtured and developed was a justification for the ideas of the Guild. In more fortunate circumstances, had he been moved earlier out of the poisonous environment in London, he might have lived a long life of great usefulness, claimed Ashbee. In any case, he had become a part of Guild mythology, featured in the Essex House Song Book as the second of 'the Guild's 3 'prentices' and appearing as one of the chorus of Guildsmen in *Widdecombe Fair*.

Bill Hardiman in fact was just one of many legends which had grown up with the Guild. In its 18 years of history, with over 100

craftsmen on the Roll, with its built-in rhythm of arrivals and departures, jobs beginning, jobs completed, the whole cycle of the workshops, together with its emphasis on communal activity, community
traditions, the Guild had accumulated countless tales and fables which
helped to give it its particular identity (3). This continuing tradition
partially explains the strong sense of attachment felt by past Guildsmen
and apprentices, many of whom corresponded with the Ashbees and
many of whom, sooner or later, found their way back to the Guild on a
visit or a holiday. Some of them, after a few years of disillusionment in
outside employment, felt a keen nostalgia for the old days in Guild
workshops. Lewis Hughes, after several years away, first in a trade
workshop, next down a Welsh coalmine and most recently, in desperation, on a London milk round, longed to join the Guild again in his
old role of blacksmith, but by now there was no room to take him back.

The years of expansion, when Ashbee could enrol almost anyone
whose ideas or whose handclasp had impressed him, were now definitely
over. Financially, the Guild was all too obviously in trouble. The
works had been on short time, off and on, for the whole of the past year.
The Annual Report for 1905 announced regretfully that for the first
time in the history of the company the Guild had made a loss. Trade
had been bad the year before, but this year was so much worse that the
loss was quite a heavy one, amounting to £958.

The official reason given was the general slump in trade and lack of
spending power among potential Guild customers. The Report also
complained that people who had previously spent money regularly on
works of handicraft were now tending to spend what resources they had
differently, on more ostentatious luxuries, particularly motor cars.
Certainly, the financial problems of the Guild were reflected by the
troubles of similar craft workshops and a sense of malaise within the
movement generally, a lack of direction and a loss of confidence which

(3) Sixty years after the Guild first
came to Campden, they still told the
tale of the day one of the craftsmen
chalked a giant outline of Ashbee on
the floor of the workshop in the Silk
Mill. 'Why is it so big?' asked Ashbee
when he saw it. The craftsmen roared
with laughter. 'It's because you're a
Big Man, CRA.'

(4) Gerald, it has to be remembered,
had always been against the Campden
scheme on grounds of practicality: 'He
says we ought to combine with other
heads of business and do the thing
cheaply', wrote Janet, adding
caustically: 'The only firms, whose
promises he holds, to try "Garden
City" when it does exist, are a small
arms factory and a soap works!'
(*Ashbee Memoirs,* 23 February, 1902)

was sadly apparent in the successive shows of the Arts and Crafts Exhibition Society, and which was to lead, a few years later, to a minor revolution by a group of younger artists and designers who broke from the Arts and Crafts to form the Design and Industries Association.

Problems of the times; troubles of the Arts and Crafts; the special difficulties of communication between Campden and London, the source of most commissions: all these extraneous reasons for the Guild's financial difficulties were real and convincing. But were they the whole answer? There was a growing feeling, as the losses became public knowledge, that at least some of the problems lay within the Guild itself.

Ashbee had no lack of candid friends, and he received a barrage of remonstrance and advice. Rob Holland wrote entreating him to suffer fools more gladly: 'for then', he said, 'instead of having so many enemies in Campden and the neighbourhood, you would have friendly sympathy with the Guild and its objects and a great deal of local work, which now goes elsewhere.'⁴ Gerald Bishop sent a long stern missive diagnosing the problems of both the Guild and Ashbee's architectural practice as the result of ineffective management (4). He poured cold water on Ashbee's latest scheme to appoint Will Hart as Manager, accusing Ashbee of having no idea of his own limitations. 'It is for this reason', wrote Gerald, 'that I urge strongly that the affairs of the Guild as a whole should be put in the hands of a gentleman of business experience, one with whom you could work on equal terms, as it were; who in managing the Guild *would also manage you.*'⁵

Gerald claimed that the disease was desperate. And so it seemed. But not so desperate as to stop normal activity. Life, for the time being, went on very much as usual. Celebrity visits to the Silk Mill still continued. At Easter-time Eliza Wedgwood brought round Arthur Balfour, whose term of office as Prime Minister had then just ended. He was easily recognized by the Guild craftsmen: 'Oh Miss Wedgwood!' said the Manager, 'You don't need to introduce your visitor – I've seen his picture so often – in the golfing papers!'⁶ Mrs Ashbee's comment was 'Came, saw and smashed a showcase!'⁷ Alec Miller reported that the ex-Prime Minister seemed specially interested in the craftsmen's tools.

Foreign Arts and Crafts enthusiasts and fact-finders were still making the same bee-line for the Guild in Chipping Campden. H. E. Berlepsch-Valendas, who came to visit Ashbee in summer 1906 and wrote a long account for *Kunst und Handwerk* a year later, was totally bowled over by the beauty of the town and the quality of life he found among the Guildsmen. His first port of call was Woolstaplers':

I had no preconceived ideas [he wrote] about the manner in which one of the best known English architects and arts and crafts men might be living. No entrance hall, no reception room, no solemn initiation in preparation for even more refined colours of other apartments – there was none of this! Two steps down from the road, and I was in the family house which gave the impression of comfort – but no sign of mysterious gimmicks or heavy symbolism suggestive of the inhabitants' spiritual domain. Nor was it a nervous lady in a modern dress-reform machine-embroidered sack-like garment, 'sicklied o'er with the pale cast of thought', who offered me her hand with a friendly smile after quickly reading the introduction from Walter Crane which I had handed to her. Her hand – it was not white, not lined with strongly protruding blue veins – no, it was brown, sunburnt, a working hand, not the hand of a drawing-room lady – this hand belonged to a female apparition whose radiant health-exuding beauty gave her an air of triumph. A moment later I was seated between her and a Hungarian Countess for whom Ashbee was building a house befitting a countess in Budapest. Here too no questions about 'where from, where to', but after a few polite welcoming words the invitation, 'let's go to the work-shops'.

Then the walk from workshop to workshop. The lady who accompanied me, Ashbee's wife, had a factual question for everyone there, everyone hammering, or chiselling, modelling or planing, and proved herself familiar with all the techniques. There was no gossiping among the working people, no counterpart of the beer jug, which had been banned in some Munich workshops only to be replaced by the beer bottle.

For the educated English workman alcohol had little or no relevance. And then looking out of the window, there were lovely views into gardens with their unimaginably lush flower beds. The silhouettes of huge trees and high steep roofs with mighty chimneys framed the picture. Here and there, through a gap, a glimpse of distant hills, of hazy-blue rolling country. All this created an indescribably pleasant impression. Presumably it must rain here sometimes, but the impression given by the way the men's work was carried out did not depend on vagaries of rain or sunshine. Could these be the results of the Toynbee Hall experiment which

---

(5) George Ives (1867–1950). A disciple of Edward Carpenter and one of the most ardent espousers of The Cause. *Eros' Throne*, his collection of Uranian lyrics, was published in 1900 and approved by Oscar Wilde.

Ives was a man of considerable mystery, even to his friends, claiming to be a Priest of a secret order founded in Ancient Greece in the time of Socrates. He had a sacred ring which he offered to bequeath to Laurence Housman if he would join the order. 'But', wrote Housman to Janet in June 1950, 'I hadn't the faith for it.' (Letter in the possession of Felicity Ashbee)

are still with Ashbee as his life's work develops further and further, leading him to self-fulfilment? One could almost believe that fate predestines some people to show others how life can be made worth living. However, the will has to be there as well.

' "Shall we go now",' said Janet, after the workshop tour. ' "By now Mr Ashbee will have finished his work and will be ready to receive you . . ." ' To Berlepsch-Valendas, the meeting with Ashbee himself was the climax of his visit: 'A tall, slim, but muscular-looking man with a springy walk', he wrote, 'stretched his hand out to me. With certain people one has only to look into their eyes to tell who one is dealing with. His calm but confident gaze, and the overall aimiability of his expression, harmonized with everything else around him. "Would you like to come for a walk with me? I have to supervise the rebuilding of a small ruined monastery." ' [8]

Guild problems, unsuspected by Herr Berlepsch-Valendas, did nothing to discourage Janet and Goldsworthy Lowes Dickinson from embarking on a complex correspondence about the Eternal Realities and Shelley. 'Shelley', wrote Goldie, 'never got incarnate. That's what gives him his unique quality, which people either love or hate according as they are more or less incarnate themselves.'

Janet replied that in that case she is certainly incarnate herself, for she greatly dislikes Shelley:

I am poles apart from him, and that is probably why the elusive soap-bubble quality – spirit – does not find any ring of answer in me. He was supernatural I think. It is very astonishing women were so fond of him: it must have been I think the physical fascination and charm, for though women are attracted by intellectual power I don't think they ever get into line with the 'children of the spirit' idea.

Goldie wrote back contentiously:

All women I think have more need of and love of matter than men. Men are the idealists. That's why they so often make a mess of things. Women would run the world more sensibly, but then so deadly sensibly. A woman's first cry is: 'How will it affect the children?' A man says 'How will it affect the soul or the race or God?' – What rot! Pray forgive me. [9]

This was the sort of correspondence Janet revelled in. She loved discussing eternal abstractions with intellectual men. Perhaps it was her lack of formal education as a girl which in her later life made her so avid for new ideas and new experiences. Her innumerable letters to Laurence Housman sparkle with intellectual curiosity. Her correspondence with George Ives (5), political and sexual anarchist – with his repeated calls for total revolution, refusing all compromise with all religious parties, all compromise with existing sexual morality, all compromise with any aspect of the class system – would certainly have made any lesser woman quail.

In May, she went off to stay with Charley Holden (6), a visit which again gave her much food for reflection. Charles Holden had worked in Ashbee's London office, as a junior architect, a few years earlier. He was then an intense and ambitious young man of 22, an enthusiastic advocate of Whitman, in particular his *Laws for Creations,* and a great admirer of Thoreau and Edward Carpenter whose ideas – surely proof of his immense determination – he succeeded in translating into architectural terms. His job with Ashbee was his first after leaving home in Bolton. His talent had been immediately apparent: he was 'manifestly born to it', Janet recollected, 'wonderful great ivory elevations rose on paper beneath his hand: we looked to great things.' For various reasons, ostensibly his marriage but more probably a clash of ideas or personality, he had not stayed with Ashbee long (7). In 1899, he had joined Percy Adams as his chief assistant. 'Ever since then', wrote Janet, 'he has ghosted for him; and under Adams' name these same strange stately palaces are rising all about, under the title of hospitals, sanatoria, libraries, and town halls. He goes his quiet way and feels glad his buildings are put up under *any*one's name: "people will know someday" – he comments.'[10]

Holden and his wife, a small grey-haired exceptionally energetic lady,

(6) Charles Holden (1875–1960). Generally regarded as the great exponent of the British modern movement in architecture, although many of his buildings are most idiosyncratic, more in the tradition of the Arts and Crafts. The best-known buildings of his early Percy Adams period include the Belgrave Hospital, Kennington; King Edward VII Sanatorium at Midhurst; and Bristol Public Library. Later, he was famous for his work on the London Underground.

(7) He recalled his days with the Guild in an obituary of Ashbee in the *RIBA Journal*: 'It was a rare experience to

work with Ashbee and to live at Essex House in the atmosphere of craftwork in metal and wood, in the design and making of furniture, the printing of books and in the delicate craft of jewellery and the setting of precious stones.

All these things came easily to Ashbee and he had a rare sense of their appropriate treatment.'

(8) Even Ashbee himself, staying in a New York hostel for problem boys, admitted: 'Carpenterism, the simplification of life, is sorely tried by the absence of a bathroom'. (*Ashbee Journals,* December 1900)

were now living at Codicote in Hertfordshire. Janet gathered that Margaret Holden had had a rather lurid past, and her son by her first marriage, an overgrown and delicate boy of 16, was part of the ménage, helping in the house in between periods of vague 'study'. Mrs Holden was now luxuriating in the Simple Life in all its ramifications. The house, with its lead glazed casements and white-washed walls, was a perfect example of the style, complete in every detail from the oak settle by the hearth to the bananas and brown bread on the table. Needless to say, there was no hot water, for the minds of the Holdens were on more important matters. Their philosophy was one of plain living and high thinking and strenuous activity for the improvement of society. Village life, for a start, had been taken well in hand. The Holdens organized clubs and institutes and drills, and of course enjoyed a running battle with the Vicar.

Janet described the Holdens' way of life with some acerbity, discounting the obvious parallels with her own household. The Holdens' regime was certainly more spartan; maybe she felt the Simple Life had gone too far. The visit prompted her to analyse her own ideas of simple living. Where *was* the Simple Life? It was surely not in Chelsea where a School of the Simple Life had been set up for sophisticated Londoners, in homespun clothes and sandals, to practise scouring the domestic copper and, in the words of the Simple Life Prospectus, to 'learn to do everything that two hands may accomplish'. Yet, easy as it was to pour scorn upon the cranks and mountebanks, Janet was very well aware of the pitfalls which awaited serious, intelligent and wholly sincere people searching for a rational and honest way of living:

Every year brings fresh attempts to attain the simple life; some think it can only be done within rough-cast and thatch in a field; others think a loose dress and a low collar will ensure it; again others believe an absence of servants makes for it; others again say 'no home; give me a hotel.' Roger Fry 5 or 6 years ago told me he had tried the simple life, but had found it so complex that he had to give it up. (8)

I think the answer to these puzzles is one with the locality of the Kingdom of Heaven. The Simple Life is within you. Not in organization of labour, not in abolition of class differences, not in cooking your own dinner or doing your own scrubbing; not in Morris hangings or white-washed walls any more than Victorian ribbons or horsehair sofas – but in the heart and the mind. In fact you cannot *lead* the simple life; it must take *you* by the hand.[11]

The Simple Life, however, was not for everybody. In Campden that same summer the Earl of Gainsborough held a grand reception for the coming of age of his son and heir, the Viscount, an occasion on which the pomp of country-house society showed up in its full glory. The guest list was reassuringly predictable, confirming all the ancient hierarchies of the county, beginning with a good assortment of the local gentry and including the few miscellaneous Americans always to be found at such Edwardian events. There were tenants – 'so called', as Ashbee felt bound to describe them – and varied hangers-on. There was the Roman Catholic priest, who said grace very nicely, and the Anglican parson, the hated Vicar Carrington, who responded rather badly for the opposition God. Everyone was there who should have been invited. Or anyway all those who had expected invitations. In his self-appointed role of spectre at the feast, Ashbee could not resist pointing out that not a single labourer was anywhere in evidence, and – while not refusing the Earl's lavish hospitality – this led him on to prophesy inevitable doom for English aristocracy.

But however imminent the demise of belted Earls, it seemed that, for the moment, things were going rather better for the capitalists and the bourgeoisie of Britain than for the builders of the City of the Sun. A Guild sing-song held in June, described by Ashbee in the Journal, a spontaneous and delightful night of favourite rounds and catches, interspersed with Mrs Dunn's newest, most spicy Campden gossip, was for many of the singers overlaid with melancholy. The decision had been taken, a serious and sad one, to disband the Essex House Press.

The finances of the Press had been a problem since the early days in Campden, and the printers had been put on half-time working as far back as summer 1904. The market for fine printing generally was receding, and sales in America, which the Press relied on, were badly affected by increasing competition both from other hand-press workshops and from machine-printed books, produced in hand-press style. The Essex House Press had had particular misfortunes since it arrived in Campden, first with the Song Books, some of which had been remaindered, and then with its major new enterprise, the Bible. This was to be a two-volume edition for use in Churches, printed in Ashbee's Prayer Book type with about sixty of William Strang's woodcuts. The original proposal for an edition of 300 was cut down, through lack of subscribers, to 200, then 100. But even at this level, the Bible was not viable. Only 40 subscribed, and the scheme had now been jettisoned.

Ashbee always saw the failure of the Bible as a decisive moment in the history of the Press. Compared with the other workshops of the Guild, the Press was of course a special liability. Because hand-printed books were produced in series, each new publication needed capital investment. If an edition failed to sell, then this discouraged further investment, for it could well be argued that a new hand-printed book would decrease potential sales of books already printed. It was partly this inherent inflexibility, and partly the fact that the Press was a small private subsidiary group within the Guild, relatively easy to discard without dismembering the whole Guild structure, which, at a time of worry, with little work in progress, made it an obvious candidate to be closed down.

But though, technically speaking, closure of the Press was practicable without much disruption of the other workshops, this was a decision with disturbing consequences in terms of Guild prestige and Guild morale. The transfer of the Press from Kelmscott House to Whitechapel after Morris's death in 1898 had been greeted at the time as a considerable triumph for the Guild of Handicraft, a feather in its cap, and when the Guild had moved to Campden, the workshop of the Press on the ground floor of the Silk Mill, with its two hand presses and its stack of hand-made paper, and the portrait of Morris which was proudly shown to newcomers, was persuasive evidence of Arts and Crafts ideas and methods. Closing down the Press meant that Ashbee, who had used it both for the circulation of his own polemics and for propagation of his best-loved literature, lost a valuable channel of communication. It also meant the end of *Giles Cockbill* and the Ballads. But most of all, the thing which must have caused Ashbee most anguish, was the obvious, dismaying contravention of basic Guild philosophy in withdrawing support from one of its own workshops and agreeing to dismiss good men who did good work.

The greatest loss to the Guild would be Old Binning, the chief compositor, who had worked for 20 years, first with Morris, then with Ashbee. Old Binning who would take his hat off to no one – man or woman. Old Binning who, according to Archie Ramage, modelled himself on Morris so closely that he was almost Morris's double, and wore an identical blue shirt. Binning had been a colleague of Morris's in Socialist League days, and always insisted it was he who had persuaded Morris of the value of political action. Binning, grim-faced but very tender-hearted, had become a Guild legend in his time. His loss was the more poignant because, doubtful as he had been at the begining about the move to Campden, he had come to love the country. He was an old man and it was a worry whether, back in London, he would find another job.

Ashbee was also especially depressed that Archie Ramage would soon be leaving Campden. Archie, a relatively new recruit, the second of the 'Scotch boys', had come to Campden from a large newspaper office and, after the soullessness of monotypes and linotypes, had responded with delight to the life of a small workshop and the ideals of the Guild. Since he arrived in Campden he had married and now had two small and bonny boys. He was naturally sorry to have to move his family back from the country to the strains of life in London, but Archie himself, an earnest and ambitious politician, found some elation in the prospect of plunging into the great mêlée of London Socialism and constructive labour organization. Ashbee, with paternal good wishes for his Socialist future and a generous present of books and money, said goodbye to Archie in the middle of the summer. The other compositor, Bill Hill, had left before him. Dick Eatley, another Guildsman who had worked with Morris, an unusually accomplished Pressman whose other claim to fame was his curious ability to drink his pint of beer perpendicularly at the morning break, also left the Guild around this time. Only Old Binning, with his usual dogged conscientiousness, stayed on. 'Binning, the Captain', wrote Archie, 'remained – I suppose – to go down with his ship.'[12]

In July, a letter came for Janet from John Masefield, inviting the Ashbees to Ireland for a holiday:

It is a bad place to get at; but when you are here, you are 'well apaid', as the Knights are in Malory, when they get a spear or so right through them. So come which week best suits you. Con is not here yet; but she bade me write to you directly I learned what room we had. There is good swimming, when the wind drops, and it is a pretty place in all weathers; *but bring thick things*, and thick boots, and macintoshes stiffened with armour plate.

I have just written an ode to a hen here.

Ode to a hen. Strophe.	Antistrophe.
You wander in the spinach;	Eat you, perhaps, and then
O hen, I greet you.	My thanks I'll render
Ere I return to Greenwich	so be not tough Oh hen
Perhaps I'll eat you.	Be tender[13]

Janet, not surprisingly, decided not to go. But Ashbee, perhaps won over by the Ode to a Hen, ignored all the ominous hints in Masefield's letter. He needed a change of scene, away from Campden worries. Encouraged by Gerald, guide and mentor to Charley as well as his wife's worshipper (a not untypical result of Simple Living), he set off for County Antrim with his armour-plated rainwear.

He stayed at Cushenden with the Masefields for a week. It was gloomy countryside, Ireland at its most squalid; a wasteland of ram-shackle houses, untilled fields and broken fences, gates tied together with bits of wire and string. The Masefields' house was an abandoned Coast Guard station with 13 sunless windows looking out to sea. The coastline around Cushenden was cold and wild and comfortless. Constant wind and rain made the whole house shake and tremble. The place was definitely full of ghosts and evil fairies. On top of all this, Masefield himself had dreadful toothache, which made him feel parti-cularly Irish and morose.

Entertainment at Cushenden was hardly stimulating. In the mornings and afternoons Ashbee and the Masefields wandered on the cliffs, dissecting Irish legends and discussing the problems of the Gaelic League, the nationalistic movement led by poets and by painters which Masefield at that time was in the thick of. Even the Gaelic League was fraught with Celtic tensions. The 'waimbfulness' of Ireland, Ashbee's word for its unadulterated melancholy, was oppressive. His relief at leaving Country Antrim seems to have been great.

Almost as soon as he returned to Campden, Ashbee had to face the sad task of the dismantling of the Press shop. He wrote about it in the Journal, very touchingly:

Rather a sorrowful afternoon – for it was to me as if I was taking the inventory of a man's life. Twenty years – perhaps it's 25 – any way 'tis the best part of a man's life! I took stock with old Binning the Father of our Chapel of printers of the goods of the Essex House Press. He handed over to me with all the great care and con-scientious uprightness which I have always observed in him, the materials with which for nearly a quarter of a century he has worked, nearly 10 years with me and as many or more with Morris.

Alas that we could not go on with our work for we all of us loved it so and I think the book collectors of a day to come will probably prize some of the books – probably the wrong ones but certainly some (9). And here they came along all these quaintly named things that the Master Craftsman once used and old Binning and I entered them up and chalked them down and set out value on them – so much for the working price and so much for the sentiment, except when we came to sizing

(9) So it turned out. For instance, Sotheby's sold 3 Essex House Press books in June 1978: Shakespeare's Poems, No.122 of 450 copies, bound in red morocco with an elaborate design of onlaid black morocco strapwork outlined in gilt, 1899, £280; Spenser's Epithalamion, one of 150 vellum copies, 1901, £110; and Ashbee's own Endeavour towards the teaching of John Ruskin and William Morris, No.4 of 350, bound in green morocco with an onlaid and tooled pattern, 1901, £250.

up the Press on which the Chaucer was printed and we raised that a full £5 above its market value. As for the racks, and the making up frames, and the 24 brass tube quarto galleys, and the wide slips and the chases and the demy folio chases and the quotations and the leads and the reglets and the super royal inking table and the expanding roller frames, I got so confused among the details that I had to chalk my own numbers on them to the old man's disgust. 'You ought to have known all their names' his look seemed to say 'after producing books upon them for 10 years' but then I was thinking of the books while he was thinking of the tools and the honour and dignity of the tools.[14]

Old Binning took his departure solemnly and stoically, with a trace of the bitterness which often seemed engrained in old-fashioned Socialists of Binning's type. Although in theory the Press had closed down only temporarily and would be reinstated when the Guild became more prosperous, it was obvious that Binning would not return to Campden, and as Ashbee shook hands with him his heart was heavy.

Yet the gloom was not so general as might have been imagined. Philippe Mairet, who arrived in August, at the time the Essex House Press was being dismantled, was almost unaware of the upheaval. To him, Campden seemed a wholly optimistic place. Ashbee had taken Philippe Mairet (10) on in London, on the recommendation of his old headmaster, who happened to be George Chettle's father, as a draughtsman to work in Chipping Campden. For the past few weeks, at Ashbee's instigation, he had been making drawings of work at the Victoria and Albert Museum, to get him into training for his job in the Campden architectural office. This entailed drawing architectural details from Ashbee's sketches and providing working drawings for

(10) Philippe Mairet (1886–1975), illustrator, stained glass craftsman, actor, editor and writer. His *Times* obituary called him 'A true European'. He was certainly a man of many diverse enthusiasms. He acted at the Old Vic in the days of Lilian Baylis; he worked with A. N. Orage on *The New Age,* and later himself edited *The New English Weekly* up to the end of the Second World War. He joined the Church of England and was active in the Christian Social Movement. He became a great Adlerian, translating several of Adler's books and

contributing *An ABC of Adlerian Psychology.* He translated Mounier, Eliade and Sartre. In spite of so many intellectual diversions, his early loyalty to Ashbee remained. In 1971, he wrote to Felicity: 'Your father was an intimate and deeply important influence in my life'.

(11) These ideas, of course, were carried further by Eric Gill and Hilary Pepler with the Guild of St Joseph and St Dominic at Ditchling, which Mairet was to know much later on.

Guild craftsmen. His starting salary was £1 a week, less 15 shillings for bed and board at Braithwaite.

Philippe Mairet (or PAM, as he soon came to be called) came from a poor, though genteel, North London family. His father, originally French Swiss, was a watchmaker; his mother came from Surrey. The household was nonconformist in its leanings, rather narrow and possessive, and Philippe, a highly-strung young man with a bad stammer, although undoubtedly both artistic and intelligent, had so far had a rather hazardous career. He had failed to qualify for the Academy Schools and had taken a job with a firm of advertisers, miserable work compared with which his tasks in Chipping Campden seemed almost total joy.

To Mairet, even more perhaps than Alec Miller, Campden came as a salvation. He threw himself into the Guild life. He walked and cycled, played hockey and played football, went swimming in the Bathing Lake. He, Alec and George Chettle, most literary of the boys at Braithwaite, spent stimulating evenings by the fire reading poetry and essays and Platonic dialogues. They also sometimes joined the friendly gatherings at Woolstaplers', when Ashbee himself would read out loud to them or lead them in madrigals and glees and catches. Philippe Mairet understood the ideals behind the Guild, respected Ashbee's emphasis on intellectual betterment. Regularly, he attended the weekly University Extension lectures at Campden School of Arts and Crafts. With the annual Guild plays, he was really in his element. His talent as an actor was discovered straightaway, and Ashbee immediately gave him leading roles. It seemed his true metier. He lost all his self-consciousness. His stammer, almost miraculously, disappeared.

He looked back on his Guild period with enormous gratitude: 'For all of us young men, mostly of some cultural talent or aspiration, who had been brought up in lower middle-class families, generally in the big built-up areas, this life in Campden was both a liberation and a rich educational experience.'[15] It had been almost a substitute for University. Mairet, as much as anyone in Campden, appreciated Ashbee's views on work and leisure: the idea that work should be a source of pleasure and the strong belief that leisure should be used for self-improvement (11).

The work itself was all that Mairet could have hoped for. He could not get over the fact that he was being paid (however little) for work which he felt it was a privilege to do. His drawings for the workshops brought him into constant contact with the Guildsmen and he later did all 200 hundred illustrations for Ashbee's *Modern English Silverwork*.

He was very much impressed by the Campden Guildsmen's attitude to work and their pride in their status as skilled craftsmen. 'To hear them in conversation about their works in iron, silver and wood', Mairet wrote later, 'was more like listening to artists discussing painting or sculpture, or to arguments between architects.'[16] His work on Ashbee's buildings kept him in close touch with the architectural projects under way. One of the chief of these, when Mairet joined the office, was the reconstruction of the Norman Chapel at Broad Campden, the 'small ruined monastery' which impressed Berlepsch-Valendas. This was being restored for Ethel and Ananda Coomaraswamy (12), who were coming to live there the next spring.

Another new inhabitant for Campden, Wentworth Huyshe, had arrived a little before Mairet. Huyshe, an expansive, generous, boisterous man, step-father of the Harts, was living temporarily with the boys at Braithwaite, looking around to find himself a house. Much of his life had been spent in the East and in North Africa as a war correspondent, and he had also lived for some time in Paris editing *Galignani's Messenger*. He collected mediaeval weapons and he was a passionate amateur historian, having just written an antiquarian history of his home town Hitchin. His curious accumulation of experience, and his enjoyment of the role of raconteur, had a mesmeric effect upon his audience at

(12) Ananda Coomaraswamy (1877–1947), mineralogist, expert on Indian Arts and Crafts, metaphysician, philosopher and writer. He came from Ceylon. His father, Sir Mutu Coomaraswamy, was a distinguished Oriental scholar as well as a lawyer, and incidentally the first Asian to be knighted in Queen Victoria's reign. His mother, Lady Elizabeth Clay Beeby Coomeraswamy, came from Kent and Ananda's middle name was 'Kentish'. He went to school and university in England. (At Wycliffe College he was especially renowned for his skill in kicking up his leg above his head.)
He had met Ethel, Fred Partridge's sister, later well-known as the weaver Ethel Mairet, on a geological expedition to Barnstaple, and they had married in 1902. They were now in Ceylon,

where Ananda was directing the Mineralogical Survey of the island, but were coming back to England in a few months' time.

(13) Hugh Seebohm, a banker, son of Frederic Seebohm, had been at King's with Ashbee and became a life-long family friend.
E. Peter Jones, a Wolverhampton manufacturer (often referred to by Ashbee as 'the ironmaster') had been a Guild patron before the move to Campden. He was now the landlord of Island House in Campden which Ashbee had restored in 1903 and which now contained the Craftsman Club and the Guild Bindery. In 1905, he commissioned Ashbee to design a scheme for workers' housing at Ellesmere Port.

Braithwaite. Philippe Mairet described him in surprise and admiration: 'His slim, neat figure with his pointed grey beard and well-curled moustaches gave him a rather french appearance, increased by his talent for emphatic discourse and gesticulation. Conversation around the dining table at Braithwaite was always brisk and copious enough, but when "father" Huyshe was present it was a brilliant entertainment.'[17] The flamboyant Father Huyshe settled at Broad Campden, where he worked – intermittently – as a heraldic draughtsman, and his son Reynell later shared the workshop of his step-brother George Hart.

But although in the excitement of beginning life in Campden Philippe Mairet scarcely noticed the Guild's economic troubles, older-established members of the Guild by now had few illusions. They realized the seriousness of the situation and were coming under pressure to reorganize the Guild on more commercial lines. A Committee of Inspection had been appointed: it included Hugh Seebohm and Peter Jones (13), as well as Gerald Bishop, and it recommended ruthless action. Rob Holland wrote a strongly-worded letter to Charlie Daniels, Guild Labour Director, explaining his view that in order to pull round, the Guild had to make itself commercially viable. In the past, he suggested, 'we have perhaps paid more attention to what we like and what we consider art, than to what our customers want. This is a wrong attitude.'[18] The Guild should from now on find out exactly what its customers required and give it to them at as low a price as possible.

This was not a principle the Guild of Handicraft was used to. But the Guildsmen did their best and so – up to a point – did Ashbee. They tried hard, against the odds, to increase the Guild's efficiency. One of the Guild's great problems, shown up clearly in successive balance sheets, had been its accumulation of stock, speculative work made to keep the craftsmen occupied. It was a vicious circle, progressively alarming. As profits fell, the stock was still inexorably mounting. It was obvious to everyone this must be put a stop to. Early in the summer, the Guild announced a Clearance Sale at both its London shops – 16A Brook Street and the Dering Yard Gallery – where a large collection of Guild furniture and silver, jewellery and light fittings and other metal-work was sold off at bargain prices. (The hand-list itemizes such covetable pieces as a Fumed Oak Sideboard, Green Stained Oak Revolving Bookcase, Ruskin Muffin Dish with domed silver cover, and buckles and clasps 'too numerous to catalogue', and also draws attention to a fine set of Hammered Bronze Altar Furniture reduced from £27 to £22.) The Clearance Sale was reasonably successful, and later in the summer, in the interests of economy, the Dering Yard showroom was given up completely, a transaction which the Guild directors reported to have been carried through on favourable terms.

In Campden itself, quite drastic measures were being taken. The shops were, in workshop parlance, now being 'screwed up'; they were run more rigidly, and the making of stock, unless it was cheap and immediately saleable, was forbidden. The decision was taken by the Guildsmen to reduce the working hours to run from 8 am to 5 pm and to shut the workshops down on Saturdays. The new régime was enforced kindly but with firmness by the new Campden Manager, James Webster (14), a man who, Ashbee commented, combined the unusual two qualities of an aesthetic understanding of good craftsmanship and commercial acumen. With the advent of James Webster, who was liked by the men and elected an Honorary Guildsman, there were general hopes that the worst crisis was now over. Figures for the second half of 1906, once reforms had been brought in, showed a definite improvement. The Guild had not precisely made a profit, but at least there had been dramatic cutting-down of losses.

Yet, considering the history of the Guild and his high hopes for it, Ashbee was hardly likely to regard the reconstruction of the Guild with equanimity. He saw that reforms and economies were necessary, but he could not help being painfully aware that a Guild reorganized on commercial lines could only contravene the principles he most believed in. If work had to be cheap, how could one maintain standard? And if work had to be fast, what would happen to the margin, the leisure, the repose which he believed essential for all civilized working? If commercial considerations were paramount, what room would there be for individual development, for the idea of education through craftsmanship? He accepted the new régime, because he had to, there was no alternative, but it dismayed him deeply. It belittled the Guild Idea, the Guild achievement. This was simply never what the Guild had been about.

(14) Later, as Managing Director of Twyfords, concerned with artefacts of a very different kind.

(15) At the age of 24, he noted a convenient aphorism in his Journal: 'There are two sorts of failure of which the higher is success.'

(16) *Narcissus* had been the first of the Guild plays, produced in 1897 and taken on a tour of public schools. One port of call was Haileybury where the vote of thanks, to Ashbee's amusement, was given by a boy who shared the same initials. This was Clement R. Atlee, Prime Minister to-be.

'It's no good your asking for an amusing letter,' he wrote to Janet from Woolstaplers' in December, 'for it isn't in me. I've heard 2 o'clock strike and I've heard 3 o'clock strike and it's tripping on for 4 o'clock and the interminable black rain of the Cotswold nights is going drip drip with that incessant thirsty gurgle down the drain pipe, my brain is like a racing clock. Add to that there's simply no news, not even the tiniest morsel of scandal!'[19]

The end of the year was unusually depressing. Many of the things Ashbee had worked for seemed in jeopardy. The unexpected gift of two pheasants for Janet from the Earl of Gainsborough even had him reflecting on whether he might have been better making his career as an opulent country-house architect instead of building cottages for families on 20 shillings a week.

But, as usual, a ray of light appeared on the horizon. Ashbee had a useful knack, all through his life, of finding signals of success even in the midst of failure (15). His morale was improved hugely by a letter which now reached him from W. A. White, ex-foreman of the metal-shop, who had resigned in March after 17 years' service as a Guildsman. White wrote to him from Sheffield, where he was now working, to ask if Ashbee minded if he performed *The Masque of Narcissus* (16) with his pupils. He was only sorry it was not to be *The Alchemist* or *Epicoene*. If a craftsman silversmith of little education could embark on a production of a Jonson play in Sheffield, hardly a stronghold of Elizabethan drama, who could say the years of the Guild had been redundant? Ashbee, in great elation, wished the enterprise God speed.

The Death of Conradin 1907

In New Year 1907, the Guild performed *The Critic,* the second play by Sheridan to be produced in Campden. The prospect of acting in yet another classic of English comedy seems to have daunted old Tom Jellife, the cabinet-maker, who said he would be in it only on condition his part could be a silent one. In a flash of inspiration, the boys cast him for Lord Burleigh. 'He had a splendid head', wrote Ashbee, 'and he shook it nobly.'[1]

For the first time in Guild history, Ashbee himself was absent on the night the Guild play opened in the Town Hall, Chipping Campden. Alec Miller was left in charge of the production while Ashbee went to Sicily to plan a marble villa for Colonel Shaw Hellier, an old client, who after a disastrous, wild, brief venture into marriage, had decided to leave Staffordshire and settle in Taormina.

The Colonel himself, although over 70, was still exceptionally sprightly, and the Ashbees spent an energetic month with him in Sicily. Part of it was work, but much of it was holiday. They took picnics of bread and eggs and wine out on the hillsides; escaping the English and especially the Americans who clustered together in Taormina, they liked to explore the remote Sicilian villages. They toured all the sites of architectural interest. ('Sicily', pronounced Ashbee, 'is a land for Architects.'[2]) They went to view the services at Monreale, where Ashbee, much impressed by the splendour of the staging, the glitter, the colour, the incense and the music, could not help feeling one element was missing. 'It is the human body that is absent . . . There are, to put it bluntly, too many men in petticoats, I want to see the limbs of the boys as they sing their hymn to Phoebus in the Palaestra – the Greeks would not have dressed up in scarlet with lace flounces'.[3]

Taormina in those days was very much a place where artists congregated. It was also something of a homosexual's haven. Its charms had been well publicized by Baron Wilhelm von Gloeden, painter and pioneer photographer, whose pictures of Taormina boys and girls had become famous. By 1900, the beauties of the town were legendary, and a succession of painters came to live there. Robert Kitson, the English watercolourist, for instance, built his own house in Taormina, Casa Cuseni, in 1905, and Frank Brangwyn painted murals in the dining-room (as well as designing the table and the chairs). Taormina was an obvious place for Colonel Shaw Hellier, retired soldier as he was with some artistic leanings, as susceptible as Ashbee – if not more so – to the glories of Sicilian boyhood, to choose to end his days.

The Ashbees liked the Colonel. He was marvellously childlike, end-lessly enthusiastic. He was military, but remarkably unpompous. He was devoted, Ashbee noted with approval, to all the little simple helpful things of life. One day he baked them each a loaf of bread; the marma-lade he made was apparently superlative; as a matter of principle, he felt it right and fitting he should always wash his socks himself, not give them to the servants. In the house he had rented while awaiting his own villa, to which he had transported his old English butler Harry, he kept two pianos, a pianola and an American organ, on all of which he played with a most erratic vigour. (His taste in music, as in people, was completely unreliable: he would switch from Chopin to the latest rag-time or worst sentimental song.) The Colonel, known as the 'Colonello Inglese', was a popular figure in Taormina. He was always giving parties, one of which, described by Ashbee, had that special atmosphere of rather frenzied gaiety which typified the entertainments of the English Colony in many a Mediterranean seaside town.

Yesterday we had a dance here, for the Colonel is perpetually young. The neigh-bours in 'the Set', the neighbours we meet now every day, Sicilian aristocrats, quaint little finely shaped people with Greek profiles and black wondrous eyes, a Calabrian Baron who organized the Contra dance, trapesing all the dancers in fantastic coils through the rooms in and out, the English Medico and his wife, an English Parson who makes good natured faces – the other very sticky starchy English just on the act of thawing but never quite, – a Danish lady, a Dutch lady with a French husband, some Italians, and a troop of rather impossible Americans. It was very amusing, and the Colonel enjoyed himself like a child, while his bevy of Sicilian boy retainers looked in at the door with large dreamy eyes and nodded their heads and twitched their fingers to the dance music. But my word, how these people can dance! It was a real thing, in the midst of the Civilized banality of the bourgeoisie. – Before we knew where we were, the Barone, who acted as Master of the Ceremonies, called the Tarantella in the midst of the Contra Danse and 2 Sicilian boys and 2 Sicilian girls danced it fit to intoxicate one, to the music of the mandolin and two guitars. There was Greek fire in it, we had hardly seemed to see it when it was all over and the whole room rang with a round of applause. Alas for those of us who can only look on !⁴

The Colonel was full of excitement about plans for his new villa. He had bought a spectacular site on the hill-side looking north-east to Calabria, incorporating both an orange grove and an olive wood, with terraces on several levels high above the sea. Behind was a genuine Greek temple of Apollo, now converted into the Church of San Pancrazio, a dilapidated building, but ineffably romantic. Ashbee spent many hours working on the site. One of his main theories – very much a precept of the Arts and Crafts architects – was that buildings should never be alien to their setting but should be related to the landscape and the history of the district. In Sicily he therefore set himself the problem of designing a building which would be recognizably Graeco-Sicilian in feeling, using local materials and employing Sicilian craftsmen. However, since both he and the Colonel were British patriots, this did not prevent them from deciding that the villa in Taormina would be called after St George (1).

Another of Ashbee's activities in Sicily was the composition of *Conradin*. 'I have been wandering about over Arkadina piecing together bits of Conradin', he wrote in his Journal, and then a few weeks later: 'I am still hammering and polishing at Conradin.'⁵ Conradin, characteristically sub-titled *A Philosophical Ballad* (2), is a poem set in mediaeval Italy, a reworking of Ashbee's favourite theme of the spiritual quest. It is the story of the golden youth, the innocent, riding out in search of the Sicilian Paradise, meeting tests and temptations along the way and finally submitting to death itself. The moral of the story – which lent itself ideally to a series of quasi-heraldic illustrations by Philippe Mairet – was that death was not an end but a beginning:

The good must die and the ill prevail
Ere the sweet new life be ushered in:
And thus it was with Conradin.

It was a poem which not only expressed Ashbee's admiration for those far-off days of sacrifice and chivalry; it was also obviously a contemporary comment on the trials and tribulations of the Guild of Handicraft.

On their way back to Campden, travelling in the train, the Ashbees met the Webbs again. By design or accident, the Webbs made their appearance in the lives of the Ashbees with peculiar regularity, providing a constant counter-balance, in their very different view of Socialist priorities, to the ideals of Ashbee's City of the Sun. Sidney was in rather a pessimistic mood. The performance of the Liberal Government, with its great majority, was undeniably depressing and the prospects for educational reform seemed to him particularly unpromising. 'Nothing will be done', he said, 'in education for 5 years now and all we can hope for is that the work we have done in London – your schools of Arts and Crafts and so forth – will not be undone.'

The Ashbees did their best to dispel the gloom with tales of Sicily. But they were fairly unsuccessful. 'I never want to go to Sicily', said Sidney dolefully, 'for I should absolutely lose all hope for human nature. There has been no Country in the world that has been so fought for, so longed for, had such chances, such civilizations, such fertility for 3000 years and what is the net product now? Tell!!'

'You measure the net product by the wrong gauge', replied Ashbee. 'Every Sicilian is a gentleman. I don't see that poverty matters so much where you have grace, happiness and good manners.'

This talk of gentlemanliness soon prompted Beatrice to scrutinize her husband. They were on their way to Stanway. Was he fit for Lady Elcho?

' "Sidney", she said, looking severely at his gloves through the points of which peeped at least 4 tell-tale fingers. "How can you go to a swagger country house like that?" '.

' "Oh that's not my department" he replied and plunged again into the blue book correcting his wife's proofs.'[6]

Although the Ashbees' weeks in Taormina had been fruitful, and the Colonel's commission had raised Ashbee's spirits greatly, it had not brought in any new jobs for the Guildsmen, since work on the San Giorgio was all to be done locally. Back in Campden, the Ashbees had to brace themselves immediately to face a rapidly-worsening financial situation. In April, Gerald Bishop, on behalf of the Directors, made a detailed statement to the Guildsmen. The reforms had not achieved the

(1) The foundation stone of the Villa S. Giorgio, the most impressive of Ashbee's remaining buildings, was laid on St George's Day 1908 'IN NOME DEL GRANDE ARCHITETTO DEL UNIVERSO'. When Colonel Shaw Hellier died, his two nieces lived there for many years. By the mid-70s, remarkably unaltered, it had become a first-class pensione.

(2) Eventually published by the Essex House Press at the Norman Chapel, October 1908, and dedicated to the Colonel.

F

recovery they hoped for. The question was now how to keep the Guild afloat at all.

Gerald's proposal was that the Guild shareholders should write down the value of their shares dramatically. This drastic measure seemed the only possibility for giving the Guild a new financial lease of life. A number of Preference Shares would be issued so that the Directors could pay back the bank overdraft. Because such a ruthless writing-down of capital would more or less obliterate the Guildsmen's individual holdings, the meeting was adjourned for the men to think it over. As Ashbee later commented: 'They took it loyally and with the English workman's humorous stoicism.' However, the Guildsmen were notably reluctant to part with any more of their resources and decided that 'in the present state of trade' they could not see their way, as a collective body, to taking up the new Preference Shares in the Guild. From now on, the taking up of shares should be voluntary, a matter for individual decision. Though understandable enough, this new ruling had a significance which Ashbee himself would have been all too well aware of: in effect it was a shedding of co-operative principles, denial of the basis of the Guild Idea.

A few weeks later, just before the Balance Sheet was issued, Ashbee sent out a personal letter to 30 of the principal Guild shareholders, imploring them to subscribe to the new issue of 6 per cent Preference Shares. He made out a good case, emphasizing the fact that the Guild had been at work for 20 years in all and for 15 of those years had paid a steady 5 per cent on its invested capital. He argued that the recent loss should be seen in its context, simply as a passing phase in the whole history of Guild endeavour, the result of the unfortunate coincidence of all the expenses and upheaval of the move to Gloucestershire with a depression of trade in general. He reiterated his belief in the Guild standard: the standard of the work ('much of its production', he said, 'will, we believe, rank as among the best English work of the last two decades') and the standard of life among the Guildsmen. He reminded the shareholders of what had already been achieved in Campden: the decaying village had been revivified, new houses and workshops had been built, new gardens and allotments had been laid out; work had been found for a number of local people who would otherwise have drifted away to the big cities; the Campden School of Arts and Crafts had been established, and now had over 300 pupils, men, women and children. He pointed out that the School, although set up under the auspices of Gloucestershire County Council, was mainly run by the workpeople of the Guild.

All these achievements, argued Ashbee, were at stake if the Guild could not find the fresh capital it needed to pay off its bank overdraft. Give the Guild another chance was the plea he put to shareholders. He felt that as far as financial prospects went, the Guild had already turned the corner, and that, with trade improving and the Guild reorganized, the next year's results would be altogether different. Finally, he suggested that although commercial considerations were undoubtedly important to those who had their shares in it, the Guild could not be looked at as a business pure and simple. Since it had a special aim it must be judged by special standards.

He ended the letter:

Had we been makers of armour plate or patent medicines, or any other of the much advertised mechanical productions that appear to be among the necessities of Modern Life, our pecuniary results so far might have been different, but as we merely make good things of individual merit, and where reduplication is impossible, cheapness and large profits are not open to us, but we still anticipate once again a steady return in our investment when we have cut our present losses, and when we have adjusted ourselves to our new working conditions; for the money that has hitherto been paid to our bankers on interest on loan, will in future go to our preference shareholders in dividend. I myself am one of the principal subscribers, may I hope that you will be another?

Yours sincerely,
(signed) C. R. Ashbee.[7]

The shareholders wrote back at considerable length. Some of them were still extremely sympathetic. 'I have a strong conviction', wrote one particularly loyal shareholder, 'that the Guild's little beginnings are destined to grow into a big thing and a solution of many problems.'[8] Many of the letters showed considerable grasp of Ashbee's aims and approval of the Guild of Handicraft attainments. One compared the Guild community at Campden with the Cadbury village at Birmingham, much to the detriment of Bournville: 'they have tried to humanize leisure, you have tried to humanize work as well.'[9] But in spite of so much individual sympathy and understanding, it appears that the majority of shareholders were disappointingly unwilling to take on any further financial commitment. The consensus of opinion, confirmed by the Guild Balance Sheet which reached them a few days after Ashbee's letter, was that the experiment had been duly tried and had not succeeded. The Guild had now lost almost all its external support.

But the Guild of Handicraft was not so easily defeated. Ashbee's own obstinacy was well known. Although the hope of paying off the

Guild's bank overdraft had to be abandoned, less than £500 of the £1000 which Ashbee asked for having been subscribed, there was apparently no feeling of immediate panic. The usual Cotswold summer programme of events and visits, incoming and outgoing, seems to have continued, with no lessening of energy.

At Easter 1907, Ashbee's Journal entry was particularly cheerful:

It is like a whiff of fresh air – when our Cockney boys come back to us. The picturesque feudalism and homely, slow moving mother grey of Gloucestershire has a tendency to stuffiness that needs constant correction. This time it was our little Jew boy 'Sammy.' Sim. Samuels (3) – Nothing could be more completely Semitic at its best, and nothing more Cockney at its best, the real right modern East End London. Healthy, happy, stoical, keen, irresponsible, inquisitive, democratic, full of snap, full of motion, full of savoir faire, enjoying his holiday, well equipped for tramping or bicycling, clean collar and dusty boots, with a positive delight in landscape and flowers – a veritable cock-sparrow of a boy with a touch somehow – a far off touch, I don't know why, of the aristophanic Athenian. Peisthetairos is for ever turning up from East London and he brings his cloud cockatoo touch with him.

Sammy and his pal – a young shoemaker, had tramped to Campden for their Easter holiday. He wanted to tell me how he was getting on, how his jeweller's shop was doing, and the world and you generally. He has been here twice before at holiday times but both times we have been away but now he caught me and the time for confidences had come. He is doing well, earning his £2 a week and still in the same shop whither he went, with some misgiving when 5 years ago the family ties were too strong and he refused to come to Campden. The Guild remains to him a central point in life and I find he measures his work by the standard it sets. We recalled every conceivable episode in workshop history, and he paid a series of house to house visits to all his workshop chums. Sammy's development was characteristic. He came to us originally as a stray hand to shift the sheets in the Press, a little printer's devil, but that was not good enough for him, and instinctively he nosed his way into the jeweller's shop. He had the inevitable eye for colours and gold, and he was excellent at arithmetic. We put him to sweeping up the lemels and then to helping the enamellers, and his natural love of metals developed a skill of fingers; also he was quick and willing, and he had wonderful bright eyes.

So I found just the same boy only better – and with one delicious addition, he

(3) Sim. Samuels had come to the Guild as an apprentice in 1898, but he decided not to make the move to Campden.

was burning to tell me of his athletics. It was still rather cold for swimming but he begged to be allowed to see the lake and so I promised him my key on the morrow. When the morrow came I was crowded up with visitors and clients, and the pledge of a tea party at St John Hankin's, where we always have to talk modern drama, which bores me intensely, not the drama but the talk about it. Sammy way-laid me in the street, he had a towel rolled up under his arm. He stood at a respectful distance to let my fashionable friends go by, and then whispered. 'Come along C.R.A. I've got a clean towel, it won't be the first time we've shared one together and *you* first taught me to swim!' Of course the invitation was irresistible. We had the lake to ourselves, for it was the first spring day of the year, and though the sun was hot the morning frosts were not yet over and the bole was barely touched with green. There were larks overhead and farmer Haines' wheat had made exactly two inches and a half. Sammy stripped, took a long breath, drew up his arms and turning his back to me said as he bent his head round over his shoulder. 'I want you to tell me how I've developed – are the back muscles good?' I specified their excellencies here and there. How do you come by these two beauties? I asked fingering two strong little fellows on the upper arm. 'Ah' said Sammy 'there's the secret of it all. That's not work, jewellers don't get muscles like that – that's pure athletics – *pure* athletics!'

Then he sprang to the board and took a beautiful dive taking care as he did it that I should observe his form, for part of the joy of athletics – '*pure* athletics' – is a healthy self-consciousness in the eye of those we care for. See Pindar! His figure was as beautiful as his dive, in fact my little Jew boy would be beautiful throughout were it not for the prodigious overpowering nose of his. A good head, eyes all afire of brown, sensitive lips and mouth – but Oh the nose! It means a lot no doubt, but it has a touch of King Valoroso after his escapade with the warming pan. Somehow I don't mind it in the least, never did, for there is a restless living flame in Sammy that plays to one and burns up all prejudice.

As we dried ourselves in the sun, Sammy unfolded to me the nature of the East London Sports Club that he had started – all good athletes. 'The Apollos' he had called them. Quite a nice name wasn't it? For if they did not sing to the lyre, they enjoyed their naked bodies in the sun, and if they could not get the sun Victoria Park way – they took the Whitechapel baths instead, and kept up their swimming the winter through. I promptly invited 7 East End Apollos down for a Polo match this summer. Nose or no nose, straight or pendulous, if they are like Sammy they will all be welcome. I got frowns from Janet for being an hour late at the aesthetic tea party – but the real aesthetics were mine![10]

Soon afterwards, the Ashbees went to Paris for 10 days. They spent most of their time on an intensive schedule of sight-seeing, covering many miles of pictures and traversing many avenues of sculpture, con-cluding that the bourgeois element in art – the 'partridge and water colour point of view' as Ashbee liked to describe it – was as prevalent in Paris as in London. But they did react with some excitement when they saw, in a dark corner of the Beaux Arts, the strange architectural dream-drawings of Garas (4), and they searched him out in his studio in a remote quarter of Paris. They found him a mild, bearded man, still young and exceptionally silent, surrounded by his drawings of transcendental temples, the meaning of which he was unable to explain.

'It is a far cry from Garas in his sordid little street to the "best part of Kensington" ', wrote Janet in the Journal on 31 May, appreciative of the incongruity of moving on from Garas's studio to the splendours of Thorpe Lodge on Campden Hill. The Ashbees broke their journey from Paris to the Cotswolds with a short luxurious visit to Montagu Norman (5), the banker: Norman had bought Thorpe Lodge three years before and was now meticulously reconstructing it, overseeing every detail of the building work, designing much of the furniture himself. But though his surroundings were the opposite of Garas's, the complete antithesis of the Parisian artist's garret, Janet noted a certain similarity of character: both were men of mystery, remote and solitary. Garas conjured up his imaginary temples; Monty Norman worked intently at creating his own real one. 'He is a strange being', wrote Janet, 'and has the air of a magician, a kind of Circe for there is the feminine touch as he prowls about his Palace and roams in this lovely garden, here, solitary, in the heart of London . . . I can imagine him with his quiet, almost Oriental, yellow-brown eyes appraising red and orange moroccos, testing with a long look the bloom on a rug, or the moulding of a frieze – feeling between the tongue and those even firm teeth whether the vol-au-vent had the right crispness of pastry or the wine the perfect flavour. "L'art de bien vivre" in its pleasantest form;

---

(4) This was possibly the artist Francois Garat, who specialized in painting views of Paris.

(5) Montagu Norman (1871–1950, later Lord Norman). Governor of the Bank of England from 1920 to 1944. A cousin of Rob Holland's and a patron of Ashbee's: the Guild had made the bedroom furniture for Thorpe Lodge. He was a fastidious collector and commissioner. As Gordon Russell wrote later: 'Norman's personal interest and active support of the craftsmen of his own day, sustained as it was over a considerable period of time, shows the delightful enthusiasm displayed by the great patrons of the Renaissance – yet with the particularly intimate character that has always been associated with the gifted amateur in England.' (Article in The Banker, March 1955)

"Live and let live", "Fais ce que tu voudras" – all the pleasant tolerant luxurious tags invented by the happy beauty loving people of the world, come to mind as one opens his cedar chests, undresses in his turquoise tiled bathroom, and eats his curds and cream.'[11]

Janet, inevitably, had certain moral scruples about such rampant self-indulgence. But a particularly uncongenial evening at a Fabian Society meeting in a hot small room in the Adelphi, where Goldsworthy Lowes Dickinson read a remarkably dull paper on Plato's *Guardians,* made her more appreciative of the comforts of Thorpe Lodge. Besides, it had to be admitted that the Guild depended on the patronage of Norman and rich discriminating clients like him. Had there been more customers like Monty Norman, the Guild would not be having such a struggle to survive.

Home in Campden, the main news was that this year Alec Miller had been elected Labour Director. This pleased Ashbee immensely, not just because he felt it a good change for the Guild to have a younger representative of Labour, after a long run of old-established Guildsmen, but also because Alec was one of his own protegés. He could not help seeing his election as a triumph for the intellectual-aesthetic view of craftsmanship, and also as a little victory for the Comrades. Where former Directors, such as Jellife, Mark and Daniels, had done their duties adequately, but without imagination, Ashbee hoped for much better things from Alec: a rarer finer quality and deeper insight. 'Whether that is going to help us', he added rather ruefully, 'in our present difficulties which are not so much aesthetic and ethical as commercial – the future will show.'[12]

The intellectual life of Campden had expanded with the arrival of the Coomaraswamys, by now installed in the Norman Chapel which the Guild of Handicraft had been restoring for them. Ethel Coomaraswamy already knew the Cotswolds through her brother, Fred Partridge, who had worked as a Guild jeweller. The days of his disgrace, when he had been ejected from Campden for philandering, were forgiven and forgotten, and it was presumably with his encouragement that the Coomaraswamys came to live so near the Guild.

Ashbee and Ananda Coomaraswamy had many preoccupations in common. Coomaraswamy's recent period in Ceylon, which was followed by a three-month tour of India, had intensified his interest in the arts and crafts of India and he had come to Campden to work on a large and very intellectual study of Mediaeval Sinhalese Art. He was much perplexed by the way in which the values of Western civilization were encroaching upon traditional Indian life and culture, just as

Ashbee was appalled at the speed and voracity with which industrialization was destroying the whole quality of life in England, attacking the old standards, demolishing the virtues of both countryside and town. But where Ashbee saw art and craft in social terms, conscious of its effect on the well-being of the individual artist-craftsman and its influence on contemporary society, Coomaraswamy's view of art was much more abstract. He was most concerned with its spiritual basis and, in Indian art in particular, the fusion of the contemplative and sensual, the sacred and profane. This element in Coomaraswamy's thinking seems to have made little impression on Ashbee, but it was of course to have a profound influence, a year or two later, on the work of Eric Gill.

The townspeople of Campden, though by this time well inured to the eccentricities of the Ashbees and their friends, must still have found the tall exotic figure of Ananda, with his pale olive skin and his shaggy soft black hair, unusual, if not positively startling (6). Ethel, too, described by Janet as a strange little thin underdeveloped woman with a predilection by day for the gaunt sack-frocks of the Godfrey Blount connection, and by night for Eastern draperies and strange Sinhalese jewellery, must have seemed the more outrageous by contrast with the current fashion of the local farmers' wives and daughters and the ladies of the Gloucestershire aristocracy.

The decor of the Norman Chapel in Broad Campden was correspondingly individualistic. It was featured in *The Studio* in 1907, and Philippe Mairet later described in his Memoirs the idiosyncratic character of the interior with its well chosen mixture of Eastern artefacts and English Arts and Crafts both from the Morris workshops and the Guild in Campden. This highly original decorative style was, recalled Mairet, best displayed in the music room:

a lofty apartment over thirty feet long and broad in proportion: at the east end of it you went up a few steps to a sort of dais, which had its own fireplace and functioned as the Doctor's study; this had a low balustrade of massive timbers and could be screened from the rest of the room by a large pair of sumptuous curtains. The grand piano just below the balustrade was enclosed in an enormous oblong case designed and made in Ceylon; it stood on four legs almost a foot square, elaborately shaped and chamfered by Sinhalese craftsmen. A big oak lectern before the embrasure of one of the Gothic windows bore a copy of William Morris's huge Kelmscott edition of Chaucer. The walls were draped here and there with Bokhara and Indian hangings and with a large Burne-Jones and Morris tapestry.[13]

The arrival of the Coomaraswamys at Broad Campden opened up

new possibilities for Guild activities. Ethel and Ananda were supporters of the Guild both in theory and in practice: they held shares in it and, even more important at a time when the workshops were so slack, they placed substantial orders. In summer 1907, Ananda bought one of the Essex House presses, which had once belonged to Morris, and prepared to use it to print his own book *Medieval Sinhalese Art*. Although the Coomaraswamys were in some ways a remote, unworldly couple – 'Both of them live in their enchanted chapel, which glows rose colour with linen and Morris hangings and Oriental crimsons, like two elves, creatures you cannot gossip with, and that yet have something more human about them than the most ordinary of us',[14] wrote Janet – they enjoyed companionship and Ananda, in particular, felt a pressing need for the stimulus of argument. The Ashbees were likely to be summoned for a walk or a meal at Broad Campden only to find themselves enmeshed in a gigantic discussion on Coomaraswamy's topic of the day.

A typical evening at the Norman Chapel in summer 1907, described by Janet in the Journal, ended with Coomaraswamy, Fred Partridge, Alec Miller and others in the party walking back across the fields to Campden deep in discussion on 'the ULTIMATE ROSE or whether the Ideal exists behind all the varieties of reality'. Since the possibilities of ultimate reality were by no means exhausted by the time they got to Campden, the debate continued for many hours at Woolstaplers'. 'We all burned in our separate corners', wrote Janet. 'AK glowed and smiled his mysterious smile. Partridge stuttered and shot sparks.'[15] They finally adjourned and began reciting Wordsworth and Shakespeare sonnets late into the night.

With the addition of the Coomaraswamys, the Guild community in Campden had in many ways reached its high peak of development. It was ironic, at a time when Guild finances were deteriorating badly, that standards of culture, which Ashbee put such faith in, were so demonstrably triumphant. Though in point of fact the Guild was by then being badly hampered by its commercial problems, which left no room for manoeuvre, the image of Campden as the bastion of freedom, and the quiet unhurried creative life, was strong.

John Masefield still regarded Campden as perfection, encouraging the Ashbees to get on with writing poetry in such ideal conditions. 'You have all in your favour', he wrote. 'You are out of London, you don't

(6) Just as the sight of Tagore in his robes, on a visit to the Rothensteins in 1912, when the cult of Indian art was at its height in England, must have amazed the cottagers at Oakridge Lynch.

have to write much prose, if any, and you have a community ready at hand, as your material, just large enough to give variety, and small enough for you to know.' He added:

I would I were on Pillicock Hill
For there I'd sit and sing my fill
Like an ousel cock with a tawny bill
Tradoodle   (This is in Beaumont & Fletcher this word is.)

I'd sing the golden stars to bed,
With the milk of song would I be fed,
And my skull would sing when I was dead
So welcome merry Shrovetide.[16]

Roger Fry, too, seemed to have a golden image of the Cotswolds. He wrote to Janet from New York in 1907 assuring her that, though he had not corresponded recently, Campden was still a place he often thought about. Sometimes, he said, amongst the skyscrapers and trolleycars, the crowded New York cityscape would seem to vanish – 'and I've been somewhere in the Cotswolds again'.[17]

The sightseers continued to arrive at the Guild workshops. In August, it was Alfred East, the well-known landscape painter (7), a neighbour of the Ashbees, another relatively new arrival in the Cotswolds. His house was at Stow-on-the-Wold and for his studio he used a magnificent old barn at Upper Swell. Janet did not take to Alfred East. She found him a terrible come-down after Rothenstein: 'A tall grizzled Englishman in a scheme of grey homespun, his vision entirely obscured by his very second-rate personality.'[18] He talked incessantly about himself, apparently seeing life entirely from the viewpoint of what would or what would not make an Alfred East canvas. She found his self-centred conversation so obnoxious that she told him she no longer took visitors around the Silk Mill these days, and handed him over to George Hart.

Janet's strictures on Alfred East are quite predictable. He was not the sort of man she could ever have been patient with. But there were other signs that Janet's tolerance was flagging. Her youthful optimism, the pioneering spirit which had helped to bring the Guild to Campden,

---

(7) Alfred East (1849–1913, later Sir Alfred). Establishment figure, Beaux Arts in background. In the year he came to Campden he was appointed President of the Royal Society of British Artists.

was by this time noticeably in abeyance. She was almost 30. Guild affairs were a constant source of worry; and the MS of *Rachel,* written a year later, shows the sadness and uneasiness of Janet's private life.

Her love for Gerald Bishop still continued. But the early days of simple elation were now over. Janet's joyful scheme of loving both Gerald and her husband, equally but differently, now seemed a bit too hopeful. The tensions of the situation continued: the dispiriting deceptions, the sexual frustrations, the lack of any hope of resolution. Not surprisingly, the weekends when Gerald came to Campden were fraught with deep anxieties, with earnest conversations. Even the many letters which Gerald wrote to Janet, cheering, tender letters, became a source of worry. What if someone found them and completely misinterpreted them? One day, impetuously, Janet took them into the Library at Woolstaplers' and burned them all.

One of Janet's sorrows, which increased as she grew older, was of course the fact that so far she had no children. This was hard to bear for someone with such strong maternal instincts, for someone whose physique itself was motherly. Janet felt her deprivation the more keenly in contrast to the child-rearing going on around her. The Nasons' massive family had multiplied still further. Rob Holland's fifth son, Richard, was born in 1907. Quite a number of the Guildsmen, even Guildsmen who had married since they came to Campden, now had substantial families. Though Janet had lavished so much protective interest on the Guild apprentices and the many stray young men and boys of Ashbee's circle, vicarious motherhood, it seemed, was not enough for her. She desperately wanted some children of her own.

Inspired by a picture by William Strang – the Ashbees' friend and incidentally a most productive father – which showed a childless woman in a state of desolation, Janet, typically, put her feelings down in sonnet form:

FOR A DRAWING BY WILLIAM STRANG

O woman, with the long dishevelled hair
And piteous eyes, and wide despairing lips,
And loose-girt gown, and beautiful strong hips,
And arm half raised to beat the pulsing air –
Around your naked shoulders hangs a cloud
Of children-souls, imploring to be born –
Ah! how your heart is desperately torn
In barren labour, crying out aloud!

You hear them whisper, though your eyes are blind
Amid warm breath you feel your temples kissed;
Your frightened fingers brushing back the mist
Can never clear the vision from your mind.
Alas, and in how many women's eyes
Your dreams of unborn babies I recognize.

The noblest man oft loathes the fleshly strife,
'Give me the children of the soul!' he cries –
And, when he takes a happy human wife,
He thinks he reads agreement in her eyes.
She, nothing doubting, enters in the bond,
She glories in his spiritual love
And little . . . as she looks beyond,
He has a life apart she knows not of.
But as the years pass, in the silent room
Where he sits dreaming of the Nation's good
She slowly knows her individual doom
Longing for children of her flesh and blood.
For woman needs her babes to keep her whole . . .
She cannot have these children of the soul.[19]

Late in the summer, hoping for a few days' respite from the now very pessimistic atmosphere of Campden, Ashbee went on an expedition to the Highlands. He was himself by now almost at breaking point and it seemed to Janet that only Alec Miller could help to reconcile him to the end of all his hopes for the survival of the Guild in Chipping Campden. The two shared a cabin in the little steamer which took them from Oban round the Orkneys and back again to Edinburgh. Those long summer days in Scotland, spent walking, talking, reading, were a poignant reminder of their earlier diversions: tramping on the wolds at

(8) In H. S. Ashbee's bequests, his immediate family was conspicuously absent. Besides his gifts of books and pictures to the nation, and his various small personal bequests, his fortune was divided to provide an income for his business partner (two-fifths), his cousin Louisa Maude Ashbee (two-fifths) and Edward Henry Montauban (the other one-fifth). Montauban's identity remains mysterious, but it has always been believed in Ashbee's family that H. S. Ashbee had a second secret family in Paris who were beneficiaries from his estate.

(9) 'Angels are cheap today', the men once chalked above the door of Alec Miller's workshop: Guild humour, on the whole, was less than subtle.

Campden, sketching in the French cathedrals. On the island of Kerrera, they read *One of our Conquerors* and Shelley's translation of *The Banquet* of Plato. They recited *As You Like It* to each other, discovering they knew the whole of it by heart. It was during this Highland holiday that Ashbee mentioned the large fortune which his father, who died in 1900, had bequeathed out of the family (8). He had not apparently referred to this before, and Alec commented that it was very much in character that Ashbee regretted the loss of the inheritance, which as the only son of a rich father he might well have expected, mainly because he thought he could have used it to stave off the demise of the Guild.

There was still a little work coming in to the old Silk Mill. 'Let us devoutly thank his gracious and fat Majesty Edward VII des. gra. rex Aug. &c. &c. and Charley Holden, the little genius turned into the thin ghost of modern architecture for giving us these scraps of a "King's Sanatorium",'[20] wrote Ashbee, referring to the work on the interior of King Edward VII Sanatorium at Midhurst, a building which Charles Holden had designed. Alec, later in the year, had a good commission for a new reredos and large carved organ case for the church at Calne in Wiltshire (9). But though the woodworkers continued to be relatively busy, other Guild workshops were almost at a standstill. Since the cancellation of plans for the grandiose new Springfield Catholic Centre, abandoned when the brewer Lawrence Hodson lost his money, Ashbee had no large-scale architectural jobs pending. As Ashbee's own commissions in the past had generated so much work for the Guild craftsmen, there is no doubt that this was another factor in the current Campden crisis.

The Guild jewellers and silversmiths were in the worst predicament. This was nothing new: right back in 1903, Janet had been complaining of the effects of commercial competition on Guild craftsmanship. ('Here is Liberty & Co.', she wrote indignantly, 'putting £10,000 into the Cymric Co., and we struggling to get our hundreds, and having to potboil with vile brooches etc., to make ends meet.'[21]) Ever since the Guild arrived in Campden, the jewellers and silversmiths had had to contend with increasingly highly-organized development by Liberty's and Hutton's and other firms producing by semi-mechanical methods work which, to the uninitiated, much resembled Guild work. As the Guild itself became less able to support them, the metalworkers' problems appeared the more acute.

Some of the jewellers made a desperate attempt to meet the competition head-on. Hoping to undercut the Birmingham trade (in which, ironically, some of them had trained), they started making their jewellery much cheaper, concentrating on traditional designs which were easy to chase and could be quickly made in batches. But although the new cut-price Guild enamel brooches sold reasonably well in the retail shop in Brook Street, this flagrant contravention of Guild precept and Guild practice, abandonment of the whole policy of standard, was more than many of the craftsmen could approve of. It led to an inevitable conflict in the workshops, with the spokesmen for commercial necessity ranged against the traditional upholders of Guild standard: as symbolic a confrontation as any in Ashbee's own romances. The consensus of opinion was very much for Ashbee. It was generally felt that any lowering of standard could only bring the whole of the Guild into disrepute.

How *could* running costs be cut? This was the question still being asked at the Guild meeting in August, 1907. It seemed that by this time all expedients had been tried. Even the rent at Braithwaite House had been raised from 15 shillings a week to £1, in the attempt to put the Guild back on a secure financial footing. But the situation showed few signs of recovery, and by now about a third of the craftsmen of the Guild had drifted off from Campden in search of work elsewhere.

Ashbee himself was always hopeful that the crisis was only temporary. He felt convinced that the Guild would reassemble and soon set itself on a new course of prosperity. He asked departing Guildsmen to publicize the Guild, a request which some Guildsmen found a little onerous. (Charley Downer, the blacksmith, was obviously worried by the parcel of catalogues which Ashbee despatched after him to St Albans: 'There is no person desirous of knowing the Guild here', he wrote to Ashbee, 'I wish there were.'[22])

But while Ashbee concentrated on the day the Guild of Handicraft would rise again, the phoenix from the ashes, Janet saw the need for more immediate action in order to forestall an imminent disaster. In autumn 1907, staying with her family at Godden Green, she wrote

(10) Professor Patrick Geddes (1854–1932), convinced multidisciplinarian. As Ashbee later commented: 'Geddes' great achievement in life has been the making of a bridge between Biology and Social Science, thus giving a fresh clue to reconstruction, to civics and to the town plan. His, I think, is one of the most synthetic minds of our time. But he is very tiresome about it . . .' (*Palestine Notebook,* Heinemann, 1923). In 1918, Ashbee had taken over from Geddes as Civic Adviser on Town Planning in Jerusalem and, unlikely as it seems, Ashbee's proposals were judged much more practical than his predecessor's.

with some urgency reminding Charley that he needed to close Braithwaite House completely. Alec and Philippe Mairet must find some
other lodgings. Braithwaite was a liability: 'It is merely piling up our
debt.'[23]

There are certain points in the history of the Guild, certain events
which pinpoint its achievements and, in a way, seem to justify its whole
existence. One of these occurred in November, 1907, at the very height
of the Guild's financial crisis. Janet, in her Journal, gave a vivacious
account of the occasion:

We have just had a visit from Prof. Patrick Geddes (10), the Edinburgh Sociolo-
gist. When Charley told me he was going to give a Friday lecture at our Technical
School on 'London, Edinburgh and Campden,' I was certainly nervous, visioning
a fire-brand who should re-ignite the dying embers of local hostility. I was reassured
however on seeing a slight wiry man of 50 step on to the platform, hardly tall
enough to see over the desk, with the beautiful vague eyes of the ineffectual enthusiast. What we heard of his lecture, for he spoke in a still small voice into his
brown beard, was quite harmless and indeed nearly disconnected – and consisted
of curious scraps of knowledge about every conceivable subject. Botany, geology –
history, religion, sociology, agriculture, romance, literature, he can talk about all,
with about as much thread as you find between A and B in Murray's dictionary.
What is really interesting about him is his versatility. He is full of lore, facts and
assumptions – assertions based on the wildest premises, but all containing a germ of
thought – an idea that sets you wondering and re-considering your previous
certainties. He is a sort of yeast, never producing anything by itself, and yet setting
everything near it agog with life. For serious argument he is no good, as he cheats;
but once started talking he will go on for hours, colouring with instances, narrating
adventures, raising hypotheses, till you are nearly giddy. I think he must be better
for men than women. Nevill's friend Douglas Davidson who was here, was
tremendously interested and stimulated – and Charley was spell bound. I felt
fatigue, and a slight annoyance which I am bound to say arose from a first-
impression of dislike to his appearance (the regular Stage Professor, shaggy hair all
over his eyes – untidy dress and unclean hands). But his wonderful benign eyes,
especially when softened by a rare smile, kindled his whole face.[24]

Geddes went to visit the Guildsmen at the Silk Mill, impressing
them with his extraordinary sense of 'mental incandescence' (as Alec
Miller later called it). To the craftsmen he seemed an amazingly
stimulating and galvanic person, and his knack of rapid but profound
generalization struck them as unique. With his typical quiet, almost
bird-like little movements, he came into Alec's workshop where the
carving of the reredos for Calne was then in progress and suggested the

3 Magi should be based on: 1, the grand old scientist Sir Francis Galton, the father of Eugenics; 2, the middle-aged Bernard Shaw; and 3, the youthful H. G. Wells, with his new interpretation of science.

Geddes's visit to Campden, and its impact on the Guildsmen, points up one of Ashbee's greatest talents. This was his ability to bring people together: people from disparate disciplines and backgrounds, people otherwise unlikely to have met. It was, in a way, his chief claim to creativity. It explains the particular atmosphere of Campden and the lasting impression made by those years on the people who lived through them. But sadly enough, in just its fifth year of existence, Ashbee's City of the Sun was almost at an end.

The plight of the Guild was by then causing great concern to Rob Holland, its chief financial adviser. His position both as a director of the Guild and friend of Ashbee's and a partner in Martin's Bank had been becoming increasingly unenviable as the debts of the Guild grew. He had been involved at every major stage of Guild development: the formation of the Guild into a Limited Company; the opening of the London shop and gallery; the move from London to the Cotswolds. It had even been Rob Holland who first suggested Campden as the place for the Guild settlement. To a man of his idealism and integrity, so closely connected with what had now turned out to be a series of mis-judgments, the demise of the Guild was a source of great anxiety. Hoping against hope to save the Guild at the last moment, he offered to go shares with Ashbee and put in the equivalent of any further capital available. Ashbee had £1000 or so of his own money. But the rest of the directors persuaded them that further investment would be folly. The principal shareholding groups – the Ashbee family and Rob Holland and Martin's Bank – then made an agreement with the Guild directors that the Guild should go into voluntary liquidation. The Guild stock should be sold off gradually, to discharge its debts.

The news seems to have spread quickly, causing some consternation, not just amongst the Ashbees' friends and the Guild shareholders but in the more enlightened artistic and intellectual circles of the time. The break-up of the Guild seemed the death of a whole principle.

Wrote Halsey Ricardo to Eliza Wedgwood:

So the Guild of Handicraft has come to an end! I am sorry – of course – for there was much in that venture that deserved support – and I am sorry to think that with all this talk of 'Art' and 'Improved Taste' people will still persist in contenting themselves with imitations, rather than pay the price which the real article requires.[25]

Wrote Goldsworthy Lowes Dickinson to C. R. Ashbee:

It was with very great regret that I learned that it might be necessary to wind up the Guild of Handicraft. From what I have seen and known of it, I have long felt it to be a piece of real civilisation in industry, combining not merely a corporate interest in the work done, but a corporate life outside work and relations which have seemed to me very charming and fruitful, in matters of amusement and general culture, between the members of the Guild and Mrs Ashbee and yourself. The Guild in short has been under your guidance a real society, not an aggregation of 'hands'. It is this I have always admired in it, and I think it a matter of very great regret that this little oasis of human life should be submerged in the unintelligent ocean of competitive industry.[26]

Wrote Cecil Brewer to his fellow Art Worker:

I only want to shake you by the hand.[27]

Wrote Arthur Wauchope, the Ashbees' friend, from India:

I am very sorry Charlie that things have not gone well with the Guild, all the same I look upon you as a success, conspicuous among many failures, just because you never stooped to alter your methods to make them 'in harmony with your environment'.[28]

Wrote Nevill Forbes, Janet Ashbee's brother:

I can't tell you how awfully sorry I am that the Guild should be coming to an end as a corporate body.

I always think of those charcoal cartoons of Capital and Labour you have on the stairs of the workshops; they first impressed me at Essex House in Mile End and it is horrible to think that Capital should be triumphant even if it is only a temporary triumph; Janet tells me some of the men are going to stay on at Campden on their own and, if so, *you* will not be left entirely high and dry. Anyway I hope and trust that you won't attempt to move from Campden. I know Janet won't. Campden means such a lot now.[29]

All these sympathetic tributes meant a great deal to Ashbee. He collected them together and put them in the Journal. But of all the many letters of commiseration, the ones which he cared most about were those from his own Guildsmen. These he saw as the justification of his efforts and the hope for resurrection of the ideas he believed in.

For instance, Walter Edwards, Silversmith and Guildsman, wrote to him from Birmingham:

Dear C.R.A.,

I was sorry I had to leave Campden without being able to come and shake hands with you and wish you goodbye, but in the bustle of moving I could not get time,

8

Echoes from the City
1908 onwards

Early in 1908, the Guildsmen still remaining in Campden met at *The Swan* for a celebration dinner. They had come to commemorate the Guild's 21st birthday. But, as Alec Miller rather wanly commented, they were also, in a way, attending the Guild's funeral. The evening was not as melancholy as it might have been. But beneath the traditional birthday entertainment – songs, catches, reminiscences of pioneering days in Whitechapel – lay the fundamental question, still not adequately answered: why, after such high hopes and such propitious beginnings, did the Craft of the Guild eventually run aground?

An obvious explanation, the one popular in Campden even now among the locals and descendants of the Guildsmen, was that the Guild had become too big and too ambitious. Administrative costs of an office staff at Campden plus a showroom staff in London were much too onerous. The paperwork involved in running the Guild as a Limited Company was disproportionately burdensome. It was generally felt that the Guild had overreached itself. The structure of the Guild, by the time it got to Campden, was seen to be top-heavy, with too many salesmen and managers and clerks in relation to the number of producers. Increasing overheads, on top of many extra problems which the Guild incurred by choosing to work in a remote town in the Cotswolds, where men could not be laid off temporarily if trade declined, meant that the Guild had little leeway, few resources, to carry it through any economic fluctuations. The commonsense view of the exodus to Campden was – and no doubt always will be – that some form of financial disaster was inevitable. By the time it got to Campden, the Guild, it was felt, was on a suicidal course.

Ashbee himself analysed the débacle rather differently. In the book he wrote on the experiment at Campden, *Craftsmanship in Competitive Industry,* he argued with conviction that the fault lay with the system. The Guild had been squeezed out of existence by a combination of direct competition from factory production and the more insidious rivalry of amateur craftworkers: the threat from 'Nobody Novelty & Co.' and the threat from 'Dear Emily', his name for the great bevy of amateur craftsladies who sold their work at less than its real value. To Ashbee, the dilemma of the Guild was not merely a question of commerce; he saw it as a test-case for civilized values. If society wanted a humane way of working, in peaceful and beautiful surroundings, with secure conditions of employment, with leisure to experiment, with scope for individual development and endless possibilities for intellectual betterment, then society would have to make provision for it, by putting a check on the productions of machinery and by regulating competition from the amateur. If the Guild had failed (though he was notably reluctant to see the Campden episode in terms of failure), if society allowed the Guildsmen to sell off for 12s 6d light fittings which had cost £5 in materials and labour, then capitalist folly must be blamed for it. Ashbee believed that, before long, society would change its tack.

Alec Miller had an altogether different explanation. He blamed the poor calibre of many of the Guildsmen. The Guildsmen themselves were the people most responsible. In a letter to Ashbee, written in some bitterness three years after the Guild break-up, he maintained that the majority had never had their hearts in it. They only went along with it to humour Mr Ashbee. 'Had you been wealthy and run the shop as your private business – a thing hateful to you – hardly one of the men would have cared a rush.'[1]

No doubt there was some truth in many of these comments. The financial control of the Guild had been ham-fisted. The altruistic bias in the workshops of the Guild was indeed unrealistic without some form of subsidy. (Seventy years later, maybe Ashbee would have got one.) It was also fair to say that many of the craftsmen and their wives had little inkling of the finer points of Ashbee's theories of craftsmanship (1); from many of his Guildsmen, Ashbee hoped for far too much.

(1) Alas for Comradeship: 'You must remember Mr Ashbee', as Will Hart, the Skipper, Ashbee's hero, wrote just before his marriage in 1909, 'we live in a very conventional age and people like yourself who I always imagine have very little use for the conventions as far as living is concerned, look at things from a totally different standpoint. What I mean by this is (and I am a little sorry) that Dora is the sort of girl whose ideal of living is preferably in a modern house with modern conveniences and among modern goings-on. Of course this is naturally not my taste but I am perfectly willing to submit my all if necessary for a happy life'. (Quoted *Ashbee Journals*, 7 March 1909)

An excess of optimism had always been his failing. It was simply in his nature to take the Guild to Campden. It was also in his nature to imagine that men could be manipulated into his own idyllic vision of society. This was, as it proved, a rather dangerous assumption. In the end, his great hopes for the Guild rebounded on him. The Great Move to the Cotswolds had increased the independence of the individual Guildsmen. After the first few years in Campden, it transpired that in a sense they no longer needed leading. They no longer needed Ashbee. In a way they had outgrown him. As he later described it in the Journal: 'They had captured the countryside, they had got the confidence of the farmers, they had made friends, they had built up a school of craftsmanship, many had found their wives locally, they had in fact made a new country life, and another generation was at hand.'2

Many of the craftsmen stayed on themselves in Campden after the Guild went into liquidation. In 1909, those still working in the neighbourhood formed a reconstituted, much less formal company of Guildsmen, still dedicating themselves and their families to living 'a healthier and more reasonable life in the country', but avoiding any financial involvement. Their workshops were to be run as private businesses. Significantly, there was no longer a Director. Those who signed the Deed of Trust were C. R. Ashbee, Architect; Jack Baily, Silversmith; Charley Downer, Blacksmith; George Hart, Silversmith and Metal-worker; Will Hart, Carver; Teddy Horwood, Jeweller; William Mark, Enameller; Alec Miller, Carver and Modeller; Charley Plunkett, Polisher and Upholsterer; Jim Pyment, Cabinet Maker and Builder; Bill Thornton, Blacksmith; W. Wall, Cabinet-Maker and Joiner.

Meanwhile, 70 acres at Broad Campden had been purchased for the Guildsmen by Joseph Fels, an American millionaire, inventor of naptha soap and a vociferous supporter of the Back-to-the-Land movement. The idea was to combine craftsmanship with husbandry: each craftsman should also have a small-holding, enabling him to feed his family and providing an alternative occupation. But except for George Hart, already an experienced farmer, the craftsmen had little taste or energy for husbandry and after a few years the scheme was left to peter out.

The Ashbees stayed in Campden until 1919. Janet's romance with Gerald by then had long since ended. Gerald had remarried and gone to live in the inevitable Garden City. He remained a close friend of the family. The episode had, in a strange way, strengthened the relationship between the Ashbees and helped to remove some of the problems of their marriage. Janet, to her joy, eventually had four daughters – Mary, Felicity, Helen and Prudence – though never the son C. R. Ashbee set his heart on.

For the final few years of their period in Campden, the Ashbees themselves lived at the Norman Chapel. The Coomaraswamys had by this time parted, Ethel remarrying the Guildsman Philippe Mairet. A little later on, Ethel Mairet's weaving workshop, Gospels at Ditchling in Sussex, was one of the centres of a new artistic colony which included Ethel's brother, the jeweller Fred Partridge, and George Chettle, once Ashbee's architectural pupil. This latter-day Arts and Crafts community at Ditchling, converging at many points with Eric Gill and Pepler and the Guild of St Joseph and St Dominic, was to become, in the expert view of Ashbee, 'a very live and happy community with a lot of old Campden and Essex House spirit in it'.[3]

The Ashbees themselves, up to the First World War, were still very much embroiled in the activities of Campden, still set on their course of enlightening the natives. The School of Arts and Crafts, under the Ashbee aegis, was continuously and successfully expanding until it was rather arbitrarily closed down, just before the war, in a reorganization of local education. It was 1921, after the Ashbees had left Campden, when the Guild of Handicraft was finally disbanded.

Ashbee's later activities were relatively desultory. He never quite lost hope of arriving at Utopia, but after his long episode with the Guild and Campden it was obviously hard for him to reorientate himself, and he never really found a new base of operations or the platform for his views which he felt that he deserved.

He took up the cause of the New Civics. His hopes for the reconstructed city are well expressed in one of his most thorough and interesting studies *Where the Great City Stands,* and at this same period got himself involved with the new town plans for Dublin. At the start of the war, he was caught up in the Peace Dream, with Goldsworthy Lowes Dickinson, and in the propaganda for a league of nations, and travelled around America campaigning for disarmament (delivering 'art messages' here and there as well). In 1917, he went to Egypt to teach English at the University in Cairo. The following year, he went to Palestine, to take up the appointment as Civic Adviser to the British military government in Jerusalem. In this post, he was responsible for restoring the old city and replanning the new. He had scope for reviving the traditional Arab handicrafts. One might have imagined it would suit him. But unfortunately the appointment was short-lived, probably because of his political intransigence. With his usual contrariness, Ashbee – although Jewish – was apt to be ostentatiously pro-Arab.

When he returned to England in 1923, much of his old energy had dwindled. Although he was still sometimes to be seen at Art Workers' Guild meetings in his old role of Don Quixote, heroically tilting at the capitalist windmills, in the main his urge to alter the whole structure of society seemed to have receded. He and his family retreated to Janet's old family home, Godden Green, near Sevenoaks, where he led the quiet life of the literary gentleman, with only the most minor eccentricities. He embarked on the vast task of editing his journals. This was completed in 1938.

Janet's memories of Campden were not altogether happy ones. She perhaps had suffered most from all the backbiting, the scandals provoked inevitably by the Ashbees' contravention of local conventions, Campden patterns of behaviour, and because of the family connections with Germany, she seems to have been ostracized during the First World War. For many years after, she refused to go to Campden, and it was 1950, when she was over 70, before she could bring herself to revisit the town. On this visit it surprised her to find that the Guildsmen were getting old as well.

Ashbee himself, whose memories were more selective and who tended to recall only the things he found convenient, had a different view of Campden, more mellow, more nostalgic. Campden came to symbolize his finest aspirations. As he wrote to F. L. Griggs, still living on in Campden (a greater friend in later life than he had been as Ashbee's neighbour): 'We both wanted a better world and were both quite out of touch with the one provided us, while the beauty of life – expressed in that Gloucestershire village – was almost all in all to us.'[4]

C. R. Ashbee, in his later years, had many opportunities for mulling over the years he spent in Campden. Not only was he occupied with working through the Journals, reliving the Great Move from Whitechapel to Campden, reflecting on the theories and the ideals which inspired it, he was also exercised with a long large book called *Peckover*, not quite fiction, not quite history, but, as Ashbee very characteristically described it, a study in aesthetics, the story of a house. Since the house was the Norman Chapel in Broad Campden and the fictional-historical characters so closely resembled actual local residents, long arguments ensued about the pros and cons of publishing. The book, finally in 1932, was published privately, and nobody appears to have taken great offence.

Ashbee never lost his deep affection for Campden nor did he ever lose his faith in the importance of the way of life and work he temporarily established there. He always insisted the experiment at Campden was ahead of its time. This, he argued, was the reason for its lack of financial viability. And in fact it was noticeable, even in his life-time, how many of the Campden ideas kept resurfacing. The concept of the working community of craftsmen, for instance, was developed at the Wiener Werkstätten and later in the foundation of the Bauhaus, with its early emphasis on Guild structure and ideals. The ideas of the School of Arts and Crafts, a local centre for community education, combining the practical, the academic and aesthetic, were to be reflected in subsequent developments in British educational policy, especially in Henry Morris's Cambridgeshire Village Colleges in the late twenties and the thirties. Ashbee's view of the work of the creative craftsman as an essential element in civilized society has to some extent in recent years been vindicated by the new policy of government support for individual craft workshops. As respect for his ideas (or at least some of them) has grown, appreciation of the work of the Guild, the actual products of the craftsmen, especially the metalwork, has increased greatly. The Victoria and Albert Museum now has a particularly fine collection of Guild silver. Prices in the salerooms continue to rise steeply.

One of the strangest things to happen recently to Ashbee's reputation, a development which he himself would surely have found puzzling, is the way in which he – prime spokesman for the individual craftsman, fervent preserver of traditional skills – has come to be acclaimed as one of the fathers of the Modern Movement, one of the prophets of mechanical production. This is surely to misunderstand his basic attitude. He did not fight machinery; he saw it had its uses to liberate skilled men from unnecessary drudgery. But, unlike his friend Lloyd Wright, machinery did not excite him. The Gods of C. R. Ashbee were other things completely.

Ashbee died in 1942. After his death Janet, always a little nervous of the possible effect of her husband's revelations, apparently destroyed his *Confessio Amantis*, written out in an old note-book. It is not known if she read it.

Janet lived on, moving up to Lancashire and continuing her massive correspondence. She was still in touch with many families of Guildsmen when she died at the age of 83. The week before her death in May 1961, Alec Miller, whose family by then had moved to California, arrived in England on a visit. By an odd coincidence, on the very day her ashes were sent down for the committal service to the church in Seal where she and Charley had been married, the date which was also

Ashbee's birthday, Alec Miller, the most faithful of the Guildsmen, himself died.

There are still many memories of Guild life around Campden. A number of the Guildsmen married into local families, and several, in spite of their quasi-revolutionary beginnings, were soon transformed into pillars of society. George Hart and Charley Downer even became Churchwardens, a turn of events which might have caused some consternation to the Carringtons. As Campden itself changed from a quiet and dilapidated town into a more consciously artistic Cotswold showplace, some of the Guildsmen were tempted to become correspondingly more bourgeois in their attitudes and values. The erstwhile castigators of iniquitous employers, as Ashbee himself noted more in sorrow than in anger, were no more open-handed than the next man – maybe less so – when it came to dealing with employees of their own.

The aura of the Guild is most strong at the old Silk Mill. The building was purchased by Jim Pyment when the Guild went into liquidation. Pyment's building firm, still run by the Pyment family, occupies the ground floor of the Silk Mill. On the top floor, Robert Welch, the industrial designer and an expert on Guild metalwork, has his studio and workshop. On the first floor, in the workshop which housed the metalworkers when the Guild first came to Campden, Henry Hart and his sons still make silver. Henry's father, George Hart, the last of Ashbee's Guildsmen, had lived and worked in Campden for over 60 years.

References

PROLOGUE

1 *Ashbee Memoirs*, retrospective note to 1901 entry, written in 1938.
2 Quoted MICHAEL HOLROYD: *Lytton Strachey*. Heinemann (London 1967).

CHAPTER ONE: FROM WHITECHAPEL TO CAMELOT

1 DENNIS PROCTOR, ed. *The Autobiography of Goldsworthy Lowes Dickinson*.
Duckworth (London 1973).
2 EDWARD CARPENTER. *My Days and Dreams*. George Allen & Unwin
(London 1916).
3 GILBERT BEITH, ed. *Edward Carpenter: In Appreciation*. George Allen & Unwin
(London 1931).
4 *Ashbee Memoirs*, 4 January 1886.
5 *Edward Carpenter: In Appreciation*.
6 *The Times* obituary, June 1929.
7 *Ashbee Journals*, 20 July 1886.
8 *Ashbee Journals*, July 1886.
9 Quoted *Ashbee Journals*, July 1886.
10 *Ashbee Memoirs*, Introduction to Vol. 1, 1938.
11 *Ashbee Memoirs*, 22 November 1886.
12 *Ashbee Journals*, 30 November 1886.
13 Catalogue of the St George's Museum, Walkley, 1888. Sheffield City Libraries.
14 Quoted *Ashbee Memoirs*, 24 January 1903.
15 Letter to C. R. Ashbee from Hubert von Herkomer, 8 March 1888. Victoria and
Albert Museum MS Collection.
16 Letter to C. R. Ashbee from A. H. Mackmurdo, 1888. Victoria and Albert Museum
MS Collection.
17 Letter to C. R. Ashbee from W. B. Richmond, 1888. Victoria and Albert Museum
MS Collection.
18 *Ashbee Memoirs*, 5 December 1887.
19 PHOEBE HAYDON. *The Memoirs of a Faithful Secretary*. Unpublished MS in the
possession of Felicity Ashbee.
20 *Ashbee Memoirs*, November 1901.

21 Letter from C. R. Ashbee to Janet Forbes, 2 September 1897. In the possession of Felicity Ashbee.

22 Quoted *Ashbee Journals*, 1900.

23 Letter to C. R. Ashbee from Canon Rawnsley 3 January 1888. Victoria and Albert Museum MS Collection.

24 C. R. ASHBEE. The Guild of Handicraft, Chipping Campden. Article in *Art Journal* 1903, pp.149–52.

25 SAMUEL and HENRIETTA BARNETT. *Practicable Socialism*. Longmans, Green (London 1894).

26 ALGERNON GISSING. *The Footpath Way in Gloucestershire*. J. M. Dent (London 1924).

27 Quoted *Ashbee Journals*, 18 September 1901.

28 Quoted *Ashbee Memoirs*, 14 November 1901.

29 *Ashbee Memoirs*, 14 November 1901.

30 *Ashbee Memoirs*, 8 December 1901.

31 Quoted *Ashbee Journals*, Spring 1902.

32 *Ashbee Memoirs*, 14 December 1903.

33 *Ashbee Memoirs*, Christmas 1901.

34 *Ashbee Memoirs*, Christmas 1901.

CHAPTER TWO: COCKNEYS IN ARCADIA

1 ARCHIE RAMAGE. *The Essex House Press*. Unpublished typescript. Victoria and Albert Museum.

2 P. A. MAIRET. *Autobiographical Notes*. Unpublished typescript.

3 Quoted *Ashbee Journals*, 1901.

4 ALEC MILLER. *C. R. Ashbee and the Guild of Handicraft*. Unpublished typescript. Victoria and Albert Museum.

5 Quoted *Ashbee Journals*, 1910.

6 *Ashbee Memoirs*, 6 March 1902.

7 E. R. and J. PENNELL. *The Life of James McNeill Whistler*, 6th edition, (Philadelphia and London, 1920).

8 Quoted *Ashbee Journals*, 1902.

9 *Ashbee Memoirs*, March 1902.

10 Quoted *Ashbee Memoirs*, 15 February 1902.

11 GORDON RUSSELL. *Designer's Trade*. Allen & Unwin (London 1968).

12 NORMAN JEWSON. *By Chance I Did Rove*. Published privately 1973.

13 *Evesham Chronicle*, 22 March 1902.

14 *Art Journal*, 1903, pp. 149–52.

15 Minutes of the School of Handicraft, Report for 1902. Victoria and Albert Museum.

16 *Art Journal*, 1903, pp. 149–52.

17 *Ashbee Memoirs*, June 1902.

18 *Ashbee Memoirs*, 12 June 1902.

19 ALEC MILLER. *C. R. Ashbee and the Guild of Handicraft*.

20 *Ashbee Journals*, 3 May 1902.

21 *Ashbee Memoirs*, June 1902.

22 Quoted *Ashbee Journals*, 1 May 1902.

23 *Ashbee Memoirs*, June 1902.

24 Quoted *Ashbee Memoirs*, June 1902.

25 *Ashbee Memoirs*, 29 October 1902.

26 *Ashbee Memoirs*, 3 June 1902.

27 Quoted *Ashbee Memoirs*, Christmas Day 1915.

28 ALEC MILLER. *C. R. Ashbee and the Guild of Handicraft.*

29 *Ashbee Memoirs*, 28 December 1900.

30 *Ashbee Memoirs*, 23 June 1902.

31 ALEC MILLER. *C. R. Ashbee and the Guild of Handicraft.*

32 Quoted *Ashbee Memoirs*, September 1902.

33 C. R. ASHBEE. *Caricature.* Chapman and Hall (London 1928).

34 Quoted *Ashbee Memoirs*, 23 February 1902.

35 *Ashbee Memoirs*, September 1902.

36 *Ashbee Memoirs*, 23 September 1902.

37 Quoted *Ashbee Memoirs*, 23 September 1902.

38 *Ashbee Memoirs*, 23 September 1902.

39 *Ashbee Journals*, Autumn 1902.

40 Local newspaper report, quoted *Ashbee Journals*, Autumn 1902.

41 *Ashbee Memoirs*, November 1902.

42 *Ashbee Memoirs*, Christmas 1902.

CHAPTER THREE: THE BUILDING OF THE CITY

1 ALEC MILLER. *C. R. Ashbee and the Guild of Handicraft.*

2 *Ashbee Memoirs*, January 1903.

3 *Ashbee Journals*, 14 January 1903.

4 *Ashbee Memoirs*, January 1903.

5 *Ashbee Memoirs*, January 1903.

6 *Ashbee Journals*, 1 October 1898.

7 *Ashbee Memoirs*, January 1903.

8 *Edward Carpenter: In Appreciation.*

9 *Ashbee Memoirs*, January 1903.

10 *Ashbee Memoirs*, September 1901.

11 *Ashbee Memoirs*, 26 January 1903.

12 *Ashbee Memoirs*, 30 January 1903.

13 *Ashbee Memoirs*, 1903.

14 *Ashbee Memoirs*, June 1902.

15 *Ashbee Memoirs*, January 1914.

16 *Ashbee Journals*, 28 February 1903.

17 *Ashbee Memoirs*, 4 May 1903.

18 ALEC MILLER. *C. R. Ashbee and the Guild of Handicraft.*

19 *Ashbee Memoirs*, March 1903.

20 Quoted *Ashbee Journals*, 1903.

21 Quoted *Ashbee Memoirs*, 11 June 1903.

22 *Ashbee Memoirs*, July 1903.

23 Quoted *Ashbee Journals*, 1903.

24 BEATRICE WEBB. *Our Partnership.* Longmans Green (London 1948).

25 Ref. *A Guide to Chipping Campden and Blockley*. Borough Guides No.92,
Cheltenham *c*.1907, pp.20–1.

26 *Ashbee Memoirs*, 1909.

27 *Ashbee Memoirs*, September 1903.

28 J. H. BADLEY. *Memories and Reflections*. George Allen & Unwin (London 1955).

29 *Ashbee Memoirs*, December 1903.

30 *Ashbee Memoirs*, December 1903.

CHAPTER FOUR: THE JOLLY CRAFTSMEN'S CHORUS

1 *Ashbee Memoirs*, introduction to history of the Masters of the Art Workers' Guild, 1938.

2 C. R. ASHBEE. *Craftsmanship in Competitive Industry*. Grant & Co. for Essex House
Press (London 1908).

3 CHARLES ROWLEY. *A Workshop Paradise and other papers*. Sherratt and Hughes (1905).

4 C. R. ASHBEE. *Craftsmanship in Competitive Industry*.

5 *Rachel*, a novel by JANET ASHBEE. Unpublished MS in the possession of
Felicity Ashbee.

6 ALEC MILLER. *C. R. Ashbee and the Guild of Handicraft*.

7 *Ashbee Memoirs*, August 1904.

8 ALEC MILLER. *C. R. Ashbee and the Guild of Handicraft*.

9 Quoted *Ashbee Journals*, early 1904.

10 *Ashbee Memoirs*, August 1904.

11 *Ashbee Journals*, 21 July 1905.

12 *Ashbee Memoirs*, 12 July 1904.

13 GORDON RUSSELL. *Designer's Trade*.

14 *Ashbee Memoirs*, 4 September 1886.

15 *Ashbee Memoirs*, 1904.

16 *Ashbee Memoirs*, September 1904.

17 *Ashbee Memoirs*, 1904.

18 Quoted *Ashbee Memoirs*, September 1904.

19 *Ashbee Memoirs*, 1904.

20 *Ashbee Memoirs*, 1904.

21 *Ashbee Memoirs*, 1904.

22 ALEC MILLER. *C. R. Ashbee and the Guild of Handicraft*.

23 PHILIP HENDERSON, ed. *Letters of William Morris to his Family and Friends*.
Longmans, Green (London 1950).

24 *Ashbee Memoirs*, 5 November 1904.

25 *Ashbee Memoirs*, 5 November 1904.

26 *Ashbee Journals*, 3 November 1904.

27 *Ashbee Journals*, 3 November 1904.

28 *Ashbee Journals*, November 1904.

29 Prospectus for *The Flower and Leaf*. Essex House Press (1902).

30 Paper *On the Need for the Establishment of Country Schools of Arts and Crafts*.
Victoria and Albert Museum MS Collection.

31 Quoted *Ashbee Journals*, 1904.

32 *Ashbee Memoirs*, December 1904.

CHAPTER FIVE: THE SONG OF GILES COCKBILL

1 Quoted *Ashbee Journals*, 1905.
2 *Ashbee Journals*, September 1904.
3 Quoted *Ashbee Memoirs*, April 1905.
4 ALEC MILLER. *C. R. Ashbee and the Guild of Handicraft.*
5 Quoted *Ashbee Memoirs*, 23 August 1905.
6 Quoted *Ashbee Journals*, March 1905.
7 *Ashbee Memoirs*, 12 April 1905.
8 F. L. GRIGGS. *Campden, 24 Engravings.* With introduction by Russell Alexander. Shakespeare Head Press (Oxford 1940).
9 Quoted *Ashbee Journals*, 1 January 1905.
10 *Ashbee Journals*, 28 June 1905.
11 *Ashbee Memoirs*, June 1905.
12 Quoted *Ashbee Memoirs*, 3 December 1903.
13 *Ashbee Memoirs*, Septuagesima 1905.
14 *Ashbee Journals*, 1901.
15 JANET ASHBEE. *Rachel.*
16 JANET ASHBEE. *Rachel.*
17 JANET ASHBEE. *Rachel.*
18 JANET ASHBEE. *Rachel.*
19 JANET ASHBEE. *Rachel.*
20 *Ashbee Memoirs*, 5 June 1905.
21 *Ashbee Memoirs*, June/July 1905.
22 *Ashbee Memoirs*, June/July 1905.

CHAPTER SIX: THE GUILD'S THREE 'PRENTICES

1 *Ashbee Memoirs*, 13 January 1906.
2 *Ashbee Memoirs*, January 1906.
3 *Ashbee Memoirs*, January 1906.
4 Quoted *Ashbee Journals*, 1906.
5 Quoted *Ashbee Memoirs*, April 1906.
6 Quoted ALEC MILLER. *C. R. Ashbee and the Guild of Handicraft.*
7 *Ashbee Journals*, 1906.
8 H. E. BERLESPSCH-VALENDAS. *C. R. Ashbee and the Guild of Handicraft.* Article in *Kunst und Handwerk*, Vol. 58 (1907–8), pp. 114–20.
9 Quoted *Ashbee Journals*, 1906.
10 *Ashbee Memoirs*, 1 June 1906.
11 *Ashbee Memoirs*, 1 June 1906.
12 ARCHIE RAMAGE. *The Essex House Press.*
13 Quoted *Ashbee Memoirs*, 17 July 1906.
14 *Ashbee Memoirs*, 31 August 1906.
15 P. A. MAIRET. *Autobiographical Notes.*
16 P. A. MAIRET. *Autobiographical Notes.*

17 P. A. MAIRET. *Autobiographical Notes.*
18 Quoted Minutes of the Guild of Handicraft, 9 March 1906. Victoria and Albert Museum MS Collection.
19 *Ashbee Memoirs*, 15 December 1906.

CHAPTER SEVEN: THE DEATH OF CONRADIN

1 *Ashbee Memoirs*, introduction to January 1907–April 1908, 1938.
2 *Ashbee Memoirs*, 9 February 1907.
3 *Ashbee Memoirs*, 1907.
4 *Ashbee Memoirs*, 8 January 1907.
5 *Ashbee Memoirs*, February 1907.
6 *Ashbee Memoirs*, 16 February 1907.
7 Quoted *Craftsmanship in Competitive Industry.*
8 Quoted *Craftsmanship in Competitive Industry.*
9 Quoted *Craftsmanship in Competitive Industry.*
10 *Ashbee Memoirs*, Easter 1907.
11 *Ashbee Memoirs*, 31 May 1907.
12 *Ashbee Memoirs*, 1907.
13 P. A. MAIRET. *Autobiographical Notes.*
14 *Ashbee Memoirs*, 25 January 1908.
15 *Ashbee Journals*, 1907.
16 Quoted *Ashbee Memoirs*, 25 July 1907.
17 Quoted *Ashbee Journals*, 1907.
18 *Ashbee Journals*, 29 August 1907.
19 Unpublished MS in the possession of Felicity Ashbee.
20 *Ashbee Memoirs*, February 1907.
21 *Ashbee Memoirs*, 9 March 1903.
22 Quoted *Ashbee Journals*, 1907.
23 *Ashbee Journals*, 1907.
24 *Ashbee Memoirs*, 20 November 1907.
25 Quoted *Ashbee Memoirs*, 7 December 1907.
26 Quoted *Craftsmanship in Competitive Industry.*
27 Quoted *Ashbee Memoirs*, 29 November 1907.
28 Quoted *Ashbee Memoirs*, 1 January 1908.
29 Quoted *Ashbee Memoirs*, January 1908.
30 Quoted *Ashbee Memoirs*, 8 December 1908.

CHAPTER EIGHT: ECHOES FROM THE CITY

1 Quoted *Ashbee Journals*, 1911.
2 *Ashbee Memoirs*, introduction to January 1907–April 1908, 1938.
3 *Ashbee Memoirs*, November 1923.
4 Letter from C. R. Ashbee to F. L. Griggs, 10 January 1924. In the possession of Mrs Nina Griggs.

Sources and Select Bibliography

The main sources of information for Ashbee and his work are of course the Ashbee Journals, the complete set (44 volumes) of which are in King's College Library, Cambridge.

A shorter version, reduced to seven volumes, edited by Ashbee himself in 1938, is in the Library of the Victoria and Albert Museum and in the London Library. (In this book, the edited version is referred to as the Ashbee Memoirs.)

There is a considerable collection of material relating to the Guild – minute books, prospectuses, reports and many photographs – in the Victoria and Albert Museum.

In addition, many of the personal diaries and letters of the Ashbee family, including Janet Ashbee's autobiographical novel *Rachel,* are in the keeping of Felicity Ashbee.

From C. R. Ashbee's own large literary output, the following books have particular relevance to the Chipping Campden episode:

From Whitechapel to Camelot. Guild of Handicraft (1892).
A Few Chapters in Workshop Reconstruction and Citizenship. Guild of Handicraft (1894).
The Treatises of Benvenuto Cellini on Goldsmithing and Sculpture. Essex House Press (1898).
An Endeavour towards the teaching of John Ruskin and William Morris. Essex House Press (1901).
The Guild of Handicraft, Chipping Campden. *Art Journal* (1903).
The Last Records of a Cotswold Community. Essex House Press (1905).
The Essex House Song Book. Essex House Press (1905).
Echoes from the City of the Sun: a book of poems. Essex House Press (1905).
A Book of Cottages and Little Houses. Batsford (1906).
Conradin, a ballad. Essex House Press (1908).
Craftsmanship in Competitive Industry. Essex House Press (1908).
Modern English Silverwork. Essex House Press (1909) and new edition Weinreb (1974).
The Private Press: a study in Idealism. Essex House Press (1909).
The Trust Deed of the Guild of Handicraft. Essex House Press (1909).
The Building of Thelema: a romance of the workshops. Dent (1910).
Should We Stop Teaching Art? Batsford (1912).
The Hamptonshire Experiment in Education. Allen & Unwin (1914).
Where the Great City Stands. Essex House Press (1917).
Peckover: the Abbotscourt Papers. Astolat Press (1932).

Of the various accounts of Ashbee and the work of the Guild, many in contemporary magazines and periodicals, these are the ones I have found most worth pursuing:

Arts and Crafts Exhibition Society reviews, *Studio*, vol.9 (1897) and vol.18 (1899–1900).
A Visit to Essex House, *Studio*, vol.12 (1898).
BERLEPSCH-VALENDAS, H. E., article on C. R. Ashbee and the Guild of Handicraft, *Kunst und Handwerk*, vol.58 (1907–8).
BURROUGH, B. G., articles on C. R. Ashbee in series 'Three Disciples of William Morris', *The Connoisseur*, vol.172 (1969).
BURY, SHIRLEY, An Arts and Crafts experiment: the silverwork of C. R. Ashbee, *Victoria and Albert Museum Bulletin*, vol.III, No.1 (January 1967).
CRAWFORD, ALAN, intr. *Robert Welch, Design in a Cotswold Workshop.* Lund Humphries (1973).
CRAWFORD, ALAN, and BURY, SHIRLEY, intr. *Modern English Silverwork* (new edition). Weinreb (1974).
FRANKLIN, COLIN, chapter on Essex House Press in *The Private Presses*. Studio Vista (1969).
HONOUR, HUGH. Chapter on Ashbee in *Goldsmiths and Silversmiths*. Weidenfeld & Nicolson (1971).
KOSSATZ, HORST-HERBERT. The Vienna Secession and its early relations with Great Britain. *Studio International*, vol.181 (1971).
MILLER, ALEC. *C. R. Ashbee and the Guild of Handicraft*. Unpublished typescript completed *c.*1952. Victoria and Albert Museum.
MUTHESIUS, HERMANN. Die 'Guild and School of Handicraft' in London. *Dekorative Kunst*, vol.2 (Munich 1898).
NUTTGENS, PATRICK. A Full Life and an Honest Place, chapter on the Arts and Crafts in *Spirit of the Age: Eight Centuries of British Architecture*. BBC Publications (1975).
PEVSNER, NIKOLAUS. William Morris, C. R. Ashbee and the Twentieth Century. *Manchester Review*, vol.7 (Winter 1956).
ROWLEY, CHARLES. *A Workshop Paradise and other papers.* Sherratt & Hughes (1905).
Suggestions for the Improvement of Sporting Cups and Trophies. *Studio*, vol.19 (1900).
The New 'Magpie and Stump'. *Studio*, vol.5 (1895).
TRIGGS, OSCAR LOVELL. *Chapters in the History of the Arts and Crafts Movement.* Bohemia Guild of Industrial Art League (1902).
WHITING, FREDERICK. A Successful English Experiment. *Handicraft* (Boston 1903). Reprinted by Essex House Press (1904).

Catalogues of exhibitions which included Guild work:

Arts and Crafts Exhibition Society Exhibitions, London, from 1888.
'An Exhibition of Cotswold Craftsmanship', Cheltenham, 1951.
'The Arts and Crafts Movement', Fine Art Society, London, 1973.
'Victorian and Edwardian Decorative Arts', Victoria and Albert Museum, London, 1952.

Other books which have provided useful background information:

ADBURGHAM, ALISON. *Liberty's. A Biography of a Shop.* George Allen & Unwin (1976).

ADLARD, ELEANOR, ed. *Robert Holland-Martin: A Symposium.* Frederick Muller (1947).

ANSCOMBE, ISABELLA, and GERE, CHARLOTTE. *Arts and Crafts in Britain and America.* Academy Editions (1978).

ARMYTAGE, W. H. G. *Heavens Below. Utopian Experiments in England, 1560–1960.* Routledge & Kegan Paul (1961).

Arts and Crafts Exhibition Society. *Arts and Crafts Essays.* Rivington Percival (1893).

ASHBEE, FELICITY. Nevill Forbes 1883–1929: Some Family Letters from Russia. *Oxford Slavonic Papers*, vol.IX. Clarendon Press (Oxford 1976).

ASHBY, M. K. *The Changing English Village.* Roundhead Press (1974).

ASLIN, ELIZABETH. *19th Century English Furniture.* Faber (1962).

BADLEY, J. H. *Memories and Reflections.* George Allen & Unwin (1955).

BANHAM, REYNER. *Theory and Design in the First Machine Age.* Architectural Press (1960).

BARNETT, HENRIETTA. *Canon Barnett.* John Murray (1918).

BARNETT, SAMUEL and HENRIETTA. *Practicable Socialism.* Longmans, Green (1894).

BEITH, G., ed. *Edward Carpenter: In Appreciation.* George Allen & Unwin (1931).

BLATCHFORD, ROBERT. *Merrie England.* Clarion Press (1908).

BOOTH, CHARLES. *Life and Labour of the People in London.* Macmillan (1903).

BOYLE, ANDREW. *Montagu Norman.* Cassell (1967).

BRANDON-JONES, JOHN, and others. *C. F. A. Voysey: architect and designer.* Catalogue of exhibition at Brighton Art Gallery and Museum. Lund Humphries (1978).

BRILL, EDITH. *Life and Tradition on the Cotswolds.* J. M. Dent (1973).

BROWN, BRYAN, ed. *The England of Henry Taunt.* Routledge & Kegal Paul (1973).

BURY, SHIRLEY. The Liberty metalwork venture. *Architectural Review*, vol.133 (1963).

CAMPBELL, JOAN. *The German Werkbund.* Princeton University Press (1978).

CARPENTER, EDWARD. *Days with Walt Whitman.* George Allen (1906).

My Days and Dreams. George Allen & Unwin (1916).

CARRINGTON, NOEL. *Industrial Design in Britain.* George Allen & Unwin (1976).

CLARK, SIR JOHN, ed. *The Campden Wonder.* Oxford University Press (1959).

CLARK, ROBERT JUDSON, ed. *The Arts and Crafts Movement in America.* Catalogue of exhibition at Princeton. Princeton University Press (1972).

CLAYRE, ALASDAIR. *Work and Play.* Weidenfeld & Nicolson (1974).

COMINO, MARY. *Gimson and the Barnsleys.* Evans Brothers (1980).

COMSTOCK, F. A. *A Gothic Vision: F. L. Griggs and his work.* Boston Library and Ashmolean, Oxford (1966).

COOMARASWAMY, ANANDA, *The Arts and Crafts of India and Ceylon.* T. N. Foulis (1913).

Why Exhibit Works of Art? Luzac (1943).

CRANE, WALTER. *An Artist's Reminiscences.* Methuen (1907).

William Morris to Whistler. G. Bell (1911).

CRAWFORD, ALAN. Ten Letters from Frank Lloyd Wright to Charles Robert Ashbee. *Architectural History*, vol.13 (1970).

DARLEY, GILLIAN. *Villages of Vision.* Architectural Press (1975).

DYOS, H. J., and WOLFF, MICHAEL, eds. *The Victorian City*. Routledge & Kegan Paul (1973).

FAWCETT, JANE, ed. *Seven Victorian Architects*. Thames & Hudson (1976).

FORSTER, E. M. *Goldsworthy Lowes Dickinson*. Edward Arnold (1934).

FURBANK, P. N. *E. M. Forster*. Secker & Warburg (1977).

GARNER, PHILIPPE. *Edwardiana*. Hamlyn (1974).

GEORGE, HENRY. *Progress and Poverty*. Doubleday and McLure (1891).

GIBBS, J. ARTHUR. *A Cotswold Village*. John Murray (1898).

HADFIELD, CHARLES and ALICE, eds. *The Cotswolds: a New Study*. David & Charles (1973).

HANSON, BRIAN. Singing the Body Electric with Charles Holden. *Architectural Review* (December 1975).

HENDERSON, PHILIP, ed. *The Letters of William Morris to his Family and Friends*. Longmans, Green (1950).

HENDERSON, PHILIP. *William Morris*. Thames & Hudson (1967).

HOLLOWAY, MARK. *Heavens on Earth. Utopian Communities in America 1680–1880*. Turnstile Press (1951).

HOUSMAN, LAURENCE. *The Unexpected Years*. Jonathan Cape (1937).
Ploughshare and Pruning Hook: 10 Lectures on Social Subjects. Swarthmore Press (1919).

HOWARD, EBENEZER. *Garden Cities of Tomorrow*. Faber (1902).

HOWARTH, THOMAS. *Charles Rennie Mackintosh*. Routledge & Kegan Paul (1952).

HUGHES, GRAHAM. *Modern Silver*. Studio Vista (1967).
Modern Jewelry. Studio Books (1963).

IVES, GEORGE. *Eros' Throne*. Swan Sonnenschein (1900).

JEFFERIES, RICHARD. *Hodge and his Masters*. Smith, Elder (1880).

JEWSON, NORMAN. *By Chance I Did Rove*. Published privately (1973).

KARPELES, MAUD. *Cecil Sharp*. Routledge & Kegal Paul (1967).

KITCHEN, PADDY. *A Most Unsettling Person: an introduction to the ideas and life of Patrick Geddes*. Gollancz (1975).

KORNWOLF, JAMES D. *M. H. Baillie Scott and the Arts and Crafts Movement*. John Hopkins Press (1972).

LETHABY, W. R. *Architecture*. Expanded edition, Oxford University Press (1955).
Architecture, Mystery and Myth. Architectural Press (1974).
Form in Civilization: Collected Papers on Art and Labour. Oxford University Press (1922).
Philip Webb and his Work. Oxford University Press (1935).

LETHABY, W. R., and others. *Ernest Gimson: His Life and Work*. Shakespeare Head Press (1924).

LIPSEY, ROGER, *Coomaraswamy, Vol.3 His Life and Work*. Princeton University Press (1977).

LONDON, JACK. *The People of the Abyss*. Journeyman Press (1977).

MACKAIL, J. W. *The Life of William Morris*. Longmans, Green (1899).

MACKENZIE, NORMAN and JEANNE. *The First Fabians*. Weidenfeld & Nicolson (1977).

MADSEN, S. TSCHUDI. *Art Nouveau*. Weidenfeld & Nicolson (1967).

MAIRET, PHILIP. *Pioneer of Sociology: The Life and Letters of Patrick Geddes*. Lund Humphries (1957).

MASSÉ, H. J. L. *The Art-Workers' Guild*. Shakespeare Head Press (1935).

MEYNELL, FRANCIS. *My Lives*. Bodley Head (1971).

MOREAU, R. E. *The Departed Village.* Oxford University Press (1968).

MORRIS, WILLIAM. *Collected Works.* Longmans, Green (1910–15).

MUGGERIDGE, KITTY, and ADAM, RUTH. *Beatrice Webb: A life.* Secker & Warburg (1967).

MUTHESIUS, HERMANN. *Das englische Haus.* Wasmuth (1904–5). English translation by Janet Seligman. Crosby Lockwood Staples (1979).

MUTHESIUS, STEFAN. *The High Victorian Movement in Architecture.* Routledge & Kegan Paul (1972).

NAYLOR, GILLIAN. *The Arts and Crafts Movement.* Studio Vista (1971).

OKEY, THOMAS. *A Basketful of Memories.* J. M. Dent (1930).

PENNELL, E. R. and J. *The Whistler Journal.* J. B. Lippincott (1921).

PENTY, ARTHUR. *The Restoration of the Guild System.* Swan Sonnenschein (1906).

PEVSNER, NIKOLAUS. *Pioneers of Modern Design.* Revised edition, Penguin (1960). *Studies in Art, Architecture and Design,* vol.2. Thames & Hudson (1968).

PRIESTLEY, J. B. *The Edwardians.* Heinemann (1970).

PROCTOR, DENNIS, ed. *The Autobiography of G. Lowes Dickinson.* Duckworth (1973).

REDDIE, CECIL. *Abbotsholme.* George Allen (1900).

RICHARDS, J. M., and PEVSNER, NIKOLAUS, eds. *The Anti-Rationalists.* Architectural Press (1973).

ROTHENSTEIN, JOHN. *Summer's Lease.* Hamish Hamilton (1965).

ROTHENSTEIN, WILLIAM. *Men and Memories.* Faber & Faber (1932).

ROWBOTHAM, SHEILA, and WEEKS, JEFFREY. *Socialism and the New Life: The Personal and Sexual Politics of Edward Carpenter and Havelock Ellis.* Pluto Press (1977).

ROWLAND, KURT. *A History of the Modern Movement.* Van Nostrand Reinhold (1973).

RUSKIN, JOHN. *Fors Clavigera. Letters to the Workmen and Labourers of Great Britain.* Hazell, Watson & Viney (1871–87).

RUSSELL, GORDON. *Designer's Trade.* George Allen & Unwin (1968). Montagu Norman, Banker Designer. *The Banker* (March 1955).

SALT, HENRY. *Life of Thoreau.* Walter Scott (1896).

SCHMUTZLER, ROBERT. *Art Nouveau.* Harry N. Abrams (1962).

SEDDING, JOHN D. *Art and Handicraft.* Kegan Paul, Trench, Trübner (1893).

SELZ, PETER, and CONSTANTINE, MILDRED, eds. *Art Nouveau.* New York, Museum of Modern Art (1959).

SERVICE, ALASTAIR. *Edwardian Architecture.* Thames & Hudson (1977).

SERVICE, ALASTAIR, ed. *Edwardian Architecture and its origins.* Architectural Press (1975).

SHAW, BERNARD. 'William Morris as I knew him', reprint of 1936 essay. William Morris Society (1966).

SIMPSON, DUNCAN. *C.F.A. Voysey: an architect of individuality.* Lund Humphries (1979).

SINGHAM, S. DURAIRAJA. *Ananda Coomaraswamy, the Bridge Builder.* Privately published, Khem Meng Press (Kuala Lumpur 1977).

SINGHAM, S. DURAIRAJA. ed. *Ananda Coomaraswamy: Remembering and Remembering Again and Again.* Privately published (1974).

SMITH, CONSTANCE BABINGTON. *John Masefield.* Oxford University Press (1978).

SMITH, TIMOTHY D'ARCH. *Love in Earnest: Some Notes on the lives and writings of English 'Uranian' Poets from 1899–1930.* Routledge & Kegan Paul (1970).

SPALDING, FRANCES. *Roger Fry.* Elek/Granada (1980).

SPEAIGHT, ROBERT. *The Life of Eric Gill.* Methuen (1966).

STANSKY, PETER. C. R. Ashbee visits Stanford University. *Imprint* of Stanford Libraries Associates, vol.III, No.1 (April 1977).

STIRLING, MRS A. M. W. *William De Morgan.* Thornton, Butterworth (1922).

SUMMERSON, JOHN. Some British Contemporaries of Frank Lloyd Wright. *Studies in Western Art IV.* Princeton University Press (1963).

TAYLOR, JOHN RUSSELL. *The Art Nouveau Book in Britain.* Methuen (1966).

THOMPSON, FLORA. *Lark Rise.* Oxford University Press (1959).

THOMPSON, SUSAN OTIS. *American Book Design and William Morris.* Bowker Company (New York 1977).

THOMPSON, PAUL. *The Edwardians.* Weidenfeld & Nicolson (1975).
The Work of William Morris. Heinemann (1967).

WARD, B. M. *Reddie of Abbotsholme.* George Allen & Unwin (1934).

WEBB, BEATRICE. *Our Partnership.* Longmans, Green (1948).

WHITFIELD, CHRISTOPHER. *A History of Chipping Campden.* Shakespeare Head Press (1958).

WHITFIELD, CHRISTOPHER, ed. *Robert Dover and the Cotswold Games.* Published privately (1962).

WHITMAN, WALT. *Complete Verse and Selected Prose.* Nonesuch Press (1938).
Democratic Vistas. Walter Scott (1888).

WOOLF, VIRGINIA. *Roger Fry.* Hogarth Press (1940).

WRIGHT, FRANK LLOYD. *Autobiography.* Faber & Faber (1942).

Index

THE CAMPDEN MAYPOLE SONG.

Words by Laurence Housman. 1904.
Air: "Peace-Egging Song," Lancashire Traditional.

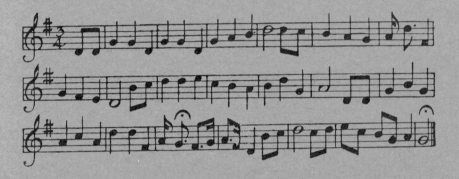

Oh, lads, where go ye on the highroad to-day?
  (On the hill, in the valley, how the green grass doth grow!)
We are going up to Campden this first morn of May,
  Where round the green maypole the pretty maids do show.

Chorus. There Broadway lies keeping her flocks under
              hill,
          There's Willersey sleeping, and sleeps with a will;
          But Campden, Chipping Campden, Broad Camp-
              den, I say,
          Is waking to life on this first morn of May!

Oh, lads, and what will ye do, when ye get there?
  (On the hill, in the valley, how the young lambs do spring!)
We will dance on the green sward, link hands with the fair,
  And round the green maypole full merrily will sing!

  V.—36